THE ALLURE OF SPORTS IN WESTERN CULTURE

The Allure of Sports in Western Culture

EDITED BY JOHN ZILCOSKY AND
MARLO A. BURKS

UNIVERSITY OF TORONTO PRESS
Toronto Buffalo London

ISBN 978-1-4875-0418-2

∞ Printed on acid-free, 100% post-consumer recycled paper
with vegetable-based inks.

Library and Archives Canada Cataloguing in Publication

Title: The allure of sports in Western culture / edited by John Zilcosky and
    Marlo A. Burks.
Names: Zilcosky, John, editor. | Burks, Marlo A., 1986- editor.
Description: Includes bibliographical references and index.
Identifiers: Canadiana 20190099089 | ISBN 9781487504182 (hardcover)
Subjects: LCSH: Sports – Social aspects. | LCSH: Sports – History. |
    LCSH: Civilization, Western.
Classification: LCC GV706.5 .A45 2019 | DDC 306.4/83—dc23

University of Toronto Press acknowledges the financial assistance to its
publishing program of the Canada Council for the Arts and the Ontario Arts
Council, an agency of the Government of Ontario.

Canada Council **Conseil des Arts**
for the Arts **du Canada**

ONTARIO ARTS COUNCIL
CONSEIL DES ARTS DE L'ONTARIO
an Ontario government agency
un organisme du gouvernement de l'Ontario

Funded by the   Financé par le
Government   gouvernement
of Canada   du Canada

MIX
Paper from
responsible sources
FSC
www.fsc.org   FSC® C016245

For Charlie, Nora, Nathaniel, and Pepper

Contents

Acknowledgments

The editors would like to thank, for their support, the Social Sciences and Humanities Research Council of Canada and – at the University of Toronto – Victoria College, the Faculty of Arts and Science, and the Department of Germanic Languages and Literatures. We are also grateful to Maral Attar-Zadeh for her editorial assistance.

PART I

Introduction

Introduction: The Allure of Sports

JOHN ZILCOSKY

It is strange to be writing about sports because, until a couple of years ago, I had never thought about them – the way that a fish does not think about water. I was born awash in sports, such that they seemed like natural events, not something to analyse. I grew up in football country – western Pennsylvania – where my father and my favourite uncle had been star players, who now viewed everything through the lens of football. My mother remembers that when I was born, the nurses took me to the nursery immediately after the difficult delivery, my head slightly flattened and deformed. My mother asked my father to check on me. "What does he look like?" she asked, eager to hear the description of her firstborn's face. "Like a middle linebacker," he said. And my father was not joking.

At that time, my father was a twenty-six-year-old assistant high school football coach – the second most important man in Kane, Pennsylvania, behind the legendary middle-aged head man. To this day, my father is proud that I, while still less than a year old, sat on my mother's lap to "watch" him prowl the sidelines during that magical 1965 autumn when Kane High School achieved its first undefeated season ever. The coaching staff also sent their first scholarship player to Penn State – a boy called John, after whom my father named me (not after John F. Kennedy, as I had always assumed). In those heady days of my early childhood, Penn State's young, vibrant assistant coach, Joe Paterno, used to drive through western Pennsylvania scouring the mill towns for talent. Nothing made my father prouder than getting a boy – young "John" from Kane, who had come from nothing – a free education. And not just anywhere, but at Penn State, where the new coach had a degree in English literature from Brown, quoted ancient Greek literature to his players, and ran the last clean program in American college sports. Paterno was my father's role model; and my uncle, the coach at a rival high school, kept a framed letter from him above his desk. God might be dead, but JoePa, as they called him, was alive and well.

As I grew up, I walked in my father's sporting footsteps, playing football, wrestling, and learning judo – eventually even gaining fascinating experiences fighting in an East Berlin judo club just after the Wall fell. I even coached one year of small-town high school football myself. While I was doing this, Joe Paterno turned down offers from the New England Patriots and the Pittsburgh Steelers, remaining instead in "Happy Valley" and coaching college kids. Along the way, he won more games than any coach in the history of big-time college football as well as the admiration of ever more young men like me.

Then came that day in November 2011, when my mother called and said, "Did you hear about Joe Paterno?" This was the year of the Penn State child sex abuse scandal, and although Paterno claimed to have known nothing about the crimes of his defensive coach, it turned out that he might have, and the university decided to fire him, now eighty-four years old. "Don't bring this up at Thanksgiving," my mother said. "It could kill your father and your uncle." Back in our old western Pennsylvania farmhouse a week later, my brothers and I did as we were told, not mentioning the man about whom everyone was thinking. And we watched the grim faces of our father and uncle. To this day, I have not known how to interpret their silence. Was it stony anger directed at the media for unfairly convicting a great man? Or was their mute rage directed at Paterno himself, for tacitly sanctioning the unspeakable?

Whatever my father was thinking on that day, this was the day when *I* started thinking about sports. I began reading stories about the Penn State scandal in the *New York Times*, *Harper's*, and *The Nation*, and then more general theories about sports. I hoped to begin to understand how they had become so important to my father, my uncle, and me (and, now, to my own son) – to the point that this disruption in our relation to sports threatened our world-view. I discovered first what I had already guessed: that my extended family and I were not alone in our devotion to sports. Sports are the most popular spectator events in the history of the world (soccer's World Cup now counts more viewers than even British royal weddings). Why?, I asked myself. I stumbled across various scholarly explanations: our love of chance and vicarious thrill, our need to release anxiety and aggression, and, most important, our sense of the "sacredness" of play – following the ancient Greek tradition. As Johan Huizinga claimed in 1938, in our otherwise godless world we create a revered space separate from the "ordinary," where we perform sporting "rituals" similar to those of religion.[1] Later thinkers developed this into a religious theory of sports: Roger Caillois argued in 1958 that fans "consecrate" and "worship" their sports heroes, and Roland Barthes claimed in 1961 that all modern sports are the heirs of "ancient religious sacrifices."[2] This seems even truer today. Fallen masses prostrate themselves weekly before their gods, whom they worship in liturgical rites of chants and songs until one side is sacrificed dramatically in defeat. This explained much of the fervency of "Friday Night Lights" in our corner of western Pennsylvania. But I resisted this as *the* explanation, not because it did not seem correct. It did. But my family's emotional response to sports seemed too complicated to be contained within one all-encompassing analogy. What is more, the religion theory did not enlighten me to the sociopolitical forces behind the ethical knot that now entangled my father, my uncle, and me.

As if to respond to my question, philosophers and sociologists from the 1970s, I discovered, claimed that sports are modernity's most effective form of social manipulation.[3] It is futile to ask why we love sports, they argued, before we understand the sociopolitical elements determining this "love." Norbert Elias, for example, maintained that the unprecedented rise of institutionalized, rule-based sports in the nineteenth century exemplified modern society's attempt to "civilize" and control bodies.[4] For Pierre Bourdieu, sports allowed these bodies to differentiate and distinguish themselves, demarcating ever more specific elites within capitalist culture.[5] Jean-Marie Brohm pointedly presented the Marxist argument that modern sports are the ruling classes' best tool for producing indoctrinated and quiescent populations.[6] More recent critics, influenced by Michel Foucault, developed similar arguments to claim that sports constitute today's most effective form of biopolitics: state power delegates itself onto each individual body, which learns to discipline itself through drills and exercises.[7] Svenja Goltermann, building on both Bourdieu and Foucault, argued that physical education in imperial Germany created the "body of the nation," and Wolf Kittler demonstrated how this same sports pedagogy – already in the Napoleonic Wars – continued the ancient Greek tradition of preparing young men for battle.[8] Finally, countless scholars and journalists claimed that sports are the new opium of the masses, fed to us by obscenely profitable media corporations.[9] And this opium's kick relies most egregiously on the exploitation of racial minorities, especially in so-called amateur sports.

Against this critical grain, the writer and activist C.L.R. James insisted already in 1963 that we love sports simply because they are beautiful. James viewed cricket, for example, as an art form on par with "theatre, ballet, opera, and the dance." We adore the former and the latter for

the same reason: they give us "aesthetic" pleasure through the "significant form" of moving bodies; and both supply a "dramatic spectacle."[10]
Joseph Kupfer concurred, arguing that sports provide a stunning dram-
aturgy. Seesaw scoring and "the delicate balance between offences and
defences" establish a theatrical "rhythm" culminating in a "climax."[11]
In 2005, Hans Ulrich Gumbrecht launched the related polemical argument that we – writers, scholars, intellectuals – deny our essential love
of this beauty because of our perceived critical obligation to reveal the
interests of the sports-industrial complex. We can no longer see athletic
bodies as what Gumbrecht calls the pure expression of aesthetic feeling,
in the classical sense developed in ancient Greece and eventually revived by Kant. Like poetry, sports please us through their "epiphany of
form." And this is precisely what brought ancient intellectuals to praise
athletes so profusely. For Gumbrecht, we need to relearn this capacity
to "praise what we love."[12] Gumbrecht's book led to a widely read 2006
debate with Hayden White in *The Chronicle of Higher Education*, where
White claimed that Gumbrecht had explained away the social and political brutality of sports in the same way that "certain ideologues in the
1930s distracted attention from the violence of war."[13] As if in partial response, Andrew Edgar has recently extended the "aesthetic" in sports
to include the "ugly." The "distorted physical gestures of athletes" and
the "ever-present threat of defeat and failure" recall the disruptions of
modern art.[14] Other critics see the lure of sports as exploding the very
category of aesthetics. Sports resemble art, Grant Farred argues, only
through a shared capacity to bring the audience into contact with the
ontologically overwhelming "event."[15]

Before discussing further the "allure" of "sports," two key definitions
are in order. What, first of all, are "sports"? Contemporary philosophers
have spilled much ink over this, most notably following Bernhard
Suits's definition of sports as a "game" marked by "skill," "physical-
ity," and a "following" (audience).[16] But critics have of course found
exceptions to this definition,[17] and the exceptions only grow when
we consider that the meaning of "sports" has changed dramatically
over time. Just 150 years ago, sports were still defined as "diversion,
entertainment, fun," related to hunting, shooting, and even amorous
play. Only the consolidation of organized sports by the end of the nineteenth century created our modern dictionary definition: "an activity
involving physical exertion and skill," regulated by "rules or customs
in which an individual or team competes against another." This semantic shift emphasizes the theoretical problem that sports historians have
long stressed. There can be no "history of sports" because today's concept has no relation to jousting in the Middle Ages or to the ancient

Greek "contest" (*agōn* or *áethlos*), especially because we moderns obsess over quantification and records.[18] Other historians have claimed that this point is overstated and that the differences between modern and ancient sports are not essential.[19] The authors in this volume do not attempt to adjudicate whether these differences are fundamental, but we do find the similarities significant enough to use the term "sports" also for ancient competitions. Generally, we use this term in the sense of "'playful' physical contests" and "regulated competition."[20] But we are careful to emphasize the often radical variations in the meaning of these competitions as they transform from ancient Greece through today.

The second term, "allure," expresses our attempt to understand what attracts people to sports. For this, the word's own origin is instructive: it was born at the crossroads of "attraction"/"fascination" and the early connotations of "sport" as hunting and lovemaking. The English "allure" derives from the thirteenth-century Anglo-Norman *aleurer*, meaning "to lure (a hawk)" back to the falconer's hand. *Aleurer* issues from the Old French *aleurrer*: "to seduce," synonymous with "*captiver*"; it implies "to attract (a person) by deceptive means." This connection of violence through hunting and seduction is at the heart of what both Farred and Gumbrecht, in their "theoretical perspectives" for this volume, understand as sports' allure. Although their emphases are different – Farred focuses on the event's ontological power and Gumbrecht on its aesthetic appeal – the two agree that sports can best be understood as a force that beguiles us. The sporting event, like the great work of art or an existential disruption, captivates us to the point of self-renunciation. For Farred, we surrender ourselves to the body of the brilliant athlete, for Gumbrecht to the "mystical body" of our co-fans in the stadium.

Such descriptions of the allure of sports have drawn censure on moral grounds. Critics have accused Gumbrecht of celebrating a religious, fascistoid ("Riefenstahl"-like) fusion with a greater being,[21] and Gumbrecht admits that ethics – in a narrow sense – is always opposed to the allure of sports. But our modern sense of ethics as "good" versus "bad" forgets the Greek *arête*, which meant both "virtue" and "excellence" and had nothing to do with empathy or compassion – asking instead simply, "Who is best?"[22] What is more, the Greek *ēthikós* comes from *êthos*, which originally meant "accustomed place" or "habitat" and, only later, "custom," "habit," and "(moral) character."[23] This connection of "place" to ethics reveals itself in Gumbrecht's argument that the fan experiences a Heideggerian "grounding" within the stadium, where "sublimely moving ethical effects" disclose themselves. Farred similarly borrows from Heidegger an ethics of "giving oneself up": the fan at the sporting event surrenders himself to the "other" playing on the field. Both Gumbrecht and Farred anchor what they call the fan's "intensity" in this accustomed place or custom of *êthos*: Gumbrecht's stadium and Farred's tradition of sports institutions, such as English soccer clubs. For both writers, this *êthos* allows the subject to transcend his narcissism and experience a commitment that is normally unavailable to him – even if this commitment always carries with it the danger of a recrudescent tribalism.

To investigate this tension within the allure of sports, we have asked our contributors – literary theorists, classicists, historians – to present historical case studies beginning with the earliest documentation of this allure: in ancient Greece. Sports were of course present in older cultures – China, Sumer, Egypt – but only the Greeks elevated sports (as *agōn* and *áethlos*) to a social and political institution.[24] In 776 BC, they founded the Olympic Games, which were significant enough to bring warring parties to mandatory truces. The period of four years between Games, the "Olympiad," even became a unit of time in historical chronologies. The Greek athletic tradition remained strong throughout most of the Roman Empire, as Sofie Remijsen describes in our volume's opening case study, fading only in late antiquity. Modern Europeans resuscitated this tradition in the nineteenth century, and some form of this – however distorted, as Charles Stocking points out – continued in Europe and the major sites of European emigration, especially North America. Because we focus on these sites, we refer to our volume's geographical range as "Western" – despite the term's inexactness and its chequered history in ideological oppression.[25] The Greeks referred to their Eastern neighbours as "barbarian" despite having borrowed from them aspects of their culture, including sports – such as wrestling, from ancient Sumer (see my article).[26] In the modern era, such borrowing became increasingly common, as when interwar Germany incorporated Japanese martial arts into their sporting ethos (see Sarah Panzer's article). And today's global soccer culture (see Gumbrecht, Farred, and Vowinckel) challenges conservative ideas of the nation-state, Europe, and the "West," as we saw in the right-wing backlash against France's 2018 "black, white, and blue" world-championship team.[27] Such phenomena undermine the descriptive value of "Western," yet we have chosen still to use that term, to alert readers that we are focusing on the major sites of the continued Greek tradition (not, say, on the long sporting customs of Asia, the Middle East, or Africa) and also to allow ourselves to reveal fissures in this conceptual monolith.

Remijsen opens our case studies with the pressing question at the heart of sports in ancient Greece: Why did the Greeks love athletics?

Even to the point of elevating them to the cornerstone of pedagogy (*paideia*) and culture? And why did this love eventually "fade" in late (Roman) antiquity? Remijsen's answer rests in allure and ethics: for the Greeks, the perfectly disciplined athletic body was both beautiful and – through the athlete's striving for individual excellence (*arête*) and honour (*philotimia*) – good. Because of Roman Christian morality and the movement to transform sports into a spectacle, this powerful conjunction of beauty, excellence, and ethics began to collapse in the fourth century. In my chapter, I pose the related question of why Plato spent so much time connecting his ethical view of the world to sports – specifically to wrestling. Seeing wrestling as the archetypal human contest, Plato disparaged mythical wrestling-to-the-death in favour of a new rule-based system. The goal, Plato insisted, was to "disentangle" bodies. This disentangled body, I argue, became Plato's symbol for the modern, moral, reasoning individual. Charles Stocking supplies an apt ending for this section by describing the dialectical relation between the ancient Olympics and their modern iteration in 1896. The modern Olympics presented the allure of the authentic Greek body, only to discover that this body was not "real." Even if, as Remijsen argues, there was an ancient coincidence of beauty and morality in the athletic body, Stocking demonstrates how this body, already in ancient times, was only an ideal. The moderns knew this, yet also disavowed this through overzealous pronouncements on the ancient marriage between aesthetics and ethics.

Our next section describes the era from the Enlightenment to the present. Rebekka von Mallinckrodt investigates the clash of spectatorial allure and morality in the popular foot races of eighteenth-century Great Britain and the Germanic Holy Roman Empire. These races were well attended for erotic and gaming reasons, but they also produced ethical questions: Should women be so lightly clad? And should servants – running as representatives of their masters' houses – be gambled on, like horses? After the revolutions of 1848, these races were often discontinued, out of fear of popular unrest. Wolf Kittler develops this social-political analysis by exposing sports' connection to warfare. In Napoleonic Prussia, a group of civilian patriots, including the poet Heinrich von Kleist, planned a guerrilla insurrection based on steeling Prussian bodies. For this, they invented modern gymnastics – thereby returning sports to their ancient role of preparing men for war. Sarah Panzer's presentation complements Kittler's by examining the importance of sports to Germany after the First World War. The Germans enthusiastically imported martial arts from Japan, hoping to create a substitute for the heroic masculinity that they had lost in the trenches.

Sports here did not prepare directly for war but rather replaced battlefield heroics through simulation, with the model of a "fair" and
"aesthetic" Eastern militarism. Developing this ancient sporting
ideal of fairness, Annette Vowinckel exposes today's hypocritical use
of the term. Cheating or "foul" play, she claims, is actually intrinsic
to sports. Using international soccer as her example, Vowinckel out-
lines accepted forms of "cheating": the tactical foul, the revenge foul,
the emergency-break foul, and so on. Cheating is indeed not outside
of sports but is *in* it, from the Greeks onward. We can now see Antilochus's unscrupulous charioteering in the *Iliad* as the predecessor of
Neymar's flops and Materazzi's successful baiting of Zidane.

If cheating is not an anomaly but is essential to sports, then might
we say the same about the broader concept of deception? Is part of our
attraction to sports our desire to see successful deception as well as
to deceive ourselves, as in the exciting seductions present already in
the etymology of "allure"? The Greeks loved to hear about Antilochus
winning through deceitful cunning (*mētis*),[28] just as we love to watch
soccer's sly divers, baseball's sign-stealers, football's ball deflators, and
track-and-field's annual superhuman record-breakers – who claim to
be clean. There may be many reasons why the viewership for the Tour
de France has dropped in the post–Lance Armstrong, "post-doping"
era, but we cannot disregard the unspoken one: that we loved the fris-
son created by the coincidence of impossible record-breaking, dangerously high speeds, and rumours of blood being injected into cyclists'
veins in the backs of RVs.[29]

Our attraction to sporting deceit is connected to our fascination with
sports' violence. We may claim to watch sports *despite* this violence, but
the history of human competition suggests otherwise. Of the many possible examples from ancient Greece, consider the unfair boxing match
in the *Iliad* between the massive Epeius and a smaller man – who both
wore the gloves of hardened leather, *caesti*, that were designed to inflict
more pain, not less. Epeius needs only one blow to knock his opponent
half-conscious, leaving him spitting thick blood. The eager onlookers
register not a wince of regret. And we barely need to mention the masses
of spectators who gathered in Roman arenas to watch unarmed people
being chased and slaughtered by wild animals (*damnatio ad bestias*).[30]
The German playwright Heinrich von Kleist shows that this bloodlust
is not just for the ancients in his 1810 true story about a crowd "shouting for joy" as one boxer kills another – with the victor dying likewise
the following day, from internal haemorrhaging. Today we have the
increasing popularity of the gory MMA, along with the endless replays
of Luis Suárez biting opponents on the soccer pitch. Does our desire

to see these bites repeatedly betray what we, from the Greeks onward, have always wanted from sports: ritualized replays of our most primitive selves? Is the dirty underbelly of sports not collateral damage that we grudgingly accept but rather exactly what we want? This offers me a hint at what was happening when my father and uncle watched Joe Paterno fall from grace. Perhaps their – and my – fascination with Penn State was never based on the belief that Paterno ran football's "last clean program" but rather on our secret knowledge, however unconscious, that something was rotten in the state of Pennsylvania. Not the actual something of Paterno's assistant abusing children in the showers, but *something* nonetheless. Is this darkness of sports what attracts us to them, regardless of how we deceive ourselves into thinking that this is not true?

This aspect of allure takes Edgar's aesthetic argument into another realm. The stakes lie in proving not that sports quench an *aesthetic* desire for ugliness in addition to an aesthetic desire for beauty (i.e., sports as modern art), but rather that the desire for ugliness speaks to a "Dionysian" allure beyond aesthetics.[31] We are drawn to hideousness on the field ("distorted faces," etc.) because we are drawn to the *absence* of a normative ethics.[32] The entire social and political ugliness of sports – cheating and gambling, brutalization of athletes' bodies, millennia-long exploitation of the oppressed – is essential to their allure. Sports thus reveal the dirty flip side of the traditional Enlightenment pairing of aesthetics and ethics. Just as athletic beauty seemed to reveal the possibility of ethical harmony, so too does the inevitable ugliness in the arena expose our desire for chaos, destruction, and limitless hedonism. It is here that we see the complexity of "allure" in sports, explaining why Edgar calls on Heidegger to elucidate it – as do Gumbrecht and Farred in this volume.[33] For allure recalls the Heideggerian mystery of locating an authentically grounded "place," an *êthos*, that can only be created through violence and destruction. *Aleurer*, we remember, was originally blood sport.

The contributions to this volume – often in direct dialogue with one another – examine this conflict within the allure of sports and demonstrate how a consistent ethics of sports is hard to locate. If it is to be found, then only in the *êthos* that allows for a new grounding of our being, as Gumbrecht and Farred argue from different perspectives, even if this founding contains within it violence, deceit, and inhumanity. This place is evocatively disclosed in our coda, where Karin Helmstaedt traces her personal history as a world-class swimmer: from the excitement of discovering her talent as a little girl, to her indignation after losing to cheating competitors, to her bliss in returning to the water, twenty years later, with her daughter. This "place" of sports – the mother-daughter swim in the Mediterranean Sea – reveals sports' oceanic essence as well as the inevitably personal feeling that they strike in many of us, including the authors of this volume. Sports are part of our lives whether we like it or not, be they experiences of joy (the fandom of Gumbrecht and Farred), ambivalence (Vowinckel watching soccer with her parents), or torture (Kittler in gym class as a boy). Sports may not be, as Plato insisted and my father always told me, the surest way to become a better person: to learn discipline, to persevere through adversity, and to accept defeat with grace.[34] For these ideals are also used by the sports industry to camouflage its brutalities and by us to hide our own desire for sports' dark side. Our knowledge of our involvement in the cruelty of sports troubles us, especially when we realize that we long for what we disavow. And we know that this longing is ethical only in the extra-moral sense of an *êthos* in which we might, intoxicatingly, be grounded. It is this ethics of desire that both excites and worries us. For it is what we will bequeath to those who come after.

NOTES

1 Johan Huizinga, *Homo Ludens: A Study of the Play Element in Culture* (Boston: Beacon, 1955 [Dutch original, 1938]), esp. 15–27. For Huizinga, not only does play contain aspects of "culture" (including religion), but culture itself is determined by and "bears the character of play" (xi).

2 Roger Caillois, *Man, Play, and Games* (Urbana: University of Illinois Press, 2001 [French original, 1958]), 122; Roland Barthes, *What Is Sport?* (New Haven: Yale University Press, 2007 [French original, 1961]), 3. Caillois tempers this position somewhat – albeit without persuasive argumentation – when claiming that "sacrifice and communion" are proper only to religion (not to games/sports). Caillois, *Man and the Sacred* (Glencoe: Free Press, 1959 [French original, 1950]), 161. Later sociologists and anthropologists followed on these arguments to describe sports – especially European soccer and American football – as new religions. See Marc Augé, "Football: De l'histoire sociale à l'anthropologie religieuse," *Le débat* (1982): 59–67; and Michael Butterworth, "Fox Sports, Super Bowl XLII, and the Affirmation of American Civil Religion," *Journal of Sport and Social Issues* 32 (2008): 318–32. For a review of the contemporary arguments linking sports to religion, on the example of soccer, see Lionel Obadia, "Does Ritual Make Religion?: The Case of Soccer in Europe," in *Religious Diversity Today*, ed. Anastasia Panagakos (Santa Barbara: Praeger, 2016), 2:281–99.

3 Even Caillois argued, already in 1958, that stadium sports could be viewed as social "sublimat[ion]" and a "harmless compensation to the masses": *Man, Play, and Games*, 97, 125.

4 Norbert Elias, "The Genesis of Sport as a Sociological Problem," in *The Sociology of Sport: A Selection of Readings*, ed. Eric Dunning (London: Frank Cass, 1971), 88–115. See also Norbert Elias and Eric Dunning, *Quest for Excitement: Sport and Leisure in the Civilizing Process* (Oxford: Basil Blackwell, 1986), which contains some of Elias's writings on sports going back to 1967.

5 Pierre Bourdieu, "Sports and Social Class," *Social Science Information* 17, no. 6 (December 1978): 819–40. Bourdieu borrows here (without acknowledgment) from Thorsten Veblen's classic critique of sports as a form of "conspicuous consumption": a self-marking of the leisure classes. See Veblen, *The Theory of the Leisure Class* (New York: Modern Library, 1934 [1899]), esp. 254–75). Bourdieu later adds to this critique the upper class's "aesthetic outlook" – in relation both to sports and to society in general – in *Distinction: A Social Critique of the Judgement of Taste* (Cambridge, MA: Harvard University Press, 1984 [French original, 1979]), 208–25. For overviews of Bourdieu's contributions to the sociology of sports, see Jean-Paul Clément, "Contributions of the Sociology of Pierre Bourdieu to the Sociology of Sport," *Sociology of Sport Journal* 12 (1995): 147–57; and Thomas Alkemeyer, "Pierre Bourdieu," in *Klassiker und Wegbereiter der Sportwissenschaft* (Stuttgart: Kohlhammer, 2006), 414–24.

6 Jean-Marie Brohm, *Sociologie politique du sport* (Paris: J.-P. Delarge, 1976).

7 For overviews of Foucault-inspired sports scholarship, see Geneviève Rail and Jean Harvey, "Body at Work: Michel Foucault and the Sociology of Sport," *Sociology of Sport Journal* 12 (1995): 164–79; and Thomas Alkemeyer and Thomas Pille, "Michel Foucault," in *Klassiker und Wegbereiter*, 431–41.

8 Svenja Goltermann, *Körper der Nation: Habitusformierung und die Politik des Turnens 1860–1890* (Göttingen: Vandenhoeck & Ruprecht), 1998; Wolf Kittler, "Erlösung aus dem Geist der preußischen Armee," in *Die Geburt des Partisanen aus dem Geist der Poesie: Heinrich von Kleist und die Strategie der Befreiungskriege* (Freiburg: Rombach, 1987), 325–75.

9 See, for example, the anthology from Brohm's journal *Quel Corps?: L'opium sportif: la critique radicale du Sport*, ed. Jean-Pierre Escriva and Henri Vaugrand (Paris: L'Harmattan, 1996).

10 C.L.R. James, *Beyond a Boundary* (London: Yellow Jersey Press, 2005 [1963]), 258, 257, 263.

11 Joseph Kupfer, "Sport – The Body Electric," in *Experience as Art: Aesthetics in Everyday Life* (Albany: SUNY Press, 1983), 127. Additional attempts to understand sports in aesthetic terms include Wolfgang Welsch, "Sport: Ästhetisch betrachtet – und sogar als Kunst?," and Sven Güldenpfennig,

"Das sportliche Kunstwerk: Die Selbstverständlichkeit des Außergewöhnlichen: Ein ästhetisches Deutungskonzept zur Sinnstruktur des Sports," both in Winfried Simmat, *Weimarer Vorträge über Beziehungen des Sports zur Kunst und Kultur* (Weimar: Bauhaus-Universität, 2000), 6–27, 28–50. For the counter-argument – that sports cannot be viewed as classically aesthetic because most are too connected to real-world results (scoring the goal is more important that *how* it is scored) – see David Best, "The Aesthetic in Sport," *British Journal of Aesthetics* 14 (1974): 201, and *Philosophy and Human Movement* (London: Unwin, 1978), 101. For a review of the arguments for and against categorizing sports as "aesthetic" (and for counter-arguments against Best), see Andrew Edgar, "Aesthetics of Sport," in *Routledge Handbook of the Philosophy of Sport*, ed. Mike McNamee and William Morgan (London: Routledge, 2015), 69–80 (on Best, 73–7).

12 Hans Ulrich Gumbrecht, *In Praise of Athletic Beauty* (Cambridge, MA: Harvard University Press, 2006 [the 2005 German translation appeared just before the English original]), 190, 34–5.

13 Hayden White, "The Place and Value of College Sports: 2 Views: They Have Betrayed Their Educational Purpose," *Chronicle of Higher Education* 52, no. 42 (June 23, 2006). Gumbrecht's response appeared in the same issue of the *Chronicle*, as "The Place and Value of College Sports: 2 Views: They Have a Powerful Aesthetic Appeal." For a criticism of Gumbrecht on historical grounds, see Ingomar Weiler, "Hans Ulrich Gumbrecht: Lob des Sports," *Sportwissenschaft* 37 (2007): 220–6. Despite this criticism, Gumbrecht has found kindred spirits, including the literary critic Günter Blamberger, who maintains that spontaneous athletic motion embodies "genius" in the eighteenth-century philosophical sense of the term; on Blamberger and genius in sports, see Thomas Alkemeyer, "Rhythmen, Resonanzen und Missklänge: Über die Körperlichkeit der Produktion des Sozialen im Spiel," in *Body Turn: Perspektiven der Soziologie des Körpers und des Sports* (Bielefeld: Transcript, 2006), 272–5. For a review of the initial German reception of Gumbrecht's book, see Thomas Schmidt, "Diskursive Lockerungen," *KulturPoetik* 8 (2008): 120–4; for the book's further resonance, see Ronaldo Helal and Fausto Amaro, eds., *Esporte e mídia: novas perspectivas: A influência da obra de Hans Ulrich Gumbrecht* (Rio de Janeiro: EdUERJ, 2015).

14 Edgar, "Aesthetics of Sport," 71. For the original explanation of this "modernist" theory, see Edgar, "The Beauty of Sport," *Sports, Ethics, and Philosophy* 7, no. 1 (2013): 100–20. Gumbrecht resists the claim of an "ugly" aesthetic in sports in his essay in this volume.

15 Grant Farred, *In Motion, At Rest: The Event of the Athletic Body* (Minneapolis: University of Minnesota Press, 2014), 3. Farred is citing here Alain Badiou's reference to the effect of art in *In Praise of Love*, which

references the Surrealists but recalls also Heidegger's claim that art shatters the limits of the "aesthetic" by revealing a shared, elemental understanding of "that which is" (in *Der Ursprung des Kunstwerkes* [1935–36]).

16 Bernard Suits, "The Elements of Sports," in *The Philosophy of Sport*, ed. R. Osterhaudt (Springfield: C.C. Thomas, 1973), 48–64. Suits's thesis here and in *The Grasshopper* (1978) was influential enough that "the following decade of *The Journal of the Philosophy of Sport* seemed scarcely to discuss much else." Mike McNamee, "Introduction to Part 1 (The Roots of Sports Ethics)," in *The Ethics of Sports: A Reader*, ed. McNamee (London: Routledge, 2010), 13.

17 See Graham McFee, *Sport, Rules and Values: Philosophical Investigations into the Nature of Sport* (London: Routledge, 2004), 15–32; McNamee, "Introduction," 13; and "What Is Sport?," in *The Ethics of Sport: Essential Readings*, ed. Arthur Caplan and Brendan Parent (Oxford: Oxford University Press, 2017), 1–2.

18 The main proponents of this discontinuity theory (shared by Gumbrecht) include Allen Guttmann, *From Ritual to Record: The Nature of Modern Sports* (New York: Columbia University Press, 1978) (see esp. 16–55) and Richard Mandell, *Sport: A Cultural History* (New York: Columbia University Press, 1984). See also Thomas F. Scanlon, *Eros and Greek Athletics* (Oxford: Oxford University Press, 2002), 7–9; and Scanlon, "The Vocabulary of Competition: *Agôn* and *Áethlos*, Greek Terms for Contest," *Journal of Sport Literature* 1 (1983): 147–62.

19 David Sansone, *Greek Athletics and the Genesis of Sport* (Berkeley: University of California Press, 1988), 6. See also David Young, who specifically counters Guttmann's theory of quantification and records in "First with the Most: Greek Athletic Records and 'Specialization,'" *Nikephoros* 9 (1996): 175–97.

20 Guttmann, *From Ritual to Record*, 7; Hajo Bernett, "Sport," *Lexikon der Pädagogik* (Freiburg: Herder, 1971–73), 4:144. With their references to play, both Guttmann and Bernett are indebted to Huizinga. For an overview of the problem of defining "sports" as well as an argument for labelling the Greek competitions *áethlos* (not "sports"), see Scanlon, *Eros and Greek Athletics*, 7–9. For various positions on the definition of sports, see the theme issue "Sport: Einheit und Vielfalt seiner Kulturen," in *Erwägen. Wissen. Ethik* 4 (2005).

21 Volker Breidecker, "Ölig reflektiert es Verschmelzungsbedürfnis: Hans Ulrich Gumbrecht über Sport," *Süddeutsche Zeitung*, 18 July 2005.

22 See Stephen G. Miller, *Arete: Greek Sports from Ancient Sources* (Berkeley: University of California Press, 2004), ix–x. As Barthes writes, sports pose the question, "Who is best?" in the ancient sense of *arête*: "Who is the best to work the world, to give it to men ... to all men? That is what sport says.

Occasionally one would like to make sport say something else. But sport is not made for that" (*What Is Sport?*, 63 [ellipsis in original]).

23 See Pedro Proscurcin Junior, *Der Begriff Ethos bei Homer: Beitrag zu einer philosophischen Interpretation* (Heidelberg: Winter, 2014); on "accustomed place" (*die gewohnten Plätze*), see 162–6.

24 On pre-Greek sports in Asia and the Middle East, see Nigel B. Crowther, *Sport in Ancient Times* (Westport: Prager, 2007), 1–33.

25 For a convincing criticism of the term "West," especially as popularized by Samuel Huntington in his *Clash of Civilizations* (1996), see Edward Said, "The Clash of Ignorance," *The Nation*, October 2001. See also Amartya Sen, "Democracy as Universal Value," *Journal of Democracy* 10 (1999): 3–17; and Paul Berman, *Terror and Liberalism* (New York: Norton, 2003), 24–6. Already in *Orientalism* (1978), Said argued that the construct "West"/"East" was a way of patronizing and dominating the "East" – extending at least as far back as Aeschylus's 472 BC play, *The Persians*, which celebrated the "Western," Greek victory.

26 On the ancient Greek construction of the East, see Said's *Orientalism* (previous endnote). As Andre Gunder Frank argues, the "West" never really existed – certainly not in ancient Greece – because "globalization" extended as far back as the rise of trade between southern Mesopotamia and northwestern India in the third millennium BC: *ReOrient: Global Economy in the Asian Age* (Berkeley: University of California Press, 1998).

On intercultural borrowings concerning wrestling in the ancient world, see Scanlon, *Eros and Greek Athletics*, 7.

27 Clint Smith, "World Cup 2018: The Black and White and Brown Faces of Les Bleus," *The New Yorker*, 22 June 2018. On a similar right-wing backlash against the multicultural German team, see "Das Tor steht links," *taz: die tageszeitung*, 24 June 2018. See also the discussion around Mesut Özil's resignation from the German team and his statement, "Deutscher, wenn wir gewinnen, aber ein Einwanderer, wenn wir verlieren": Christian Spiller, "So viel mehr als ein Rücktritt," *Zeit Online*, 23 July 2018.

28 On Antilochus's tricky "cunning" (*mētis*), see Marcel Detienne and Jean-Pierre Vernant, *Cunning Intelligence in Greek Culture and Society*, trans. Janet Lloyd (Atlantic Highlands: Humanities Press, 1978), 12–23.

29 https://www.statista.com/statistics/229087/people-who-watched-the-tour-de-france-on-tv-within-the-last-12-months-usa.

30 See Garrett Fagan, who views the allure of the Roman gladiatorial games social-psychologically: as a desire for violence and brutality that continues, despite historical and cultural differences, to the present day. *The Lure of the Arena: Social Psychology and the Crowd at the Roman Games* (Cambridge: Cambridge University Press, 2011), esp. 274–86.

31 Edgar refers to the "Dionysian" element of sports but only in the specific aesthetic sense, as "something akin to modernism in the arts" ("Aesthetics of Sport," 71).

32 For a critical review of philosophical attempts to ally sports with moral value, see Sigmund Loland, "Normative Theories of Sport: A Critical Review," in *The Ethics of Sport*, ed. Caplan and Parent, 6–18.

33 Edgar, "The Beauty of Sport" (101, 112–18), and "The Aesthetics of Sport" (81–2), both in *Sports, Ethics and Philosophy* 7, no. 1 (2013).

34 For an appeal to these and other ancient ideals, despite their continual manipulation and abuse, see Daniel A. Dombrowksi, *Contemporary Athletics and Ancient Greek Ideals* (Chicago: University of Chicago Press, 2009), esp. 7–9 and the chapter titled "The Process of Becoming Virtuous" (125–48).

PART II

Theoretical Perspectives

1 Sports/Allure

GRANT FARRED

The theory of allure, out of absolute (theoretical) necessity, has no proper disciplinary location. That is to say, it has no home, it does not belong in this realm of thought (let us name it "discipline") or that (that other "discipline," whatever that might be). That is to say, it is difficult to "trace" – in Jacques Derrida's sense, where the "trace" is understood as both a "remnant" (what remains, along the lines of "cinders"[1] or "ashes") and a "marking" (that mode of inscription that makes legible a line of thinking, of thought) – the "origins" of allure as a theoretical project. This chapter does not attempt either to provide a theoretical point of first articulation (we would be remiss to name it a "beginning") or to fix thinking on allure within a certain disciplinary orbit.

Instead, this chapter takes the "lack" (the lack of disciplinary "specificity" is precisely what "Sports/Allure" utilizes; revels in; we could even say exploits, more or less shamelessly) of a named disciplinary home as an open-ended invitation to reference and engage as many of the "fields" or modes of intellectual inquiry as possible, where allure constitutes an important part of the projects. Most importantly, and without seeking to resort to social-scientific epistemologies (it may in fact be that the theoretical argument, such as it is, stands determinedly against quantification or "proof" as the means through which allure as such can be grasped), this chapter theorizes allure in its relation to sport. This must be understood as part of the more encompassing work of thinking sport philosophically; that is, apprehending sport as being able to explicate philosophical concepts more eruditely – and passionately, one hastens to add – because of the visceral and thought-provoking ways in which sport animates philosophical concepts; it is through thinking sport that philosophical concepts obtain a new "life" and political saliency. To that end, this chapter uses the work of a range of thinkers, from Brian Massumi to Lauren Berlant and Elspeth Probyn, scholars who work in distinct but by no means disconnected registers, to provide an entrée for theorizing allure. That is, to offer an abstraction – the "theory" – that neither exists nor operates by itself but still enjoys a certain, always provisional and conditional, mind you, "sovereignty" (or, independence and singularity, we might say).

However, proffering this theorization, this thinking, is by no means allowed to disrupt or undermine the proclivity, my proclivity I should say, for infusing the theorization with explicit turns to moments in sport (or sport's history) or modes of being in relation to sport (especially, the experience of fandom). This chapter, as such, is entirely speculative. It roams theoretically wide, it plumbs the depths of fandom (it turns to the nominal fan in order to advance the argument or to "test" a particular way of thinking), and it imagines, loosely speaking, a discourse, a mode of thinking, that might do justice to the ways in which sport produces, experiences, and illuminates a concept such as allure. In strict but never too stringent terms, this chapter is a critique of the extant relations among these various modes of being in relation to sport. The affects, a theoretical debt this chapter happily acknowledges, that sport produces (how it makes fans, players, commentators, political figures, and so on and so forth feel) can only be properly or adequately comprehended if the relations among these various constituencies are recognized and an attempt to write the effect of these affects is undertaken. Risked, theoretically posited, in order to grasp, however imperfectly, how, why, and in what moments particularly, these relations work. And what kind of work it is they do. And do, one should add, with such repetitive force that they, at more than one level, demand to be thought, to be taken up as a philosophical difficulty or as a series of questions that sport poses to philosophy and challenges philosophy to address, to engage, to provide, however speculatively or concretely, answers for, answers that will, in their turn, invariably raise an entirely new set of inquiries. The answer lies in the problem.

Appropriate then, that we should begin our discussion with the question of relation.

A Theory of Relation

[T]here is no correspondence or conformity between quality and intensity. If there is a relation, it is of another nature.

– Brian Massumi[2]

The theory of allure, as thought with regard to sport, can only be understood as a matter of relation. So conceived, this raises Brian Massumi's proposition as, first, a "scientific" question: it is a precise query that asks, "in/a relation to what?"; and second, a categorical question. It frames an ontological inquiry that wonders about the "nature" of this relation. Constitutively, the question becomes: what makes up this relation, what are the various elements that combine to form this incommensurate or unequal relation between "quality and intensity?" Or, more directly for the purposes of this chapter, what is the relation between ethics and allure?

Historically, at stake is how this relation is established and how it is maintained. Massumi offers a key insight for sports fans, for whom the relation between "quality, intensity" and ethics might have a more visceral, everyday appeal. In this regard, Massumi's address might speak more immediately to fans than to theorists of sport, especially those theorists who are quantitatively inclined. As sports fans (and here I have in mind partisans rather than casual or fair-weather supporters) know only too well, the "intensity" of commitment to one's club or team often exceeds the "quality" that one's club possesses. That is, there is a disjuncture between the level of performance a group of players are "objectively" capable of and the ways in which they pour their metaphorical "hearts" out for their club either during a single game or over the course of a season. Given their druthers, fans would almost always go for "heart" over uncommitted talent.

Regarding inter-city football derbies (Glasgow Celtic and Rangers; Liverpool–Everton, Boca Juniors–River Plate, and so on) or long-standing rivalries, there is no necessary equivalence between the level of athletic performance (Was it a good game? Did the sides play well?) and the a priori political investment that characterizes, say, rugby matches between the All Blacks (New Zealand) and the Springboks (South Africa). In sports contests of this nature, "quality" can be entirely disarticulated from "intensity"; because of the history between the teams, the latter in fact matters infinitely more than the former.[3] (The only way for the players to show that they grasp the politically inflected affective consequences of the contest is to demonstrate it by playing with the requisite "intensity.") Understood as such, it is possible to posit "intensity" as an ethics (fidelity to a history; immersion in the lifeblood of a club or a nation; how the fan or the player is integrated into – the force of allure, we might say – the club or country that s/he is representing), but for the purposes of this chapter, the more pertinent line of inquiry turns on the relation between ethics and allure.

"Intensity," as such, is probably best apprehended historically. It is the sustained commitment, which can last over a lifetime or even for generations, to a particular sports institution. We might name such a commitment "loyalty"; or, if one were less generous, it could be labelled "pathology." After all, one has to be just a little deranged to remain faithful in the face of season after season of futility. In the American context, long-suffering fans of the Chicago Cubs baseball team best demonstrate this propensity, and as such, no one could have begrudged them their 2016 World Series title. If, as the wags say, "the Cubs are gonna lose again," then it was cause for universal joy when the Cubs finally broke their curse and triumphed. Still, this is where the domain of the pathological obtains, because no matter their record, Cubs fans have always continued to pack their home stadium, Wrigley Field. An entire culture has grown up around Cubs fandom: the seeming inevitability of losing, the famed curse of the goat, Murphy,[4] the unfortunate ability to snatch defeat from the jaws of victory, that sad, poetic promise to the future: "Wait 'til next year." It was, until 2016, a promise rooted less in expectation than in the postponement of this season's pain. It was an almost Sisyphean promise that was always, of course, girded by the knowledge, the inevitable expectation, that "next year" would be, as it had for so long been, much like this infernal year.

And then along came 2016, an important year if you were a Cubs fan in baseball or a Cleveland Cavaliers fan in basketball.[5] Might it then be only a little mischievous, a little naughty and playful (but never entirely playful, of course), to wonder out loud if pathology is the most ethical form of fandom? Who else keeps the faith as absolutely, as unwaveringly, as the pathological fan? Who else keeps hope alive so relentlessly, in the face of such daunting odds, in the face of such a cruel history? Is pathology the most extreme, but felicitous, form of fandom? Is the pathological fan the very incarnation of sports truth?

As loyal Cubs fan and octogenarian Ron Juffer phrases it, "Any team can have a bad century." Or, if you really want to be picky, it was a bad 108 years. Take that, you Cardinals fans. How does one argue against such a funny, self-indicting, unshakeable, and irrefutable logic? How does one not admire such loyalty? How does one not bequeath such intensity to one's offspring? It is only in this way, Hegel might suggest, that an absolute relation to the other (child, spouse, grandchildren, and so on) is established. Such is the intensity of pathos; such is the pathos of intensity; in the absolute fidelity of the Cubs fans, intensity meets its equal in pathos. This is nothing if not, as Jacques Lacan puts it, a "deeper dimension of analytical thought, work and technique that I am calling ethics."[6] To think the relation of the self to the other (football or baseball club; cricketing or rugby nation) through sport is the political "work" and the technical apparatus as such through which the "ethical," in Lacan's sense, is accessed; is achieved. It is ethical to do the work of thinking the relation, to render Massumi in a Lacanian discourse.

Cubs fans may be, in the United States, the very incarnation of the pathological/ethical power of allure, but they are by no means unique. (The pathological – unswerving loyalty, often flying in the face of the fact of losing, every year, for more than one hundred years – must be apprehended as the sports fan's deepest commitment to a constitutive truth: the decision, and the praxis that emanates from that decision, to remain faithful over the course of a lifetime to one team and one team only. No matter the psychic costs, regardless of the pain of defeat or the humiliations that are endured in the course of such a life. The ethicality of the pathological; the radical kernel of ethics lodged at the core of the pathological.) Not, that is, if we define allure as what it means to be drawn, by an unruly mixture of (1) personal overidentification: the self sees something of itself, whether this amounts to, as a certain brand of psychoanalysis would have it, projection or not, in the club or the team s/he supports, or whether this is wish fulfilment or desire or not; (2) the quirks of history: the fan "inherits" the team from a parent, a sibling, or another family member or a friend; or, the fan randomly picks a team; or, the fan is motivated by the politics that marks a team;[7] and, (3) geography: where location is sports destiny; born in Cleveland, there is no choice but to be a Browns, Indians, or Cavaliers fan. Or, to recognize the work of the dialectic, it is possible, out of a sense of native oppositionality, bloody-mindedness, or the commitment to difference for its own sake, that the fan could emerge as a response to all the extant forces, loyalties, histories, and predispositions that surround her or him. Out of such resistance, innocent or not, sports rebellion is born. All these factors, in some combination or another, bind the fan to a sports institution for life.

The force of allure is from the first understandable only as philosophical encounter. The force of allure is the "event" insofar as it signifies, in no uncertain terms, the declaration of fidelity. The first effect of the event is such that, in Alain Badiou's terms, in its "supplementarity"[8] it cannot be grasped as anything other than an overwhelming of the self. The force of allure, as will be discussed later, cannot be thought without some notion of "losing control"; that is, for the sports fan, with whom this chapter is primarily but not exclusively concerned, allure amounts to "giving the self up" to its "object." The fan cedes, routinely, her or his self to the football club, the cricket team, the basketball franchise, the national rugby side. The sports institution is the "object" that can in no way be understood as "inanimate." The team, the club, the franchise, "lives" because it is very much alive for the fan; it is, often, the very lifeblood of the fan. The requirement that the self give itself up is rarely considered a form of "sacrifice" for the fan. Rather, for the fan, "giving the self up" is more akin to deepening, strengthening, intensifying the commitment to its "object." Through "giving itself up," the self becomes, in fact, more bound to, more invested in, its object. Through the work of "giving itself up" the self becomes, if you will, more truly itself. The act of "giving oneself up" evokes Martin Heidegger's notion in *Was heißt Denken?* of being willing and able to "receive" thinking because one is already "open" and willing to open oneself up to thinking. In Heidegger's terms, all that remains is for the sport's *Sein*, the Being, the self that is made by allure, to "reach out and turn toward what desires to be thought."[9]

The Intimacy of Allure

When we talk about an object of desire, we are really talking about a cluster of promises we want someone or something to make to us and make possible for us. This cluster of promises could be embedded in a person, a thing, an institution, a text, a norm, a bunch of cells, smells, a good idea – whatever.

– Lauren Berlant[10]

In her theorization of affect,[11] Lauren Berlant offers an insight, one that is eminently and immediately recognizable to athletes and sports fans. Berlant argues that "whatever the *content* of the attachment is, the continuity of the form of it provides something of the continuity of the subject's sense of what it means to keep on living on[12] and to look forward to being in the world" (Berlant, 94). The "continuity of the form" is, of course, relationality of the self to that "object of desire" Berlant names a "promise." Sports fans, journalists, and theorists of sport are, needless to say, already intimate with Berlant's "person," which could be a favourite player or "institution," a favourite club, or even her "good idea." Transcribed into the terms of allure and sport, Berlant's "good idea," the *raison d'être* of fidelity to the club, can be thought as the politics of affiliation. Sport is replete with such "good ideas," from the Catholic/Protestant divide that has historically riven Glaswegian football to the deep nationalist investment that makes FC Barcelona, for players, fans, and Catalans the world over, "mes que un club," "More than a club," to the animus that has marked the baseball rivalry between the Boston Red Sox and the New York Yankees.

Indeed, so much rides on Berlant's formulation of the "promise," made by and to affect theory, that it is possible to posit allure, at least in this regard, as a form of bodily and psychic investment that cannot be quantified or even named properly. Allure cannot be measured: how does one quantify psychic investment? And so, towards that end, it must, out of conceptual necessity, be theorized. Allure must be given its own language so that a mode of inquiry can be produced that enables theorists to think what attracts players, fans, the viewing public, so powerfully to sport. To continue this imprecise mode of thinking, it remains possible to claim in regard to the allure of sport that "something happens" to us. Allure is that "something" beyond any metric of measurement that we make happen to ourselves, it is something that produces an affect in us, an affect that contains both emotional form and content while retaining a certain enigmatic inscrutability.

Understood as such, Massumi's critique of affect, that it is neither "activity nor passivity," is useful.[13] Not because allure is neither "active nor passive" – it is surely comprised of both in that we both do something and something happens to us because of our commitment to the promise – but because Massumi's designation allows us to locate allure in a zone of theoretical indetermination. Allure at once belongs to the broad field of affect theory and does not; and, as such, in order to think allure it has to be thought as an abstraction first. To begin with the question already offered: what is the form and content of allure?

Lack

Allure, as such, has a form deriving from the relation of not only, as we shall see, Self and Other, but also Self and Self. The more important recognition, however, might be that even if it is difficult to stipulate the formal structure of allure, it is unarguable that the form of allure is created out of affective content. Allure originates with the inexplicable force of attraction. Allure is that magnetic force that draws us, with or without our volition, towards another "body." What that body is, as Berlant makes clear, can take various shapes so that we might experience it in regard to a particular player, that team we name "ours," an icon or an institution. Call it "fatal attraction," if you will, because once the commitment is made, it is almost impossible to renege on that promise the Self made to itself.

Because of the imprecision of its theoretical apparatus, allure is always in search of a reliable, usable language that can describe and account for what the self is undergoing, is committing itself to, is immersed in, all without, and this is critical, anything like full authority over the self. In fact, it may be possible to argue that allure marks one of the limits of self-authorizing because allure *writes*, it refuses to be written. It is only possible to, in part, "author" one's relationship to allure, one is in part authored, guided, controlled by it; this is how "activity and passivity" functions in relation to allure. Any notion of agency, no matter how inflected by Foucault's critique of structure, belongs only marginally and tangentially to the experience of allure.

We give allure a language in the process of negotiating the relationship of the Self to this "body," to this force that participates in the process of defining the Self. Parenthetically, in this way, there is the temptation to understand allure as sovereign and as belonging foremost to itself; and, as such, to the Self. Such a notion of sovereignty would, of course, require the negation of the Self that can anticipate the re-emergence of the Self once it has "passed through" the encounter with the "object" of allure; here, the "object" does not point to a necessarily inanimate object such as the fan's club but serves rather as a way to designate the Other. Allure begins with or as an attraction to the Other, the object of desire.

However, the force of allure is most obviously manifested as a lack. Allure, in short, emerges out of what the Self does not possess: the Other has what the Self does not. As a lack, allure articulates as a painful athletic truth. It is the recognition that the body of the Other that we are attracted to, give ourselves to, possesses some capacity that we desired, or once desired but now acknowledge we never will possess. Fans will never, because of their athletic deficiencies, to phrase the matter cruelly, represent their favourite team; what they are, fans, is the most they'll ever be in relation to the object of their affection. The lack, as such, of the requisite athletic talent is what the fan intuitively, from the very beginning, already knows. Lack is what distinguishes the athlete from the fan: the one who plays from the one who pays to watch the athlete play. This is the facticity of constitutive athletic difference: A > B. *Entre nous*: between A (athlete) and B (fan) is the incontestable truth of athletic ability.

Here, rendered in the vernacular of sport, Berlant's promise might be posited as stipulating a set of talents and circumstances that we, as fans or amateur duffers, patently lack. These include (1) a set of skills such as dribbling, passing, batting, fielding; (2) a history that includes, no doubt, momentous victories and heroic defeats; and (3) a tradition that can also be understood as a mode of being – say, a way of playing, such as the Liverpool five-a-sides of the 1960s through the 1980s, and Barça's "tiki-taka" of the Pep Guardiola years for which the sublime touch of a Messi can stand as exemplar. There is also, to indulge just a little, the unselfish brilliance of a LeBron James, or Joe Montana's aptitude for making the right play at the right moment in the big game; not so big, maybe, as "The Catch" made by the late Dwight Clark in the dying moments of the 1982 NFC championship game. The ball, with fifty-eight seconds left, seemed destined for the clouds as Montana rolled to his right and released it under a barrage of pressure from the Dallas Cowboys defence; Clark's fingertip catch made it one of the most iconic moments in the history of sport. As fans we can talk all we want about "The Catch," but we can only dream of executing such a play in such a moment.

In these terms, then, allure must be figured as a form of attraction that requires something in excess of admiration. It demands the giving of the Self to this Other. The Self pledges itself to this other body or institution, it commits itself to this tradition in which the Self wants to be situated, it is the terms upon which this "new" relation is established. This is where allure and fandom might be said to conjoin, in Stuart Hall's sense of the conjuncture, and disaggregate: the fan is committed and as such is the subject who is in thrall to the object of his or her affection. The fan gives her- or himself over to this Other body out of a positive sense of affiliation grounded in lack. The Other has, too often in abundance, what the Self so patently and painfully lacks.

The Other is an athlete, a professional athlete. The Other possesses a range of talents that encompass everything from the ability to execute the crossover dribble like Allen Iverson to the fourth-quarter heroics of Michael Jordan. Temporally, then, it is possible to invoke Berlant's notion of "cruel optimism" as the "condition of maintaining an attachment to a problematic object in *advance* of its loss": we already know at an early age, too early maybe, not even the prospect of cruel optimism, because as fans we have come to the cruel realization about the Self as an athletic lack. Also, to reiterate lack as universality: the fan knows that her or his physical lack constitutes allure as the limit of what is possible for the fan for all time (Berlant, 94). The scratch golfer does not miraculously, out of nowhere, stride onto Augusta's Amen Corner and suddenly negotiate the twisting fairways and greens with Tiger Woods-like accuracy and ingenuity. To phrase this dialectically, allure is a form of expressed inexpressibility. Allure is the declarative, final word on the fan's athletic lack.

To render this lack formulaically: "I am < and so I give myself up in/ to this body, this other." It is at the meeting point of conjuncture and disaggregation that, we might say, the ethical question, when it is raised as a question of Self, or, more precisely, as the question of "in-voluntary" submission, becomes intensely political: what is at stake, what kind of violence (Zizou's *coup de boule* in Berlin 2006), and, yes, beauty (Jake deGrom's tailing fastball, John Olerud's swing, truly a Keatsian thing), the sublime (for me, John Barnes's goal at the Maracana in June 1986), in the giving of the Self? What is the cost of identifying so closely, over the course of lifetime, with the body of the Other? What is evinced in writing the event of this Other? What is revealed in so admiring it?

The Governing Question: What Is the Political Cost of Allure?

In response to this question, to the series of interrogatives enumerated, there can be only one answer. Allure is, if not autoimmune, then auto-generative. It produces, because of its inveterately dialectical nature, because of the tension that is endemic to the meeting point, its own discomfiture: that is, there is already incipiently an ethical component. One cannot give oneself to a body without drawing into question that body, as well as the body of the Self, and the act of giving up of the Self.[14] There is, it could be argued, a direct correlation between the intensity of the commitment, which we might name admiration for the object or the force of being drawn to that object, and the intensity of the ethical: the more intense the commitment, the more potentially self-indicting or self-affirming (that is, if lack is understood as constitutive of affirmation) the philosophical and political difficulties that emerge from that relationship. (How does the self stand in relation to the truth of its commitment? To the truth of its affective and political life, which might very well be marked by transgressions such as racism, homophobia, violence, to name just three?) As we well know, every affiliation, every expression of fidelity to (fandom), to this other body, is fraught; and it seems to be fraught on an almost daily or game-by-game basis.

The true force of allure is, finally, a matter for thinking. Allure can never stand by itself; it can, as it properly should, overwhelm us in moments, on the occasion of a historic victory or a life-shattering defeat, but it can never suppress our capacity for thinking. Sport, in this way, is exemplary. No other mode of life is predicated so intensely and so personally on the event: on the impossibility of knowing that we watch for the unexpected, again, the *coup de boule*, the Suárez bite followed by the Suárez bite followed by the Diego Costa bite. We know that we will have to think sport and our deep psychic investment in the "object" of pathology, our love, our loyalty, again and again. We will have to theorize it, to make sense of it, to explain to ourselves, to, at the very least, raise your hands, Liverpool fans, Denver Bronco fans, Chelsea fans, Sidney Crosby fans, why it is that the objects of our allure do what it is they did. Why did Suárez bite Branislav Ivanovic and bring such shame on the club and, in a later moment, his national team Uruguay? Why is Sidney Crosby so widely reviled, except by those in Pittsburgh and Canada, of course, as a cheap player?

Allure is that mode of thinking sport that emerges out of the most intimate relationship, that bond born and forged in love, admiration, and self-definition, which borders precariously on self-sacrifice and rationalization of the most painful and often extreme variety. Sport, we can conclude, has the power to "make" subjects of us, but it can also, as is true of all forms of autoimmunity, threaten (or affirm) our very Being. Allure is that articulation of autoimmunity that has the capacity to entirely undo the Self, so much so that a catalogue of inquiries almost invariably follows. Questions such as: What has allure done to me? What have I allowed it to do to me? What have I done to, with, myself?

In his theorization of affect, Massumi refers to the tendency of self-abnegation as "irreducible excess" that emerges out of the "lines of action [allure] and reaction [what I am naming 'thinking']."[15] In the following way, at least, allure is different, in no small measure because of how it compels – even as we rely on relationality and its first cousin, the dialectic – a theorization on its own terms. If, as has been argued, allure is marked by and has its own magnetic force, if allure draws us towards it in full cognition of our inveterate lack, then we must acknowledge the following: in return, allure demands, asks for, nothing and everything. We do not need to "do," as such, anything; which is why, one can argue, it is simultaneously different from and commensurate with, say, ideology: no submission of Self is required, at first glance, but allure is nothing without some mode of submission, that is, the Self subscribes to some mode of Being, to some set of prescriptions about that being's Being.

The figure who is the object of allure (that figure who inspires desire, loyalty, the desire to emulate – the self wants to play like LeBron James or Kyrie Irving – in the self) has no prefiguring, hence its inexplicability. This figure, whom I have also proffered as the object of affection (and, as such, following the argument about desire, of intense psychic investment), asks for nothing, yet there is nothing it does not ask for. It can be, but it does not need to be, a showman; it can be a highly successful club or franchise, but that is by no means an absolute demand. We know this as the allure of fandom whose first principle is absolute, incorrigible, and often frustrating fidelity. One is a fan for a range of reasons, some of them entirely subject to the force of *logos* such as legacy when we inherit our fandom from a parent or loved one; or geography: it is where we live and grew up. We are fans because of the allure of success, romance, or a special player, and that player can be talented, a failure, a rogue, or just plain average. In other instances *logos* does not apply and we cannot, for the life of us, account for our choice, but we are nevertheless absolutely bound by it. In this way, again, allure is intellectually auto-generative: we must think allure, at least, say, the figure or logic of allure, again, as if for the first time.

Allow me to make this point by way of Massumi's conception of the body as a "situated site" because it is instructive. Massumi argues that the "body doesn't just absorb pulses or discrete simulations; it infolds *contexts*, it infolds volitions and cognitions that are nothing if not situated."[16] The body is only part, less than half, I would say, of the storehouse of allure; the other half is entirely thought: and thought is absolutely subject to critique, to our thinking our response, our accounting for, our argument with ourselves and others about our allure. Allure is in itself a critique of, very narrowly conceived, our "passions." Or, as Bergson puts it, the "brain is the center of indetermination; on consciousness as subtractive and inhibitive."[17] The brain is the very source of our "not knowing," as it were, which makes it possible to render, at the risk of repetition, allure as the attraction and the expression of inexplicable attraction, in part non-volitional. It is the condition of sport. There is no relationship to sport that can ever claim complete control over the object of attraction. We might call it fandom, we might name it a pathology or fanaticism, but, let us be honest, it has only one proper name and that is love. It is for this reason that we can understand the politics of allure as the inability to predetermine, articulate, explicate our inability to renounce our response to the phenomenon (that psychic construct at the core of our political and affective beings): our first response to the phenomenon is always love. And it is love understood as precisely a phenomenon, which, as Jean-Luc Nancy reminds us, is "not appearance" but the "lively transport of self and leap into manifest existence."[18] It is love alone, the absolute relation of self to self, that can provide a true accounting for why it is that you support the team you do, or the player you admire, or why it is you invest your entire psychic and often material life in this institution; rather than, say, that one, yes that one over there, the one to whom you are morally opposed. (Love is the act of making "manifest" the self's fidelity to the other; love is the unalterable commitment to the other, that commitment that began, in one way or another, with the "leap," a term whose Heideggerian history emerges with a new vivacity in Nancy's – Hegelian – argument.) Provoke the fan in this way, and it would be best to get out of the way of the answer. Under such provocation, the fan cannot be held accountable for their response. It is a response to which I am fully sympathetic. Don't poke the tiger in search of *logos*. Ask any true partisan and you'll get the same response: Bad idea, wrong strategy and wrong subject, in both senses of the term.

In short, allure demands another relation, what might be conceived as the simultaneous twofold. The relation to the Self and to the Other, to the Other through the abnegation/submission of the Self.

Part of the relation is that it puts us in touch with ourselves and each other, no doubt, in an entirely novel, unpredictable, self-fulfilling and self-sacrificing way. The language of allure is, as such, a blend of the theory of affect, fandom, and what we might name, however inadequately, because it has the benefit of pointing us in the right direction, popular sports philosophy. The latter is a strange, potentially volatile mix of the peculiar language of love and sacrifice, the ontology of attraction and self-interrogation, always haunted by questions such as Why am I doing this? and How often or how long will I endure this?

It is impossible, for this reason, to "originate" allure. It is something that we come into, that overwhelms us, that we give ourselves to; and, to use the language of courtship, dating it, as such, seems much like a search for fool's gold, only much more fun and, yes, at least as pathological. That is why, as Massumi says, affect puts one "outside of oneself" so that it constitutes the "very point at which one is most intimately and unshareably in contact with oneself and one's vitality."[19] Again, we know, broadly speaking, what is happening and why it is happening, but we do not know exactly how this transmission from self to other is effected; or, how we effect it even though we may have only a basic grasp of what the effects of allure are.

In thinking allure we are left to remark on what happens to the boundaries, already taken apart so ruthlessly and incisively by deconstruction, between Self and Other, so that allure introduces us, once more, to the utter porousness of the world, the infinite permeability between Self and Other, the unforgiving transparency and opaqueness of the Self.

To recall the epigraph from Lauren Berlant: "When we talk about an object of desire, we are really talking about a cluster of promises we want someone or something to make to us and make possible for us. This cluster of promises could be embedded in a person, a thing, an institution, a text, a norm, a bunch of smells, a good idea – whatever."[20] Allure is, finally, nothing but the most intense relation to the Self that is founded upon an incalculable, inarticulable, reaching out to the Other in the hope of rearticulating the Self. That Other who is at the very core of the self's affective life, that Other who so indelibly marks love, limit, passion and lack, all in equal, or, unequal, measure.

NOTES

1 See Jacques Derrida's *Cinders*, translated by Ned Lukacher (Minneapolis: University of Minnesota Press, 2014), in which Derrida draws on the politics of the Shoah, or, to phrase the matter differently, uses the Holocaust

to confront that which is, despite history's best efforts, impossible to erase. It is also, of course, closely connected to Derrida's efforts to think death – "there are cinders here"; "cinders there are"; "*il y a là cendre*": *Cinders*, 3.

2 Brian Massumi, "The Politics of Systems and Environments, Part II," *Cultural Critique* 31 (Autumn 1995): 83–109.

3 As sports fans know, there is no necessary correlation between the quality of an athletic contest and the quality of the performance. The intensity can derive from a range of other sources, not least of which are political ones. The intra-city rivalry between Glasgow Celtic and Glasgow Rangers is riven with a history of religious conflict, pitting Catholics (Celtic) against Protestants (Rangers), and the intra-*autonomista* rivalry between Real Madrid (Castilla) and FC Barcelona (Catalunya) incarnates a history of political antipathy that can, for the Catalans, be traced back to the eighteenth century. Cricket matches can be equally fraught – and politically freighted – affairs, grounded in religion (India–Pakistan), a battle for regional supremacy (again, India–Pakistan), or the ever-enduring aftermath of colonialism (England–Australia). No matter the quality of the fare on display, the political stakes are always high in such contests, guaranteeing a certain level of intensity.

4 To wit: in the 2015 National League pennant series between the New York Mets and the Chicago Cubs, the Mets player who was most responsible for beating the Cubs (4–0, it turns out) was Daniel Murphy – as if, that is, to add contemporary insult to historic injury. Only the Cubbies, one imagines, could be so cruelly treated – taunted – by fate. The goat of old had returned as a big-hitting second baseman.

5 The Cavaliers' NBA championship was, of course, massively overdetermined by the city of Cleveland's athletic dearth. No championship since 1964, when the Browns won one. Mainly, however, there was the matter of it being delivered by the commitment and loyalty of a native son, a certain LeBron James, who had returned from Miami in order to secure precisely this outcome. After a failed 2015 finals, Cleveland rallied from 3–1 down to bring the city – or "Northeast Ohio," as everyone kept referring to it – what it so badly wanted. Loyalty, passion, love, and geography, all constituents of allure; all of which, we might say, lured LeBron back to his native land – Northeast Ohio.

6 Jacques Lacan, *The Ethics of Psychoanalysis: 1959–1960,* bk 7, ed. Jacques-Alain Miller, trans. Dennis Porter (New York: W.W. Norton, 1992), 203.

7 It is understood here that "politics" as such includes within its ambit what can be named "progressive," "retrograde," or worse. "Politics" then is best conceived as the power of affiliation – the force of commitment to the team, the unrelenting force that inspires loyalty, in the many forms such loyalty may assume.

8 See Alain Badiou's *Ethics: An Essay on the Understanding of Evil*, trans. Peter Hallward (New York: Verso, 2001).

9 See Martin Heidegger's *Was heißt Denken?*, especially "Lecture I," for a discussion of the importance of "receiving" and being ready to receive thinking. Heidegger, *What Is Called Thinking?*, trans. Fred D. Wieck and J. Glenn Gray (New York: Harper and Row), 1968.

10 Lauren Berlant, "Cruel Optimism," in *The Affect Theory Reader*, ed. Melissa Gregg and Gregory J. Siegworth (Durham: Duke University Press, 2010). · Berlant develops her argument more fully in her monograph of the same title. See also Lone Bertelsen and Andrew Murphie's essay, "An Ethics of Everyday Infinities and Powers: Félix Guattari on Affect and the Refrain," in *The Affect Theory Reader*. Bertelsen and Murphie's essay is especially useful for raising the question of how capital manifests itself in relation to affect, an issue that has purchase in considering the relationship between allure and sport. What is, to phrase the matter bluntly, the cost of allure? How much does our partisanship cost? What is our contribution as partisans to the machines of capital? Some of these difficulties about the politics of affect are raised most adroitly in work on shame – that is, shame as an affect. In this regard, see Eve Kosofsky Sedgwick and Adam Frank's essay, "Shame in the Cybernetic Fold," *Critical Inquiry* 21, no. 2 (Winter 1995): 496–522; and Elspeth Probyn's *Blush: Faces of Shame* (Minneapolis: University of Minnesota Press, 2005).

11 I must acknowledge, as is surely patently obvious by now, that this essay draws on the work done in affect theory by figures such as Berlant and Massumi. The effect of thinking affect, as it were, proved useful in working towards a theory of allure, a field, allure, in which it is much more difficult to encounter a theorizing *qua* theorizing; theorizing, that is, for its own intellectual sake.

12 There is a rhetorical redundancy that speaks affectively through the repetition of the preposition "on."

13 Massumi, "The Politics of Systems and Environments, Part II," 86.

14 Cf. Hans Ulrich Gumbrecht's discussion of "the body" and fandom in this volume, "'Allure' Constrained by 'Ethics'? How Athletic Events Have Engaged Their Spectators."

15 Massumi, "The Politics of Systems and Environments, Part II," 87.

16 Ibid., 90.

17 Quoted in Massumi, "The Politics of Systems and Environments, Part II," 92.

18 Jean-Luc Nancy, *Hegel: The Restlessness of the Negative*, trans. Jason Smith and Steven Miller (Minneapolis: University of Minnesota Press, 2002), 33.

19 Massumi, "The Politics of Systems and Environments, Part II," 96.

20 Ibid., 93.

2 "Allure" Constrained by "Ethics"? How Athletic Events Have Engaged Their Spectators

HANS ULRICH GUMBRECHT

Whoever tries to describe, with serious intellectual ambition, the multiple dimensions in which athletic events have engaged their spectators will soon discover a surprising lack of both open-minded and closely considered positions from the past to connect with. For if the history of modern sports, as an institutional continuity, began around 1800, with professional boxing events in London and with new forms of physical education at exclusive British colleges, its trajectory has been accompanied, for more than two hundred years, by a steady flow of ill-humoured and condescending commentaries from intellectuals. For them, until recently, sports were the absolute Other, and a despicable Other at that. There were a few exceptions to this rule, among them some authors who desperately tried to be "original" by going against the mainstream of their peers (like the German playwright Bertolt Brecht, who did his best to convince the world that boxing[1] really mattered to him), or representatives of different ideological stances who wanted sports to function as a medium of moral betterment (as was the case with the soaring vision of a cosmopolitan athletic elite that inspired the Baron de Coubertin[2] to found the modern Olympics, or with Carl Diem, a teacher of classics who went on to become the protagonist in charge of inventing the rituals[3] for the Nazi Games of 1936).

Much more abundant and repetitive (and at least equally shallow) have been the mostly left-wing discourses of a "political" critique of sports. Three obsessively recycled motifs are dominant among them: the view of sports as a spectacle essential for the production of bourgeois ideologies, that is, for keeping their fans in a state of "false consciousness"; the view that sports are an alienating activity, one that averts the viewers' attention from their own "objective" concerns and interests; and, finally, the image of sports as a cash-making machine of capitalist exploitation, based both on overpriced tickets to be paid by humble fans and on skimming off the larger part of the revenues produced by performing athletes. Not one of these accusations is specific to what we call "sports" – nor did any of them ever provoke the true excitement of intellectual innovation.

But now, within only a few years, the tide has turned, both dramatically and grotesquely. Back in the late twentieth century a young academic or an emerging artist was often expected, in this context of his or her professional environment, to keep mum about any possible passion for an ongoing World Cup or national championship; today, the situation is reversed: not exhibiting at least a certain degree of sports awareness makes people look antisocial and hopelessly old-fashioned. This change in attitude does not seem to be a response to any explicit intellectual shift or progress. A palpable embarrassment, however, surrounds the now inevitable question about the intellectual merits or the legitimacy of this new compulsory fascination. For lack of better answers, intellectuals claim to be talking about sports as a symptom of contemporary social structures or of ongoing social change; as a paradigm for a new type of economy; as an expression of national or regional identity; or, quite pretentiously, as a practice to be improved upon by the contributions of their thinking. All the while, the most visible and least artificial relationship between sports and their spectators hardly ever gets mentioned. I am of course referring to the sheer pleasure of watching sports, of sports as a modality of aesthetic experience, which is its most popular modality today. The appearance of words like "allure" and "fascination" may be quite telling in this context, for on the one hand they evoke the raw and often irresistible attraction of athletic events for so many millions of spectators, while on the other they keep sports at a distance from a certain connotation of exclusiveness attached to the concepts of philosophical aesthetics.

Where does this apparent need for a distance between aesthetics and sports come from? Why is it so difficult to take seriously the pleasure of watching sports? Why does such a question have the ring of an oxymoron? Why is it so difficult to say that we enjoy going to the stadium? My best guess is that many intellectuals are still struggling with a heritage rooted in the nineteenth century, a time when aesthetic experience and its intentional objects quite literally developed into a secular version of those sacred functions previously covered by religious rituals. Even today, we tend to breathe deeply and to feel elevated during moments of aesthetic experience – and this specific status may well be the reason why many of us still have a hard time associating aesthetic experience with those proverbial fans from the supposedly lower educational or financial strata who fill the stadiums (although rising ticket prices are now beginning to exclude such fans from stadiums). At the same time, I imagine that those old-style fans, paradoxically for identical reasons, would show a similar resistance to being associated with aesthetic experience.

This strange situation – that an aesthetic experience does not want to admit to its own existence – has the potential to result in an additional – aesthetic – quality. For if athletes and spectators in general are part of these events of aesthetic experience and do not demonstrate the otherwise typically "dignified" attitude, we can say that, quite often, they embody grace, in the sense of a specific touch of beauty belonging to those who are not aware of it. This might also explain why athletic events that have an explicit "aesthetic component," such as gymnastics, diving, and figure skating, have never been among the most popular sports.

Our initial reflection triggered by the surprising degree of resistance to a serious and unprejudiced way of thinking about sports of course does not yet fully account for the – spontaneously plausible – intuition regarding their role as objects of aesthetic experience. Are there really parallels between watching a baseball match and listening to a Beethoven symphony? And what, precisely, is it about a baseball game or a track-and-field competition that so fascinates us, in the literal sense of freezing our entire apparatus of attention? I will begin my answer to this question by explaining, step by step and with some conceptual rigour, how the specific phenomena behind the allure of sports indeed correspond to some of the most canonical descriptions of aesthetic experience. Like all other forms of aesthetic experience, watching sports has had a multitude of impacts on spectators' everyday lives. We can refer to this impact as the "ethics" of sports (in the most open sense of the concept) – and these ethics tend to have a potentially stifling effect on the allure of sports as soon as the open variety of their effects undergoes any transformation into explicit sets of values and rules of behaviour with normative claims. Two chapters in the present volume – Wolf Kittler's analysis of gymnastics as training for war and Sarah Panzer's documentation of the reception of Japanese martial arts in Germany between the two world wars – illustrate, from different historical angles, that long-term tension between the allure and the ethics of sports.[4]

Over the past few decades, however, the status of sports as a specific (and specifically informal) enclave for aesthetic experience seems to have undergone a deep transformation in the larger socio-historical context. Almost unnoticed, the roles of the athlete and of the spectator as well as the status of aesthetic experience have become gradually less socially eccentric than they had been in the early nineteenth century.

This change may account for the new, increasingly central position of sports in present-day societies and for a different attitude among intellectuals; furthermore, it has made the athlete and the spectator less exceptional and more paradigmatic figures in the present day, thus easing the traditional tension between the allure and the ethics of sports. This indeed is the observation and the thesis that I will try to describe and to comment on towards the end of this chapter.

Athletico-Aesthetic Dimensions

Given how infinitely far from sports Immanuel Kant's everyday life must have been, it is astonishing, not to say funny, that the three central features comprising his concept of "aesthetic judgment" fully converge with the involvement of our cognitive apparatus when we are in the role of sports spectators. First, what Kant refers to as the "disinterestedness" of the aesthetic judgment is its distance from our everyday intentions and concerns, a distance synonymous with what the eighteenth century began to describe as "aesthetic autonomy" (and structurally similar to the status of religious sanctuaries as typical sites of athletic competition in classical antiquity, as Sofie Remijsen[5] shows in her chapter in this volume). We care intensely that our teams win – yet no one's livelihood or personal reputation depends on it. Second, we have no quantitative or clear conceptual criteria for what strikes us as beautiful or sublime in a moment of classic aesthetic experience – or in sports. A high-scoring game is not necessarily a good game, for example, and there is no evidence or consensus regarding which qualities of a boxing event we find more impressive than others. Finally, and despite this lack of objective criteria, it is difficult for us to imagine that anyone could not agree with how we see and evaluate an artwork – or, for that matter, an athletic performance. They both presuppose and thus require a consensus of taste.[6]

Another perspective that is often implied in speaking about "aesthetic experience" has to do with a specific conception of its object of reference (we may therefore call this angle "ontological") and also with why aesthetic experience did not start to become a separate dimension in society before early modernity. Only from that time on did human self-conception and our relation to the objects of the world became predominantly spiritual within European culture, meaning that men began to see themselves as outside observers and interpreters of their physical environment, even while the (mostly spatial) relationship between human bodies and their material environments was increasingly bracketed. Ever since (and until recently), we have been calling "aesthetic" and considered exceptional those situations where the material dimension of an object of experience seems to impose itself on our attention and to exist in oscillation with our interpretation of it. When we listen to a song or when we concentrate on a painting, these acts are more complex than the mere deciphering of what the song or the painting may "mean" – for they include a focus on the sensory perception of their sound and their colour respectively. The same is true for our relationship with sports. Some movements of a player in a certain position will fulfil specific functions for his team that we can identify – and they will give him an individual position within the game. At the same time, however, we entertain a spatial relationship and a corporeal affinity with the athletes whom we watch – and this is precisely what has made their status eccentric within the mind- and interpretation-centred world of modernity.

A third dimension of the role of sports spectator refers to our psyche. I like to associate this with the legendary butterfly swimmer Pablo Morales, who once spontaneously described his attachment to sports as "the desire of being lost in focused intensity." These words from an athlete seem to subsume, quite perfectly, the experience of the spectators. "Being lost" of course corresponds to the situation of "aesthetic autonomy." But the spectator is also "intensely focused," which means that she expects a certain type of movement or event whose specific form she does not yet know – and this expectation can make her existence more intense, that is, more incisive, fuller, and more captivating than other moments of life. The appearance of the yet unknown play or movement may take quite long to happen (as is, for example, quite normal in baseball games and even part of their specific beauty) – and it may not happen at all. If, however, such an appearance occurs, we often call it "epiphanic," because what we perceive is embodied and will only happen suddenly, that is, without the frames of predictability that characterize most of our everyday lives. But how can we describe the objects of our attention that are specific to sports and that, by showing themselves, provoke aesthetic judgment? How are they related to certain "ethical" effects that the aesthetic experience of sports may produce in our everyday lives, outside the margins of aesthetic autonomy?

Athletic Events and Their Forms

What we see in athletic events is of course always and invariably human behaviour – but human behaviour experienced under the premise of aesthetics, and that means behaviour not only (or mainly) interpreted in terms of the possible intentions or strategies of those who are embodying it, but also perceived as presence, that is, as behaviour that relates to other bodies and to other material objects in space. As for its motivation, athletic behaviour is typically driven by a convergence of "agōn" (competitiveness) and "arete" (self-improvement); the *agōn* and *arete*, however, are set apart ("aesthetic autonomy," "being lost") from everyday interests and intentions. As for the forms of behaviour we associate with sports, I don't believe there is any natural or primary selection. In other words, under the premise of aesthetic autonomy and within the oscillation of *agōn* and *arete*, any behaviour can be perceived as "sports." But over the centuries a broad variety of different events have emerged, received specific resonance, and thus come to represent the complex phenomenon of sports as we know it, a phenomenon always supplemented and changed by a steady flow of innovations (recently, it appears, such innovations have occurred above all in winter sports).

All of these different athletic events are staging bodies in multiple situations and under different rules – producing different types of competition and drama, with subsequent variations in spectator interests and in the modes of participation, and whose only common denominator, besides a broad and rather incoherent range of "ethical" effects, is indeed a specific intensity that one feels while watching sports. As I just said, there is neither a limited range of possible athletic events nor a basic formula that one might consider to be their foundational matrix. In order to illustrate the variety in play here, and without any claim to completeness, I will briefly describe a few of them. Only since the mid-nineteenth century have team sports begun to occupy the international centre stage of athletic events, and I believe that at the core of the attention they provoke is less the winning or the losing of the two opposing teams (or those short moments that seem to "count," such as goals, touchdowns, or baskets) and more the beauty of individual plays. Beautiful plays can be described as the emergence of forms consisting of different bodies in movement, that is, forms articulating themselves against the resistance of the other team (its "defence"); forms that are also events because we always seem to see them for the first time and can never know ahead of time whether they will actually happen; forms, finally, that begin to vanish from the moment they begin to appear. In the end, we will always enjoy or at least appreciate a game with many beautiful plays – even if our favourite team is losing. Being on a team and performing beautiful plays cannot of course fail to have an ethical impact on those who play and on those who are watching. That said, there is empirical evidence that, when turned into a coherent and explicit structure of normative rules of behaviour, "team spirit" will yield neither success nor beauty – as shown by the flagrant pre-1989 failure of the Communist states, which wanted specifically to excel, according to their ideology, in team sports.

By contrast, boxing, wrestling, and other confrontational sports are certainly not about the emergence of beautiful plays. One part of their fascination without a doubt lies in the exhibition of violence (under conditions of mutual agreement that make violence largely unproblematic). But rather than producing the much-feared effect of giving to violence an aura of normalcy in everyday life, there is evidence in the history of these sports that what spectators most admire about them (and profit the most from) is the athletes' capacity to face physical threats that could be lethal for them. Inevitably, the legends of the greatest boxers of all time include great moments of defeat – like those suffered by Muhammad Ali, Jack Dempsey, and Marcel Cerdan.

The allure of boxing is again different from those events – mainly in track-and-field – where an individual body tries to maximize its efficiency in relation to a function that remains strictly within the world of sports: throwing a javelin, jumping high, and running fast are sports and can become beautiful to the degree that they are disconnected from practical purposes – exactly like the eighteenth-century running races described by Rebecca von Mallinckrodt in this volume,[7] and, by contrast, very different from the military function of gymnastics in early-nineteenth-century Germany. Or consider horseback riding, car racing, and shooting as events that converge in the structure of a human body trying to achieve an always precarious balance with an animal body or a complex technological device. It is a balance that cannot be achieved by the absolute will to dominate and control, but only through a much more subtle negotiation between dominance, on the one side, and, on the other, the adaptation of one's own body to an animal body or to a technological array.

I end here, although, as I said, we are far from having covered the full range of athletic events. What remains stunning above all is their dynamic diversity – and the corresponding variety of their potential ethical effects. If we go back for a moment to Kant's canonical description of the aesthetic judgment, then we can further ask, using his concepts: to which of the two general modalities of aesthetic experience do athletic events seem to have a greater affinity: to the sublime or to the beautiful? The sublime, as the more popular (and more highly esteemed) option today, refers to those objects of attention that, during certain moments, can become overwhelming for us. The beautiful, by contrast, is defined as "purposiveness without representation of an end," that is, as an object or movement that looks functional although, due to aesthetic autonomy, it does not have a functional place in the everyday world. All sports fans of course remember some breathtaking, overwhelming, and thus sublime moments that they experienced in the stadium. In the long run, however, I believe that the modality of the beautiful dominates the sublime in sports. For the beautiful ("purposiveness without purpose") has an affinity with the basic condition of most athletic events, as being staged around different intrinsic purposes – purposes that are all suspended from the everyday world, outside aesthetic autonomy.

Likewise, all athletic events have their intrinsic temporalities that set them apart, as forms with a beginning and an end ("sixty minutes," "five sets," "six attempts" etc.), from the endlessly running everyday time. Each specific temporality of course produces specific temporal economies that athletes must take into account and that they can use in more or less sophisticated ways. From this persepctive, athletic events are similar to most other – religious, juridical, or political – rituals in human culture. A clear awareness and economy of time, therefore, is essential for those who want to win. Yet I do not see any single or specific aspect of temporality that brings together all types of sports and separates them from all other rituals.

Finally, is there anything that we would call an "ugly athletic event" – as opposed to the beauty expected (unknowingly or in full awareness) when we go to the stadium? In some sports, we do speak of "ugly fouls" – but in such cases we are referring to the intention of an athlete to hurt another athlete (or to accept this risk) rather than to any specific feature in his body movement. By contrast, a pass in a team sport may not reach its targeted goal, or a gymnastic routine may not manage to embody the form demanded – yet we would not call them "ugly." If, however, an athletic performance ultimately does not provide the type of form or the type of drama for whose epiphany we have been waiting "in focused intensity," then we will be disappointed and say that our time in the stadium was boring, tedious, or flat – even if our favourite athlete or our favourite team ended up winning (and even if we learned something practical from their behaviour).

History

Is it possible to explain why, around 1800, the development of modern sports started to take place on different levels, after almost two millennia during which, since the vanishing of Greek and Roman antiquity described by Sofie Remijsen, sports had occupied a comparatively marginal position in different societies? We certainly don't have a broadly accepted answer to this question. But it may be worth imagining a link between the beginning of modern sports and the emergence, around 1800, of a new collective frame of mind that we normally refer to as the "historical world view." In this new attitude towards the world and in its discourses, the purely consciousness-based human self-image, as it has been developing since early modernity, found its ultimate institutional consolidation. So we can speculate, in the first place, that a more intense allure of watching and of practising sports might have been a non-programmatic reaction to, and compensation for, a way of everyday life that, in a growing number of social contexts, was becoming almost exclusively spiritual, to the neglect of the corporeal. Another innovation related to the historical world view was a future that appeared to be an open horizon of possibilities, a horizon that men believed they could shape. Based upon *agōn* and *arete*, sports had always presupposed this type of open future as its internal structure – but we can speculate that its appeal in a much larger social context may have helped bring sports into a culturally central position. After all, betting on the outcome of athletic events – which amounts to reacting to their open future – became part of the modern phenomenology of sports, right from the start.

It is within the framework of this new historical world view that sports developed during the nineteenth and early twentieth centuries in Europe and in America, and subsequently began to spread all over the world to become a truly global set of rituals. But as I believe that the historical world view is no longer the dominant frame for our cultures today (let alone the only one), I want to ask whether we can identify an impact, on sports, of such a possible transformation in our cultural frame conditions. At least within our everyday existence, we no longer presuppose the future to be an open horizon of possibilities that we can shape. Rather, our new future seems to be occupied by multiple threats that are slowly (or not so slowly) coming towards us. At the same time – and partly due to new electronic technologies of knowledge storage – the past, more than ever before, seems to be invading the present. Between this aggressive past and the new congested future, our present seems to be expanding into a broad dimension that contains absolutely everything and thus confronts us, collectively and individually, with a new, unheard of degree of complexity. For the first time since the Middle Ages, we no longer see ourselves as pure minds confronting and interpreting the world from outside. Rather, we feel surrounded by (and part of) that ever broadening and ever more complex present, and we thus try to reintegrate, both practically and theoretically, the body into our self-image. Early-morning jogging as well as the contemporary intellectual attempts to bring together the neuro-sciences and philosophy could be symptoms of this ongoing change.

As for sports, the new temporality seems to have only accelerated and strengthened the expansion and allure of athletic culture as it had begun to emerge around 1800. But this change may also have modified the premises under which we practise and watch sports. If the aware-ness of having and of being a body is now becoming less exceptional again, then athletes should become more paradigmatic for our contem-porary self-understanding. At the same time, the new broadening pres-ent, in its overwhelming complexity, provides us with a new freedom and with more choices of behaviour. While this increases our agency and our power over the world, it may also trigger an unprecedented existential desire for situations and institutions that give us security, for situations and institutions to hold on to, for moments in which we are exempted from the freedom and burden of choice. Without any doubt, being part of a crowd in a stadium belongs to these moments.

In other words, both from the athletes' side and from the side of the spectators, sports may appear closer today to our self-reference and to our existential concerns than they used to. Although nobody has yet thought through this historical transformation in its full complexity and in all its consequences, it may explain why the allure of sports has only grown and become more central than ever before. But this new intensity of athletic allure may also be less distant from our everyday practice as an ethical dimension than ever before. Perhaps the insist-ence on keeping sports separate from politics and from the economy, for all of its good intentions, is no longer really adequate, as sports have developed to the point that they are positively intertwined with our everyday lives, rather than autonomous from those lives. All of these dimensions are in flux now – but it is still impossible to see where ex-actly this complex movement may lead us.

Athletico-Aesthetic Dimensions, Changing

As the awareness of having and being a body is becoming less eccentric, we no longer find it to be out of the democratic order, for example, if a gold medallist profits from her fame to run for an office in politics; nor does the transition from a world-class career in sports back into normal life appear as precarious and as difficult as it used to. Without being its one and only "cause," electronic technology once again appears to play a complex role here, a role of accentuating and enforcing certain effects in this process. On the one hand, it has pushed to an ultimate limit the long-term development towards a lopsidedly mind-based form of human existence, by making a fusion between consciousness and software the predominant working situation in many (if not in the majority of) contemporary professions. This status produces a broader desire than ever for activities that involve and engage our bodies and thus accentuates the allure of sports. At the same time, the quantitative leap in computational power, together with the push towards a recuperation of our existence's physical dimension, has profoundly changed our relationship to the material and natural environment. There is no comparison, for example, between our present capacity for predicting and even, to a certain degree, manipulating the weather and what was possible in this context only a few decades ago. Although it may seem strange for a technology-mediated transformation, I think we have become endlessly more "familiar with" (and also much more attuned to changes in) our environment than in the past, we have indeed rediscovered ourselves to be part of the environment rather than its outside observer.

To use a key distinction in the philosophy of Martin Heidegger, we seem to have moved from a "present-to-hand" relationship to the physical and biological world, a relationship that had been typical for the natural sciences, to a "ready-to-hand" situation as it characterizes the hands-on attitudes of such professionals as engineers, surgeons, gardeners – and athletes. Their embodied existence lived in closeness and in familiarity both with other bodies and with the material world is less eccentric than it used to be – and, seen from the perspective of the fusion between consciousness and software, also more eccentric and more desirable than ever. This complex duplicity (of being both more exclusively spiritual than ever and, at the same time, closer to the material world) can perhaps explain why athletes, today, are more admired than they used to be as well as more paradigmatic for the latest state of the human condition. Within this historical transition, our views on how a person can and should be productive or even "creative" are now changing. Under present-at-hand conditions, we admired as "genius" fellow humans who, from an outside position, were able to interpret the world in unforeseen ways, obtaining true insights and thus motivating the hope for incisive changes in the future. Albert Einstein and "Relativity" are but the most proverbial example here.

The person, by contrast, who has arguably had the most sustained and sustainable impact on the global everyday during the past decade – Steve Jobs – did not fit the pattern of the present-at-hand. He never produced any new insights that we would celebrate as "truthful," nor did he invent any truly unprecedented products or forms of behaviour.

Constant variation under the premise of a ready-to-hand relation to the world of objects was the formula through which Jobs, profoundly and in multiple ways, transformed the attitude of a new generation towards our environment. And this precisely has long – if not always – been the attitude of the most outstanding athletes. Paavo Nurmi and Jessie Owens, Jack Dempsey and Muhammad Ali, John McEnroe and Roger Federer, Giuseppe Meazza and Lionel Messi changed their sports through accumulated (but individually small) variations – with non-dramatic variations whose practical relevance and lasting impact became obvious only in retrospect.

The question is whether we will be able to learn, for our "ethical" lives outside the autonomous world of sports, from the athletes' new ways of using space and engaging with other bodies; whether we will be able to learn from them to the same extent that we have finally begun to appreciate the beauty of their movements. Some new perspectives and discourses that analyse, put to good athletic use, and celebrate athletic achievements (like most of those brought together in this volume) may be but first steps in this very direction – we have begun to write about Champions League games with a sophistication that nobody was even able to imagine a quarter century ago, and not only military strategists are discovering that sports are a promising and practice-oriented object of study. Here, perhaps, lies the reason for the ever more vehement and less productive storms of protest about different methods of physical enhancement in sports. Granted, trying to preserve the athletes' bodies in a state of ideal purity (and thus in grotesque contrast to contemporary everyday life) was the present-at-hand attitude of Coubertin's age. But can we not imagine a radical change for the better, a change of direction towards a ready-to-hand situation where research and methods towards maximizing the athletes' performances could converge with concerns for their health and where, in the long run, the effects of athletic competition could become "ethically" beneficial outside the world of sports? This scenario may seem unlikely (and therefore all too provocative) at this point – but I do not see why it should be considered a vision impossible to achieve.

As for sports spectators, the most literally eye-catching developments within the past few decades have been the stadiums, which are fuller than ever before – even though television enables us to see and understand endlessly more about any athletic event. Those sold-out stadiums belong to a larger contemporary desire to be part of gatherings that bring together tens of thousands of human bodies, a desire that also accounts for "public viewing" events, for open-air masses read by the Pope, and for rock concerts on the beach. We can therefore safely assume that stadium crowds are symptoms of the already mentioned new collective longing for rituals, in the function of social frameworks "to hold on to." Using the oldest self-description of Christianity as "Christ's mystical body," I like to refer to the substance of such rituals as (secular) "mystical bodies." With these words, I want to emphasize that, unlike the typical modern concepts of sociability that are based exclusively on shared interests or life conditions (i.e., "society," "class," or "club"), and as a counterpoint to individual existence under the burden of constant freedom of choice, such crowds include and emphasize human existence as being a body. This is how they provide us with a sense of concreteness and relevance and with that reassuring impression of having "something to hold on to."

Not unlike sports during its earlier modern history, such "mystical bodies," labelled "crowds" or "masses," have had the worst possible reputation among intellectuals. To automatically associate them with fascism is one of the milder standard reactions whenever they get mentioned (especially when they get mentioned without the – in some circles redeeming – adjective of being "proletarian" masses). To argue for a more differentiated view of "mystical bodies" appears to be an approaching challenge, to which some contemporary philosophers have now begun to react – among them the philosopher Judith Butler, whose approach is nevertheless quite different from mine in its conceptual underpinnings. In her *Notes Toward a Performative Theory of Assembly*, Butler develops her much debated critique of gender studies' and continental sociology's fixation with describing collective human bodies as mere "mental constructions," by claiming that we have to take into account, from a non-metaphysical perspective, their physical substance and articulation in real space if we want to fully understand the political roles they are capable of playing.[8] Starting to develop an aesthetics of the crowds that occupy stadiums during athletic events could be a complementary step in the same intellectually productive direction.

Similar to some other organic phenomena and not only on a microscopic scale, mystical bodies in the stadium may adopt different shapes. They can consist, particularly in moments when the flow of athletic events gets interrupted or derailed, of all spectators minus the performing athletes (these are the moments when "the wave," as a collectively produced form, becomes the symptom of happy boredom); they can split into two antagonist bodies when the players of one team, together with their fans, stand against the players of the other team together with their fans (here, obviously, lies the greatest risk of violence);

and there are finally those rare and often sublime instances when all athletes and all spectators in a stadium become one single body, a body whose outer shape moulds itself to the stadium's architectural shape.

It is always possible (much more for traditional low-income fans than for the new-age dwellers of VIP boxes) that rhythms of collective movement, but also words and songs performed together, will give additional internal structures and contours to crowds as mystical bodies. Being part of a collectively embodied rhythm will lower the individual "tension of consciousness," to borrow a concept from Husserl, of those who stand in the crowd, and it will also reduce to a minimum their individual agency (if only due to the sheer physical impossibility of having full control over one's own body in such narrow proximity with so many other bodies). Needless to say, "lower tension of consciousness" and "reduced agency" are the two main reasons for the crowds' (or the mystical bodies') bad reputation among intellectuals and other heirs of the Enlightenment.

As a counterbalance, I like to invoke the unique intensity of lived experience that being part of a mystical body can facilitate. We certainly know, from many accidents not only in the history of sports, that such intensity always implies a risk of violence. On the other hand, crowds are well capable of producing sublimely moving ethical effects. Towards the end of the German professional soccer season 2015–16, the famously raucous standing-only part of the crowd in the stadium of my favourite team, Borussia Dortmund, remained completely silent during the second half of a home game. Then, ten minutes before the game ended with a 2–0 victory of the home team, close to thirty thousand fans intoned the song "You Never Walk Alone" – to commemorate, honour, and mourn a fan in the crowd who, during halftime, had died of a heart attack. There was no conductor, let alone a "committee" that had decided on this collective action – one that, at least for a few weeks, changed the tone in which commentators talked and wrote about stadium crowds.

Part of this particular intensity, which we sometimes sense even before the actual event begins, may have to do with a normally overlooked (although reiterated) structure of contrast. It is quite remarkable that, for the past two or three decades, stadiums have been returning from the periphery of the cities to more central neighbourhoods, to those zones indeed where the real estate prices are particularly high – although they are only being used during very limited time spans each week. Such locations have the effect of underscoring the contrast between, in the first place, the rush of downtown everyday life and the empty stadium, and, in the second place, between the mostly empty stadium and those few hours when it is filled with high-intensity action and its crowd's mystical body. The same motif makes up for the contrast between the field as stage of the game and the empty field before and after the players' warm-ups, during half-time, and after the game.

When I think about the allure of the stadium, about my never-ceasing desire to be there, and about the unique pleasure this framework of contrasts never fails to provide for me, I often associate it with another intensity-producing contrast from a different existential dimension. I am referring to the question that, according to Heidegger, is both systematically and historically at the origin of all philosophy as an ex-istential practice, that is, the question why there is Something (at all) as opposed to Nothing (at all). Due to the reiterated contrast between emptiness and plenitude that belongs to the stadium ritual, we can be-come part of precisely this question and this condition – by embodying and by being it, without being its representation or living allegory. We certainly do not actively think about this implication while we are part of an athletic event – and why should we? For wanting to represent this ontological contrast, instead of just being it, would certainly weaken the specific intensity it is able to produce in us.

Our description of the historical emergence of aesthetic experience may help us grasp what is specific about being in a stadium. From this perspective, it would indeed appear as yet another case of the oscil-lation that characterizes aesthetic experience, that is, of the oscillation between being a physical part of the world and making sense of the world, between being and interpreting as the two elementary modes of our existence. But what is at stake in this intellectual step, what do we (or anybody) gain from describing the stadium experience as a case of aesthetic experience? As I said earlier, I do not believe that we make the experience of sports any better, any more intense, or more socially acceptable by calling it "aesthetic." But doing so helps us understand why so many of us find sports truly and irresistibly fascinating. Both for athletes and for spectators, being in a stadium, because it gives them back to the physical part of their existence, can become a situation that assigns a concrete place and a grounding to their existence. However unaware stadium spectators may be of this effect, it often produces an atmosphere of serenity in the crowd, an effect where allure and ethics begin to converge.

Meanwhile and in an even larger context, it seems likely that what Western culture has been calling "aesthetic" since the seventeenth century is becoming less eccentric and autonomous again – if the impression is true that we increasingly manage to reintegrate the body into our self-image. At the same time, more and more instances of aesthetic experience are permeating the everyday (without much "autonomy"), ranging from the technologically facilitated omnipresence of music in our individual lives, to design, fashion, and a new ambition in the production of food, to the world of sports. There is a larger market for aesthetic experience – and for sports in particular – than ever before, and a greater supply of it.

As a consequence, active sports and spectator sports have ceased to occupy a marginal place in our individual existence and in our social environment. On the contrary, almost everywhere sport occupies a central place today, and it is increasingly intertwined, on multiple levels, with politics, with the economy, and with the production of knowledge. Rather than interpreting all of this as a symptom of crisis and trying to push sports back to its formerly eccentric place, we should try to face, to understand, and to react to this new situation. Sometimes we begin to feel and to fear that, due to its new centrality, omnipresence, and perhaps also oversupply, the allure of sports may lose some of its former intensity. An attempt towards resisting this tendency could lie in trying to redraw a new and clearer line of separation between the allure and the ethics of sports. If it is not realistic to assume that politics, business, and research will refrain from using athletic events and their allure for their own purposes any time soon, all we can do is to emphasize their difference – and to return to organizing and celebrating athletic events as time outs from the everyday and its ethics. In this context, I find inspiring John Zilcosky's intuition that an active engagement with the ethics of sports as a realm of analysis, distinctions, and transparency, might in the end enhance their allure as the intoxicating, Dionysian, and existentially fulfilling effect of being open towards being a body as the ground of our existence.[9]

NOTES

1 See, for example, Meg Mumford's *Bertolt Brecht* (Routledge: New York, 2009), 16.
2 See John J. MacAloon's *This Great Symbol: Pierre de Coubertin and the Origins of the Modern Olympic Games* (Routledge: New York, 2008), especially the chapter "The Mighty Working of a Symbol: From Idea to Organization."
3 John E. Findling and Kimberly D. Pelle, eds., *Encyclopedia of the Modern Olympic Movement* (Westport: Greenwood Press, 2004), 109–10.

4 See Wolf Kittler, "A Well-Trained Community: Gymnastics for the German Nation," and Sarah Panzer, "Importing a German *Kampfsport*: The Reception and Practice of Japanese Martial Arts in Interwar Germany," in this volume.

5 See Sophie Remijsen, "The Fading Allure of Greek Athletics," in this volume.

6 See Immanuel Kant, *Werke in zwölf Bänden*, vol. 10: *Kritik der Urteilskraft* (Suhrkamp: Frankfurt am Main, 1977), 158–60.

7 See Rebekka von Mallinckrodt, "Attractive or Repugnant? Running Races in Eighteenth-Century Germany and Britain," in this volume.

8 See Judith Butler, *Notes toward a Performative Theory of Assembly* (Cambridge, MA: Harvard University Press, 2015), esp. 9–11 and 83–5.

9 See John Zilcosky's "Introduction: The Allure of Sports" in this volume.

PART III

The Ancient World

3 The Fading Allure of Greek Athletics[*]

SOFIE REMIJSEN

Introduction: The Longevity of Ancient Athletics

Although it may often seem that in the present day we are more obsessed with sports than ever before, one could easily argue that the allure of sports was even more deeply embedded in ancient Greek culture than it is in modern Western society. Whereas in both modern and ancient society, sport is explicitly present in domains such as education, international relations, bodily ideals, and everyday small talk, ancient athletics even pervaded domains that today remain mostly sports-free, such as poetry or religion. Modern sport is also a fairly recent phenomenon – most of its disciplines were developed in the nineteenth or twentieth century – whereas Greek athletics could boast of occupying a central cultural role for over a millennium. The importance of this long athletic history even in the collective memory of the Greeks is nicely illustrated by the ancient habit of dating historical events with the names of Olympic victors.[1]

The term Greek athletics covers a set of individual competitive sports that remained fairly stable from at least the sixth century BC until the fourth century AD: several running events of which the *stadion*, *diaulos*, and *dolichos* were the most common distances; three combat sports, namely wrestling, boxing, and *pankration*; and a combined event called the *pentathlon*, which included the long jump, discus throwing, javelin throwing, sprinting, and wrestling.[2] Most contests or *agones* also included equestrian races for single horses with rider, for two-horse chariots, and for four-horse chariots. Regional differences and historical changes to the program were minute: an extra running contest over the distance of four stadia, called *hippios*, is, for example, known for a limited number of contests; the attire for the running contest in armour changed lightly over the course of the centuries; and two additional equestrian races, called *apene* and *kalpe*, were added in 500 and 496 BC respectively but cancelled shortly thereafter in 444 BC. The geographical span of Greek athletics gradually increased: from Greece and the neighbouring Mediterranean coasts it had spread to the large area from Italy and northern Tunisia to Syria and Egypt under the Roman Empire.[3] The basic set of disciplines, however, remained the same at several hundreds of contests, as did the custom of practising these sports naked and the habit of commemorating athletic victories for eternity on stone monuments.[4] When one compares depictions of athletes on archaic and classical amphorae with the athletes on late Roman mosaics, the greatest difference is in fact the hairstyle of the athletes, not their technique.[5]

How exactly athletics maintained such a central position in the social life of the ancient cities for about a millennium is a complex question. Explaining the allure of Greek athletics across this period would require that we examine by which different qualities this particular style of athletics could appeal to people during a millennium of changing historical circumstances – a task that lies far beyond the scope of one article or the expertise of a single historian. Instead of focusing on the continuity of the allure of athletics in antiquity, this chapter will focus on the moment it faded. Having reached an absolute high point in the second century AD, when there were more than five hundred *agones*, the number of athletic contests remained more or less stable until at least AD 300. Less than 150 years later, however, in the early fifth century, only a handful of contests had survived, which, given the long history of the contests, is a remarkably quick disappearance.[6] By looking at the factors that led to the end of this custom, we can get closer to what constituted its allure in the first place.

The allure of athletics is understood in this chapter as the reasons for which people within a certain social field are attracted to an engagement with sports (whether as active participant, as promotor of events, or as spectator, or in a combination of these various roles). As in many other chapters in this volume, here too the allure is closely connected to ethical considerations about why sports are something morally "good" and about the perceived danger that sports will degenerate through what is perceived as immoral behaviour. Until the 1980s, scholarship on ancient athletics focused primarily on an imagined decline of Greek athletics from the fourth century BC on, and attributed this decline to the rise of professional athletics. The pure amateur athletes who competed solely for the honour of the victory, an honour symbolized by a mere crown of leaves, supposedly degenerated into brutal professionals who competed for monetary gain. Over the last thirty years, this discussion has gradually been abandoned, since it has been established that valuable prizes were an aspect of ancient athletics from early on and were not in fact incompatible with the Greek understanding of honour. The ideological distinction prevailing in Greek athletics was that between a positively interpreted prize (even one as prosaic as a bag of coins) and negatively interpreted daily wages. The idea that a valuable prize was worse than a purely symbolic one reflected a nineteenth- and early twentieth-century ideal that was wrongly projected onto antiquity.[7] This does not mean, however, that one cannot understand the development of Greek athletics, and in particular its final phase, against the background of ancient considerations about morality. That for more than a millennium cities held athletes in high esteem and parents considered athletic training an essential part of the education of their boys, whom they wanted to see grow into good men, implies that they made a strong connection between athletics and moral qualities. For this reason, this chapter will focus on the changing perception and valuation of athletics in late antiquity.

The central question, therefore, is what looking at athletic contests meant to men of late antiquity. This particular question of course neglects the female experience, but that perspective is impossible to deduce from the ancient sources anyway. It also ignores the political and economic factors that contributed to the disappearance of these contests. Regarding the political context it is important to note, before proceeding to the spectator experience, that athletic games were never banned. The end of the ancient Olympics is traditionally blamed on the Christian emperor Theodosius I, and often dated to 393, which was the first Olympic year after a number of important anti-pagan laws were issued. Those laws, however, did not actually mention anything about games. In the last ten years, several scholars have shown that imperial policy in late antiquity was generally supportive of games, even when the emperor was a fervent Christian. They did not see games as an affront to piety, because pagan sacrifices were no longer held in connection to athletic contests after the mid-fourth century. This means that such contests could be accepted as secular, even if originally they had a strong religious component. Against this background, it is not surprising that there is good evidence for the continuity of some athletic contests after the reign of Theodosius I.[8]

A different political and financial development did have a detrimental effect on the games, namely, the reorganization of the Roman administrative structures. The institutions that took the lead in organizing athletic contests were the cities, whose councils and officials decided on these contests' programs and managed the funds. From the fourth century, provincial governors increased their dominance over life in the provinces: independent decisions and financial management were no longer possible.[9] In these circumstances, minor cities found it difficult to keep their contests going. Games in provincial capitals, by contrast, were generally supported by the governors. This suggests that the total collapse of the contest circuit could have been avoided through a centralization of athletic contests in the provincial capitals. There is evidence that this evolution started, but it was never completed, which suggests that there was a lack of will to adapt the organizational structures that underpinned the contests and thus maintain the games.[10] In order to understand why this willingness failed, we need to get inside the minds of the men of late antiquity.

The Identification of the Spectator with the Athlete

Each spectator experience is (and was) unique, for it is influenced by the individual's personal history, temperament, and state of mind; but to a certain extent it is (and was) also biologically and culturally predetermined. This chapter takes a closer look at the ways in which ancient spectators identified with athletes on the psychological as well as the sociocultural level.

Human beings generally experience emotions in similar ways. Taking insights from psychological research can therefore help throw a different perspective on ancient spectacles, as Garrett Fagan has recently shown in his book on the allure of the arena. It should of course be noted here that it is dangerous to project modern psychological experiences of spectacular events directly onto past cultures. Although more research on how connections are built in the brain needs to be done, neuroscientists generally acknowledge that the environment in which one grows up has a strong influence on the development of the human psyche.[11] It does not contribute anything to our understanding of antiquity to ask what feelings modern people experience when they watch sports, but since some more general psychological processes can be observed in diverse cultural groups, it is interesting to look at the ways in which their emotions are created.

An important element in the psychological experience of all kinds of entertainment (be it a book, a play, or a sports match) is self-substitution: one imagines that one is the protagonist, in this case a sportsman on display. Experiencing the contest from the imagined perspective of a contender, the spectator feels the emotions he expects the protagonist to experience, such as fear, pain, anger, or confidence. It is these shared or parapathic emotions that make the whole experience exciting. But the spectator is experiencing these emotions at a remove – that is, within a protective frame. He does not physically feel the pain and exhaustion experienced by the athlete, and therefore even negative emotions are for the spectator a source of pleasure and excitement.[12] Precisely this detachment frame is essential to the experience; it means that the spectator identifies with the performer only emotionally and only during the act of spectating.

The psychological process of self-substitution does not predetermine how the spectator's perception of the athlete (with whom he identifies during the match) is transferred outside this context, since he emotionally experiences the action *as if* he is this person in the match rather than identifying himself with the athlete as a fellow member of society. For this different type of identification, a sociological perspective is more interesting. A late-antique man watching an athletic event had been socialized into a culture that imbued him with a set of values that coloured his interpretation of what he saw. His precise reaction to the games was in no way pre-programmed, but it was structured by what Bourdieu calls his *habitus*, a set of dispositions generating typical behaviours and resulting from the spontaneous internalization of the practices and norms of his social field(s).[13] One can even say that *all* people involved in the games were performing the culture into which they had been socialized; the games were an enactment of cultural and social norms and an instrument to pass these on.[14]

Sociologists like van Nieuwkerk, whose monograph (1995) discusses the status of female performers in twentieth-century Egypt, examine perceptions of social actors by asking questions such as these: Would you want to see your daughter married to such a person? Do you want your children to start such a career? And so on. By focusing on social practices, such questions aim to go beyond the norms explicitly expressed in the spoken and written discourse on performers. The answers illuminate how the interviewees see the performers' place in society in relation to their own place. They also show that perceptions of the morality of performers depend on the social status of the spectator in relation to that of the performer. For the ancient spectators too we can examine whether they saw a participant in public events as their social peer or as an inferior, by looking at their willingness to have their children engage in similar activities or to connect themselves to such participants. Although it is obviously impossible to interview the ancient spectators, the Greek source material does give clear indications about the family connections of athletes and about the personal engagement of the spectators with the competitive sports that were displayed during public events. Ancient sources generally give a distorted picture of society: the urban elites are put in the limelight, and all others are barely distinguishable in the shadows. For this particular study, however, this is not such an issue because this overrepresented layer of the population contains those people who were in a position to choose how to spend their leisure time and their money, and hence those people on which the allure of ancient athletics most depended. At least for them, we are in a position to examine whether they saw the sportsmen they watched as their social peers and whether they could imagine themselves taking part in contests. Translated again in terms of Bourdieu, we will only examine the *habitus* of a specific social field, namely, the elites in the later Roman *poleis* of the eastern provinces, and for this group, we can investigate which types of engagement with athletics could imbue individuals with social prestige, or "symbolic capital," as Bourdieu calls it. Under the term "ancient elites" I understand a broad propertied class, whose tangible possessions ranged from rather modest workshops and residences to vast estates and who can be distinguished from the majority of the ancient population living around (and occasionally under) subsistence level.

Both types of identification processes – psychological self-substitution during the act of spectating, and a more general social identification with performers as social superiors, peers, or inferiors – were at work in the ancient world, but led to different perceptions of different types of contests. We can take as a first example gladiatorial contests, which were also popular in the eastern provinces, where games of Roman and Greek origin existed side by side.[15] Watching gladiatorial combat was an intense emotional experience; the best description of this can be found in Augustine's *Confessions*. He describes how his friend Alypius was dragged to the games by others, but refused to watch. Then, however, "at a certain fall in the fight, when a huge roar from the entire crowd struck him powerfully, he was overcome by curiosity ... for when he saw the blood, he drank in the savagery and did not turn away but fixed his gaze on it ... He looked, he shouted, he was fired up, and he carried away with him the madness that would goad him to return, not only with his original companions but even as their leader dragging others along."[16] Successful gladiators were heroes lauded for their brave feats: the spectators could share in the victory and bask in the reflected glory. Unsuccessful gladiators, by contrast, who in their weakness could no longer uphold the Roman ideal of virtue, were allowed to die. That such a dramatic ending of the show was accepted by the crowd indicates that the spectators, while emotionally invested in the show, at the same time maintained a protective distance from the gladiator as a real person. Socially, gladiators were not the peers of the upper classes that formed a disproportionate number of their spectators, that paid for their performances and wrote about them in literary texts. Gladiators did not intermarry with the urban elites; like many other performers, even non-slave gladiators were forbidden to do so by law on account of their legal status as "infamous," which limited their civic rights.[17] Nor were the technical skills of gladiators taught to upper-class boys as part of their education. Roman gladiatorial shows were hence experienced mainly as pure entertainment: the parapathic emotions during the fight were enjoyed intensely, but the upper-class spectators did not identify with gladiators as their social peers. Organizing these shows for his peers to enjoy them increased an elite man's symbolic capital, whereas associating with gladiators as social actors in their own right decreased it.

This was different when it came to athletics. Athletic exercises and competitions had long been part of upper-class boys' education in the eastern Mediterranean. This was even institutionalized over the course of the Hellenistic period, when it became the main activity of the ephebate, an educational program for future citizens organized in the *gymnasia* of most cities in Greece, Asia Minor, Syria, and Egypt.[18] This means that a spectator at an athletic contest not only recognized the quality of the athletic techniques on display, like any devoted sports fan would, but had often personally tried these techniques and could imagine that it could have been him in the middle – if only he had been a little younger or more talented or had trained harder as a boy. A particularly good move in a fight may have created the same kind of emotional response in spectators of a gladiatorial combat as in spectators of a wrestling contest, but on the level of social identification the differences were great. The athlete in the spotlight came from the same social milieu as those people among the spectators who had invested in the physical education of their little boys, and who mingled with the athletes in various other social contexts, such as local government. If the spectators of an *agon* had been asked whether they saw the athletes as suitable partners for their daughters, many would have answered this question positively.[19] Several aspects of this specific experience of athletics changed, however, in late antiquity, and here we can find some reasons why the allure of Greek athletics eventually faded.

The Spectator as a Potential Athlete

After the third century AD – which was about two centuries before the final collapse of the ancient circuit of athletic contests – the cultural role of athletics started to change gradually. For the urban elites involved, this change seems to have remained largely invisible. There is no clear shift in the discourse on athletics in the third century – critical voices on practising these sports were not becoming louder, for example.[20] Even in Christian milieux, it remained a perfectly acceptable option for parents to hire a private trainer for the athletic education of their sons.[21] What did disappear, however, was the widely shared view that the community had to provide sports infrastructure and sports education. As people hardly noticed this change, we can find no evidence of it in literary texts, but the architecture of bathing complexes and the abandonment of an educational institution do bear witness to this transformation.

A typical institution of Hellenistic and imperial-age cities in the eastern Mediterranean was the *gymnasium*. In these large publicly funded complexes in the middle of the city, the citizens met to bathe, to exercise, to see and to be seen. Many of these complexes had been built or renovated by rich individuals as a benefaction to the community, but even these were not private business enterprises. It was the city that managed the complexes and appointed magistrates to finance the wood for the hot baths and the oil for the athletic exercises from their own pockets – taking up this office was an obligatory tax-like service for the richest citizens.[22] The central courtyard that defined this sort of complex as a *gymnasium* (instead of mere baths) was the wrestling area or *palaistra*. This was one of the areas frequented by the elite to meet their peers. Even if they were not particularly sports-minded, they would have felt a certain social pressure to regularly spend time here, for their peers did as well. And even when they spent most of their time chatting instead of training strenuously, they may still have insisted that their sons exercise vigorously, as part of their socialization within this group.

A typical *palaistra* was designed with the training of wrestling and other combat sports in mind. The central courtyard was covered with sand to break the athletes' falls, water basins were set up for refreshment during exercise, and the courtyard was surrounded by a shady gallery, from which athletes could enter smaller rooms to undress, rub themselves with oil, and then sprinkle themselves with sand (a wrestler was not supposed to be too slippery) or work on their hitting and kicking techniques with a punching bag.[23] Long before the later imperial period the *palaistra* had become multifunctional; still, wrestling training continued to determine its design. It seems that by the third century, however, suitability for athletics was no longer the dominant criterion for the layout of this area.[24] New bathing complexes often omitted the *palaistra*. The benefactors apparently assumed that the inclusion of this large feature would not increase their symbolic capital. In older complexes that still had a *palaistra*, this area often saw major renovations during the fourth century. For example, pavement was frequently installed, which made training in a sport like wrestling very hard, in the literal meaning of the word. Young men with a natural fondness for physical activity would still meet up in these courtyards, but to enjoy themselves with ball games instead of traditional athletics.[25] The architectural changes reflected new uses of the *palaistra* that had probably already become common for the people involved. Therefore, those changes were not perceived as drastic. Modern scholars generally avoid the word *gymnasium* for baths without a *palaistra*; yet for visitors in late antiquity this distinction seems to have mattered little, for they used Greek words like *gymnasion* and *loutron* (bath) interchangeably.[26] The urban elites still visited these complexes to see and be seen, but clearly, it was no longer important to be seen practising athletics.

In the city's main *gymnasium*, young men could be registered for the ephebate. When this educational program for future citizens started to spread across the Greek world in the Hellenistic period, there was still a link between this program and the military education of citizens, but – although never disappearing completely – this aspect quickly lost its centrality.[27] Under the Roman Empire the training of ephebes was voluntary – hence mainly supported by the elites – and focused on athletic exercise and communal festivals. Therefore, the continued popularity of this program of physical education cannot be explained by its practical value, which was very limited indeed. One needs to ask what other competences the ephebes gained. Today, parents want their children to participate in sports not only because it is good for their health but also to learn about teamwork or to gain physical self-confidence. In antiquity, athletics and specific body types resulting from athletic training were similarly linked to mental and moral strength. The aspiration to be the best was far more central among these qualities than it is today: the sports the ephebes trained in and the prizes and honours they could gain were all individual. This ambition to stand out – referred to as *philotimia* (the love of honour) in Greek – also played a central part in the later life of elite citizens, when they competed with the splendour of their benefactions rather than with athletic feats. The ephebate was, in other words, a highly valued way of imbuing young men with the mixture of communal ideals and exceptional competitiveness that characterized the local government of the ancient cities, and in this way functioned as training in citizenship.[28]

The ephebate was still popular in the mid-third century but had disappeared by the later fourth century. Unfortunately, we have very few sources from the intermediate decades to date the decline more precisely. From Athens, for example, many inscriptions set up by ephebes in the mid-third century have survived because they were reused in a defensive wall built in response to the Herulian invasion of 267. That we have no inscriptions from after this date does not prove the disappearance of the *ephebate*: it just means that later *ephebes* felt no incentive to put up further inscriptions, either because the financial situation had worsened, or because the epigraphic tradition had been interrupted by the removal of the older monuments, or because inscriptions in general had become less popular as new ways of honouring individuals became dominant, as can be seen throughout the empire.[29] Only in Roman Egypt, where references to gymnasium officials in documentary papyri are relatively continuous, is it clear that the *kosmetai*, the officials directing this program, had disappeared by the mid-fourth century.[30] This is not surprising, given the aforementioned architectural changes and the customs they represented. At a time when the urban elites no longer felt social pressure to engage personally in athletic exercises, they also no longer felt that their sons needed a formal athletic education in order to become successful members of society.

Because private trainers for children are attested even after the fourth century, one cannot say that all members of the elite lost touch with athletic training when the *ephebate* was abandoned, but personal experience with athletics certainly became less common and stopped being regarded as typical of the average good citizen. This change preceded the decline of the big agonistic festivals: whereas non-professional athletic exercises had started to decline in the third century, the latter only declined from the second quarter of the fourth century. This means that the elites of the Greek cities were still watching athletics while they themselves were no longer engaged in athletic practice. The removal of athletic exercises as a standard feature of upper-class life did, however, affect the spectator experience. Until at least the mid-third century, many of the people watching athletic matches would have had personal experience with athletic techniques – in particular, the ancient combat sports were highly technical. They knew from their own experience which wrestling grips were particularly difficult and how the score of the pentathlon was kept. They were, in other words, all potential athletes. By the later fourth century, however, the average man in the public did not have personal experience and may have appreciated the results of a champion athlete irrespective of the level of his technique. Nor did the spectator automatically think it could have been him competing in the contest, as his ancestors would have done.

The Spectator's Perception of the Moral Qualities of Athletes

The lack of personal experience with athletics could certainly increase the distance between the athlete and the non-athletic spectator; but a social identification between the two could still take place, at least in certain types of games. Most athletes participating in games such as the Olympics were still members of the elite – on average probably even richer than their predecessors, as private training was now the only way to end up in an athletic career. But even when spectator and athlete belonged to the same socio-economic group, more and more spectators would have found it difficult to view these athletes as virtuous men as a consequence of their identity as athletes. By circa AD 400, perceptions of athletics had indeed changed, which made it more difficult for the spectator to identify with the athlete.

To understand this development, we should ask why the social pressure to engage in athletics had diminished. As explained before, one of the main moral qualities that athletic training in the Greek style was meant to teach the young sons of elite citizens was the ambition to stand out and to be the best; this seems to have been one of the most enduring ideals in ancient Greek culture. The fact that this ideal was no longer passed on through an institutionalized system of physical education does not necessarily mean that this ideal was gone. Excellence could also be promoted in other areas of life and by means of private athletic training. The decline of the ephebate and of daily exercises in the public gymnasium may suggest, however, that competitiveness was now considered less essential for the lower ranks of the elites and/or was now disconnected from a specific body type. Changes in political culture confirm the former: especially after the administrative reforms around 300, civic duties such as procuring oil for the gymnasium seem to have become more and more an unwanted burden for the less fortunate of the elite; meanwhile, the more fortunate increasingly focused their energy and financial means on levels of the administration above that of the city.[31]

The link between certain body types and the ambition to be the best deserves further investigation. A prerequisite for attaining excellence in athletics (and in other fields) was mastery of another quality, namely, self-control. Career athletes with a long list of victories could be seen as embodiments of this ideal. A good illustration of the association between champion athletes and virtues is Dio's praise of Melankomas, a famous boxer who died in the prime of his life around AD 70: "He had the good fortune to be from an illustrious family and to have beauty, and moreover courage, strength and self-control, things that are truly the greatest of blessings. Indeed the most admirable thing in a man is not only to be unconquered by one's opponents, but also by toil, heat, hunger and libido."[32] Around AD 300, champion athletes could still be associated with these qualities. In the same vein as Dio, Pseudo-Dionysius, who authored a handbook of rhetoric in the third or fourth century, observed that athletes became famous champions through self-control, self-discipline, and training. Clearly, then, these were still the principal virtues associated with athletics.[33]

The moral strength needed to ignore physical signs such as tiredness and to continue training was of course only one possible type of self-control. The avoidance of all types of luxury, including rich foods, was another, to which the Greek word for physical training, *askesis*, was similarly applied. In the modern term "asceticism" we find the root of this Greek word. Until the early third century, asceticism was interpreted by most of the population as a kind of subversive behaviour, practised only by some philosophers criticizing society but not by model citizens[34] – quite unlike athletic *askesis*. Over the course of the third and fourth centuries, however one can see a clear shift towards a wider acceptance of an ascetic lifestyle as admirable among pagans and, especially, Christians.[35] By the late fourth and fifth centuries, extreme ascetics such as hermits and stylites had become popular heroes. People were excited to meet them and asked their advice on all matters. Even children glorified them, playing out scenes with a hermit as the protagonist.[36]

At first glance, this new positive perception of asceticism may seem easily combinable with a positive perception of athletics, in that self-control was central to both. But whereas the ascetic fought his body and subjected it to his mind, the relation between the body and the mind of the athlete was ambiguous. On the one hand, he subdued his body through constant training and a controlled (even if rich) diet; on the other, he was obsessed with the perfect body and muscles. The two lifestyles aimed at opposite effects: the athlete suffered in order to become a victor in physical contests, while the ascetic suffered in order to win a metaphysical contest. Although many early Christian criticisms of athletics were inspired by traditional philosophical concerns – for example, the image of the athlete as a glutton – the striking new element in these texts is their objection to the athlete's vanity. For Tertullian, for example, the athlete tried to outdo God's work with his obsession for his own physical shape.[37]

The inception of the idea of athletics as a vain pursuit can be traced to the third century; at that point, however, the competitive drive to be the best was not yet under intense scrutiny. Although the inter-elite competition for honour shifted from the local city arena to more central levels of the Roman administration, this essential character of the ancient political culture changed only very gradually. From the fourth century on, however, a debate developed between on the one hand Christian thinkers, who presented humility as the highest virtue and pride as the worst sin, and on the other the lay elite, who continued to pursue glory, for example, by financing lavish games.[38] Although the Christian discourse often focused on the most ostentatious acts of self-promotion by benefactors, the criticism of worldly ambition could also be applied to athletic competitions. The most explicit link between *agones* and the sin of pride can be found in Augustine's *Confessions*, written circa AD 400. Augustine was never an athlete, but as a young man he did participate in contests for performers, in which highly educated men competed with their own literary compositions. Augustine, being a talented writer, even won such a competition around AD 380 at an important contest in Carthage, where the victory crown was awarded to him by the provincial governor. After his conversion to a Christian lifestyle, however, he confessed this juvenile love for winning contests as a sin.[39]

By the fifth century, a spectator of athletic games who was socialized in this Christian world could easily interpret an athlete as vain: vain in the sense that the athlete seemed overly obsessed with his body, as well as in the sense that he attached a misplaced importance to his own excellence. This negative perception did not arrive in the Roman cities fully formed. Because asceticism and humility gradually gained their place in the late-antique value set, without being able to immediately change the culture of competitiveness among the elite, the late-antique athlete was certainly not universally perceived as immoral. The athletes from elite backgrounds were first and foremost ambiguous figures – even in the works of clerics, who could combine criticism of games with positive athletic metaphors in the same work. As late as the sixth century, we find authors – now all Christians – who take pains to explain that the particular athletes they describe are admirable men with a chaste lifestyle.[40] In iconography, too, artists developed strategies to allay potential suspicion. From the later third century on, mosaics with busts of athletes became ever more popular, but such depictions emphasized their fame rather than their bodily activities.[41]

The Spectator's Experience of the Event

Thus far I have argued that the increasing lack of personal experience with athletics and the increasing suspicion about the moral qualities of the athletes created a greater distance between spectators and athletes and that this inhibited social identification: the spectator no longer automatically saw the person on display as his peer. This tendency was reinforced by the fact that elite athletes saw their opportunities to compete disappearing as the contest circuit collapsed. Athletes from a lower social background – who did not look down on receiving wages rather than prizes – were growing in number, because Roman circus games became popular in the eastern provinces in the fourth century and the circus directors were increasingly hiring such men for athletic interludes between the horse races.[42] This increasing distance between elite spectators and athletes affected the former's perception of contests. The difference between the Greek elite's experience of an athletic contest and that of a Roman arena show, as described in the second section, faded. This can be seen in the language used for public games.

Modern scholars commonly use the neutral-sounding term "games" for all mass events in antiquity, including Roman spectacles and athletic contests. This term is a translation of the Latin word *ludi*, which did not, however, carry this broad meaning. *Ludi* were technically only chariot races and theatrical performances. The Latin term covering all sorts of games, including arena shows and athletic contests, was *spectacula*, "spectacles" or "shows." Such Latin terms did not, however, cover the categories used by people in the athletic sector, since the main language of this sector, and of the elite of the eastern provinces, was Greek. Hence we have to look at Greek usage to understand how spectators in the eastern Mediterranean categorized their experiences of different games.

Although arena shows and other forms of entertainment imported from the West were popular in the eastern provinces throughout the imperial age, the Greek language did not develop an umbrella term equivalent to *spectacula*, as long as the spectator experiences of these Roman shows were sufficiently different from the experience of *agones*. The Greek word for "shows," *theai*, shares its derivation of the verb "to watch" with the Latin term *spectacula*, but despite the semantic similarity these words are not perfect translations of each other, because *theai* was used only for shows that were not *agones*. Interestingly, however, usage changed from the fourth century on. Around AD 400, several authors socialized in the Greek world do start to use the word *theai* for all kinds of games, including athletics. This change in terms, which moved the focus from the participant in the games to the spectator, coincided with a shift in the discourse about games towards the show's dangerous effect on the spectator's behaviour.[43]

By the fifth century, in other words, the crowd perceived the contests as mere spectacles. They no longer saw peers displaying their talents. The contest was now primarily an emotionally engaging show that had to compete with other shows, such as the increasingly popular circus races, for the attention of spectators. There were few traditional *agones* left by now. Although the last known celebration of an *agon* was in AD 520, most had disappeared at least a century before that.[44]

As a side event in circuses, athletics survived longer, because these games better fit the new emphasis on spectacularity. Unfortunately,

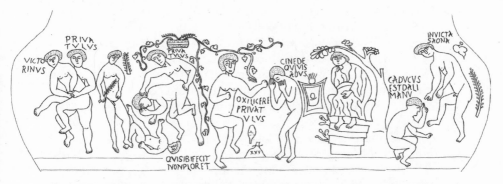

Figure 3.1. Figurative scenes on a late-antique bronze vase (drawn by Willy Remijsen on the basis of photographs by Hartwig Hotter)

only one late-antique depiction of an athletic context did certainly not document a traditional *agon*. It consists of a series of scenes from a *pankration* match on a bronze vase, with a reference to the Green circus faction on the neck.[45] The show element is obvious in all of these scenes (Figure 3.1). Whereas most imperial-age mosaics with athletic scenes depict matches as ongoing or refer to victory by focusing on a single athlete holding prizes, this vase is as much about defeat and even humiliation as it is about victory. One athlete is always depicted as a loser, never fighting back. In the second, third, and fourth scenes respectively he is trampled, thrown like a sack of flour, and hit in the face. In the first scene there is a possible insinuation of sexual abuse; in the final scene he holds up his finger to the judge as a sign of defeat. Captions insulting the loser are added to the scenes; even if it is entirely possible that abusive language had long been a feature of stadium events – there are too few descriptions to generalize about the atmosphere in *stadia* – this vase is certainly unique in adding those captions to the scene as an additional means of glorifying the defeat.

The language of these images and their depictions of a *pankration* match, which are different from traditional depictions of *agones*, are surprisingly close to the famous description of French wrestling (*le catch*) by the French philosopher Roland Barthes in his essay *In the Ring*: "In judo, a man who is down is hardly down at all, he rolls over, he withdraws, he evades defeat, or if defeat is obvious, he immediately leaves the match; in wrestling, a man down is exaggeratedly so, filling the spectator's entire field of vision with the intolerable spectacle of his powerlessness."[46] "Nothing can signify more clearly and more passionately the exemplary humiliation of the vanquished. Deprived of all resilience, the wrestler's flesh is nothing but an obscene mass spread on the ground and vulnerable to relentless insults and relentless jubilations."[47]

A traditional *agon* was, just like Barthes's description of judo, all about the victory, with defeat almost erased from view. The late-antique contest on the vase, however, looks more like a professional wrestling match, where violent defeat and humiliation are central to the experience.[48] On the vase as well as in Barthes's description, defeat is underscored with theatrical gestures: the loser remains stretched out on the ground and thus gives the victor an opportunity to place his foot on him and to debase him. French *catch* was staged, and the wrestler played out certain roles: a fat effeminate figure, for example, was bound to lose.[49] The purpose of this role-playing was to exemplify justice. "But what wrestling is especially supposed to imitate is a purely moral concept: justice."[50] Social psychology has shown that violence is indeed more easily perceived as justified when the victim is regarded as a "lesser" person. Such prejudices allow for an emotional distance when we see people suffer; indeed, they can give licence to revel in it.[51] On the ancient vase too we find evidence for typecasting: although the losing athlete is ironically called "Victorinus" (the winner) – against the unassuming name of the champion "Privatulus" (the little *privatus*, a man without an official function) – he is depicted as an effeminate weakling and cry-baby: in the first scene, he tries to protect his genitals from the grabbing hand of Privatulus, and the caption under the second and third scenes reads "he who does this to himself, shouldn't cry." The caption where he is shielding his face starts with the insult *cinaede*, "sissy!" I do not exclude the possibility that the "overacting" on the vase represents actual role-playing by athletes in the circus: they cooperated in troupes that hired themselves out as a whole, which means that these athletes were very well acquainted with one another's moves. These troupes were eventually incorporated into the so-called circus factions, large corporations that controlled all the entertainment in a city.[52]

French *catch* was more entertainment than sport. In the words of Barthes, "[s]ome people consider that wrestling is an ignoble sport. Wrestling is not a sport, it is a spectacle ... a wrestled performance of Suffering."[53] Similarly, the *pankration* match between Privatulus and Victorinus is a spectacle or *thea*. The scenes do not raise the question of which of two peers will win the match. On the contrary, the body language of Victorinus and the abuses inflicted on him give the spectator licence to revel in his defeat from the start. But these parapathic emotions have little to do with the allure of traditional Greek athletics.

This chapter started from the observation that the allure of Greek athletics depended on its perception as a custom reflecting and imbuing moral qualities, among the elites who sponsored the contests and paid for specialized training for their sons. From the third century on, the qualities of the athlete, trained in the gymnasium, were no longer identified with the qualities of the good citizen. Increasingly, athletics came to be seen as a vain pursuit performed by inferior men. When this millennium-long custom lost its strong connection to moral qualities starting from the third century, its allure irreversibly faded, and the willingness to organize the contests disappeared.

NOTES

* I would like to thank John Zilcosky for the invitation to present my research among a group of scholars with such wide-ranging expertise. This chapter further explores some ideas published in my monograph on the disappearance of athletic games in Late Antiquity: Sofie Remijsen, *The End of Greek Athletics in Late Antiquity* (Cambridge: Cambridge University Press, 2015), esp. 252–88 and 321–42; and in a paper on the different perceptions of athletics among people from Roman and Greek cultural backgrounds: Remijsen, "Looking at Athletics in the Fourth Century: The Unification of the Spectacle Landscape in East and West," in *East and West in the Roman Empire of the Fourth Century: An End to Unity?* ed. Roald Dijkstra, Sanne van Poppel, and Daniëlle Slootjes (Leiden: Brill, 2015), 121–46, so some repetition has been unavoidable.

1 For the time-reckoning in Olympiads and its cultural role, see, for example, Paul Christesen, *Olympic Victor Lists and Ancient Greek History* (Cambridge: Cambridge University Press, 2007).

2 There are many handbooks introducing these basic aspects of Greek athletics. The widely translated work by M.I. Finley and H.W. Pleket, *The Olympic Games: The First Thousand Years* (London: Chatto & Windus, 1976), remains a good starting point, certainly when supplemented by a source book such as Stephen Miller's *Arete: Greek Sport from Ancient Sources*, 3rd and expanded ed. (Berkeley: University of California Press, 2004), the convenient short lexicon of Mark Golden, *Sport in the Ancient World from A to Z* (London and New York: Routledge, 2004), and a companion with more recent scholarship such as Paul Christesen and Donald G. Kyle, eds., *A Companion to Sport and Spectacle in Greek and Roman Antiquity* (Chichester: Wiley Blackwell, 2014).

3 A brief overview of Greek athletics in the Roman period can be found in Thomas F. Scanlon, *Eros and Greek Athletics* (Oxford: Oxford University Press, 2002): 40–63, with tables and a graph documenting changes in the geographical spread of Olympic athletes.

4 Luigi Moretti's *Iscrizioni agonistiche greche* (Rome: Angelo Signorelli, 1953)
   and Joachim Ebert's *Griechische Epigramme auf Sieger an gymnischen und hippischen Agonen* (Berlin: Akademie Verlag, 1972) are two classical *corpora* with
   a selection of agonistic inscriptions from the archaic to the Roman period.
5 The most beautiful depictions of archaic and classical athletes can be found
   on the so-called Panathenaic vases. For an overview, see Martin Bentz,
   *Panathenäische Preisamphoren. Eine athenische Vasengattung und ihre Funktion
   vom 6.–4. Jahrhundert v. Chr.* (Basel: Vereinigung der Freunde antiker Kunst,
   1998). For a recent catalogue of all Roman wall paintings and mosaics with
   athletics, see Anke Bohne, *Bilder vom Sport: Untersuchungen zur Ikonographie
   römischer Athleten-Darstellungen* (Hildesheim: Weidmann, 2011). A characteristic hairstyle of imperial-age athletes, absent in the earlier depictions,
   is the short pony-tail called a *cirrus*: see Jean-Paul Thuillier, "Le cirrus et la
   barbe. Questions d'iconographie athlétique romaine," *Mélanges de l'École
   française de Rome. Antiquité* 110 (1998): 351–80.
6 For an estimate of the number of *agones* in the Roman Empire, see Wolfgang Leschhorn, "Die Verbreitung von Agonen in den östlichen Provinzen
   des römischen Reiches," *Stadion* 24 (1998): 31. For a summary on the disappearance of the *agones* after the third century, see Remijsen, *The End of
   Greek Athletics in Late Antiquity*, 164–71.
7 A standard work on the impact of modern ideologies on our understanding of ancient athletics is David C. Young's *The Olympic Myth of Greek
   Amateur Athletics* (Chicago: Ares, 1984). Young is keen to deny the aristocratic character of Greek athletics; Henri W. Pleket gives a more nuanced
   picture of the social background of athletes and the character of the ancient ideology concerning prizes. See Pleket, "Zur Soziologie des antiken
   Sports," *Mededelingen van het Nederlands Instituut te Rome* 36 (1974): 57–87;
   and Pleket, "Athleten im Altertum: Soziale Herkunft und Ideologie,"
   Nikephoros 18 (2005): 151–63.
8 For a full discussion of the evidence and recent scholarship, see Ingomar
   Weiler, "Theodosius I. und die Olympischen Spiele," *Nikephoros* 17 (2004):
   53–75 and Remijsen, *The End of Greek Athletics in Late Antiquity*, 47–50,
   184–7, 212–17. The religious legislation referred to (often implicitly) are
   the laws recorded in the *Codex Theodosianus* 16.10.10–12. For an English
   translation of the Theodosian code, see Clyde Pharr, *The Theodosian Code
   and Novels and the Sirmondian Constitutions: A Translation with Commentary,
   Glossary, and Bibliography* (Princeton: Princeton University Press, 1952),
   esp. 473–4 for the relevant laws.
9 For an introduction to these administrative changes, see, for example,
   John H.W.G. Liebeschuetz, "Government and Administration in the Late
   Empire (to A.D. 476)," in *The Roman World*, ed. John Walker (London:
   Routledge, 1987), 1: 455–69; and Jean-Michel Carrié, "Developments in

Provincial and Local Administration," in *The Crisis of Empire: A.D. 193–337*, ed. Alan Bowman, Peter Garnsey, and Averil Cameron (Cambridge: Cambridge University Press, 2005): 269–312, esp. 301–2 for the cities' finances.

10 See Remijsen, *The End of Greek Athletics in Late Antiquity*, 289–320, for changes to the financial organization of games.

11 See, for example, the review of Fagan's book by Christian Mann, "Review of: Fagan, Garrett G. *The Lure of the Arena. Social Psychology and the Crowd at the Roman Games*. Cambridge: Cambridge University Press, 2011," *Nikephoros* 24 (2011): 291.

12 Garrett G. Fagan, *The Lure of the Arena: Social Psychology and the Crowd at the Roman Games* (Cambridge: Cambridge University Press, 2011), 197–209.

13 Pierre Bourdieu, *An Outline of a Theory of Practice*, trans. Richard Nice (Cambridge: Cambridge University Press, 1977), 72.

14 For a good example of how the concept of cultural performance can be applied to ancient games, see Jonathan C. Edmondson, "Dynamic Arenas: Gladiatorial Presentations in the City of Rome and the Construction of Roman Society during the Early Empire," in *Roman Theater and Society*, ed. William J. Slater (Ann Arbor: University of Michigan Press, 1996), 69–112, esp. 73–4.

15 The standard work on gladiators in the Roman East is Louis Robert's *Les gladiateurs dans l'Orient grec* (Paris: Champion, 1940, republished in Amsterdam: A.M. Hakkert, 1971). Robert was the first to prove that these violent Roman games were also popular in areas dominated by Greek culture. For a recent work on the more subtle differences in perceptions of gladiators in the East, see Christian Mann, *"Um keinen Kranz, um das Leben kämpfen wir!" Gladiatoren im Osten des Römischen Reiches und die Frage der Romanisierung* (Berlin: Verlag Antike, 2011).

16 Augustine, *Confessions* 6.13. Translation quoted from Fagan, *The Lure of the Arena*, 291–3.

17 On the gladiator as personified *virtus*, see Keith Hopkins, *Death and Renewal* (Cambridge: Cambridge University Press, 1983), 1–30. For a good study on the social background and self-representation of gladiators in Roman Nîmes, see Valerie Hope, "Negotiating Identity and Status: The Gladiators of Roman Nîmes," *Cultural Identity in the Roman Empire*, ed. Ray Laurence and Joanne Berry (London: Routledge, 1998), 175–95. For an introduction to the legal status of *infamia* for performers, see Hartmut Leppin, "Between Marginality and Celebrity: Entertainers and Entertainments in Roman Society," in *The Oxford Handbook of Social Relations in the Roman World*, ed. Michael Peachin (Oxford: Oxford University Press, 2011), 671–2. For the social composition of the spectating masses, see Fagan, *The Lure of the Arena*, 96–120.

18 For a recent study on the ephebate and its spread in the Hellenistic period,
    see Andrzej S. Chankowski, *L'éphébie hellénistique. Etude d'une institution
    civique dans les cités grecques des îles de la Mer Egée et de l'Asie Mineure* (Paris:
    de Boccard, 2010). For a register of all sources, documenting its spread
    in the Roman Empire, see Nigel M. Kennell, *Ephebeia: A Register of Greek
    Cities with Citizen Training Systems in the Hellenistic and Roman Periods*
    (Hildesheim: Weidmann, 2006); and for a more in-depth analysis of the
    role of the ephebate in imperial-age Athens, see Hans-Ulrich Wiemer, "Von
    der Bürgerschule zum aristokratischen Klub? Die athenische Ephebie in
    der römischen Kaiserzeit," *Chiron* 41 (2011): 487–537.

19 For the importance of athletics in the education of the elite, for the social
    background of athletes, and for the role of athletics in the formation of an
    elite identity, see especially the following works of Onno van Nijf: "Local
    Heroes: Athletics, Festivals, and Elite Self-Fashioning in the Roman East,"
    in *Being Greek under Rome: Cultural Identity, the Second Sophistic, and the De-
    velopment of Empire*, ed. Simon Goldhill (Cambridge: Cambridge University
    Press, 2001), 306–34; "Athletics, Andreia and the Askêsis-Culture in the
    Roman East," in *Andreia: Studies in Manliness and Courage in Classical An-
    tiquity*, ed. Ralph M. Rosen and Ineke Sluiter (Leiden: Brill, 2003): 263–86;
    and "Athletics and Paideia: Festivals and Physical Education in the World
    of the Second Sophistic," in *Paideia: The World of the Second Sophistic*, ed.
    Barbara E. Borg (Berlin: De Gruyter 2004), 203–27.

20 Cf. Alan Cameron, *Circus Factions: Blues and Greens at Rome and Byzantium*
    (Oxford: Clarendon Press, 1976), 216: "The gymnasium died a natu-
    ral death unlamented even by the few remaining Hellenes of the day."
    Tertullian's treatise *On Spectacles*, the first systematic Christian polemic
    against Greco-Roman festivals, written ca. AD 200, can of course be
    regarded as an innovation in the ancient discourse on games. Such Latin
    treatises, however, would not have influenced the discourse of the main
    group participating in athletic culture. Tertullian wrote for the Christians
    in the West, where athletics had always had a different role than in the
    East – in the West, people liked to watch, and to train leisurely, but they
    always remained reticent about competing in public. In the culturally
    Greek East, Christian criticism of athletics was far milder – for example,
    Clement of Alexandria (*Paedagogus* 3.9–10) did not approve of visiting the
    baths purely for pleasure, but did consider it healthy for boys to wrestle in
    the *palaistra*. A similar tradition of systematically argued polemics never
    developed in the East.

21 We know of several young athletes from elite backgrounds who excelled at
    the games. Cf. Remijsen, *The End of Greek Athletics in Late Antiquity*, 264–5.
    For every boy who excelled, however, many more did not. A nice illus-
    tration of this principle, and of the fact that athletic training for boys was

apparently not considered something typical of pagans, is a letter (No. 1671) from the collection of Isidore of Pelusium, an Egyptian ascetic from the early fifth century, who remarked to his acquaintance Agathodaimon, a schoolteacher, that not all boys training with a private trainer became athletes (as an illustration that not every child can become very competent).

22 For the character of the main city magistracy in the imperial-age gymnasium, the gymnasiarchy, see Peter Scholz, "Städtische Honoratioren-herrschaft und Gymnasiarchie in der Kaiserzeit," in *Das kaiserzeitliche Gymnasion*, ed. Peter Scholz and Dirk Wiegandt (Berlin: De Gruyter, 2015), 79–96, 82–91.

23 See Fikret Yegül, *Bathing in the Roman World* (Cambridge: Cambridge University Press, 2010), 155–9, for a fuller description of imperial-age gymnasia.

24 For a discussion of these changes, with examples, see Fikret Yegül, *Baths and Bathing in Classical Antiquity* (Cambridge, MA: MIT Press, 1992), 307–13; and Yegül, *Bathing in the Roman World*, 181–3.

25 Himerius, a fourth-century teacher working in Athens, assumed that his students would spend their time off with ball games (*Oration* 69.7). An early-Byzantine inscription (SEG XXXVI 1343, l. 5) from Hammat Gader (near the Sea of Galilee) mentions the creation of a "playground" in a renovated bathing complex.

26 Later Greek *lexica* explain the word *gymnasion* as a synonym for baths. See, for example, Suda, s.v. Γυμνάσια • ἀλειπτήρια ἤ βαλανεῖα ἤ λουτρά. The Suda is the largest of the Byzantine *lexica*: it dates from the tenth century but includes much information from earlier texts.

27 See Chankowski, *L'éphébie hellénistique*, 319–82, for the military aspect of the Hellenistic ephebate; and Wiemer, "Von der Bürgerschule zum aristokratischen Klub?" 491–95 for the remainders of this aspect in the later Athenian ephebate and 497–98 for the typical activities of the imperial-age ephebes.

28 For a good discussion of the political culture of these cities see Arjan Zuiderhoek, *The Politics of Munificence in the Roman Empire: Citizens, Elites and Benefactors in Asia Minor* (Cambridge: Cambridge University Press, 2009). For the role of the ephebate in the socialization of the youth in imperial-age Athens see Wiemer "Von der Bürgerschule zum aristokratischen Klub?," 500, 505–8, 513–14.

29 A clear indication that the Athenian ephebate was still very popular at the time of the Herulian invasion is the sheer length of the most recent lists of ephebes (for the numbers, see the table in Wiemer, "Von der Bürgerschule zum aristokratischen Klub?," 219). On the chronological distribution of inscriptions, the so-called epigraphic habit, see Ramsay MacMullen, "The Epigraphic Habit in the Roman Empire," *American Journal of Philology*

103 (1982): 233–46; and for placing the third-century decline in the wider context of new means of self-representation, see Barbara E. Borg, "Bilder für die Ewigkeit oder glanzvoller Auftritt? Zum Repräsentationsverhalten der stadtrömischen Eliten im dritten Jahrhundert nach Christus," in *Statuen in der Spätantike*, ed. Franz Alto Bauer and Christian Witschel (Wiesbaden: Reichert Verlag, 2007), 43–77.

30 The latest reference to a *kosmetes* in a papyrus text (P.Ant. I 31) from Roman Egypt is dated to AD 347. The previous sources on the Egyptian ephebate are two decades earlier: P.Sakaon 66, another papyrus with a *kosmetes*, dates from 328, and P.Oxy. I 42 documents a contest for ephebes in 323.

31 Cf. n9 for these administrative changes.

32 Dio Chrysostomus, *Oration* 28.12

33 Pseudo-Dionysius, *Ars rhetorica* 7.292. This passage belongs to a chapter teaching the student of rhetoric how to praise an athlete. An English translation of this little-known rhetorical handbook can be found in Donald A. Russell and Nigel G. Wilson, *Menander Rhetor* (Oxford: Oxford University Press, 1981), 377–81.

34 See James A. Francis, *Subversive Virtue: Asceticism and Authority in the Second-Century Pagan World* (University Park: Pennsylvania State University Press, 1995), esp. xiii–xvi, for the term "subversive."

35 Peter Brown, *The Body and Society: Men, Women, and Sexual Renunciation in Early Christianity* (New York: Columbia University Press, 1988), 190–2, 202.

36 The standard work on the popularity and authority of such ascetics or "holy men" is Peter Brown's "The Rise and Function of the Holy Man in Late Antiquity," *Journal of Roman Studies* 61 (1971): 80–101. For children playing demon and monk, see Theodoret's *Religious History* 9.9.

37 The image of the professional athlete as a glutton goes back to classical Athens. Cf. Zinon Papakonstantinou, "Ancient Critics of Greek Sport," in *A Companion to Sport and Spectacle in Greek and Roman Antiquity*, ed. Paul Christesen and Donald G. Kyle (Chichester: Wiley-Blackwell, 2014): 324. For Christian authors repeating this argument, see, for example, Tatian, *Address to the Greeks* 23; Tertullian, *On Spectacles* 18; and Novatian, *On Spectacles* 8. The passages of both Tertullian and Novatian also use the word *vanus*. It is important to note that the nudity of the athletes is not an important issue in these texts. Male nudity would only become an issue by the fifth or sixth century AD – too late to have influenced the decline of nude athletic exercises. Cf. Remijsen, *The End of Greek Athletics in Late Antiquity*, 275–7.

38 The roots of the famous list of "seven deadly sins" lie in a late fourth-century list of evil thoughts by Evagrius of Pontus. He considered pride the greatest temptation of all. Cf. Evagrius Ponticus, *Practicus* 13–14. A famous description of the vainglory of the presidents of games can be

found in a treatise by John Chrysostom (ca. AD 400) called "An address on vainglory and the right way for Parents to bring up their children," esp. 4–5 (most easily accessible in the 1951 translation by Max L.W. Laistner, *Christianity and Pagan Culture in the Later Roman Empire: Together with an English Translation of John Chrysostom's Address on Vainglory and the Right Way for Parents to Bring Up Their Children* (Ithaca: Cornell University Press, 1951).

39 Augustinus, *Confessions* 1.10: "I loved the conceited victories in contests." See *Confessions* 4.2–3 for the fact that he indeed won a competition for poets as a young man and was awarded the victory crown by the governor.

40 The description of Olympic athletes in John Malalas's sixth-century *Chronicle* (12.10) is explicit, as well as insistent on the fact these were noble and chaste youths, and is intended to counter the negative expectations of his readers. A new German translation of this work was published in 2009 by Johannes Thurn and Misha Meier, *Johannes Malalas. Weltchronik* (Stuttgart: Hiersemann, 2009).

41 Examples are collected in Bohne, *Bilder vom Sport*; see nos. K1, K23, K51, K55, K56, K61, K85b, and K100 of this catalogue.

42 For this type of athletes see Remijsen, *The End of Greek Athletics in Late Antiquity*, 224–30, 249–51.

43 For a fuller discussion on the terminology for games and its changes in Late Antiquity, see Remijsen, *The End of Greek Athletics in Late Antiquity*, 326–34.

44 The last surviving contest was the Olympic contest of Antioch (currently Antakya on the Turkish–Syrian border). For its disappearance, see John Malalas, *Chronicle* 17.12.

45 This vase, which is in a private collection, was first discussed by Dietrich O. Klose and Thomas Klein, "Werbung für den Wettkampf in spätantiker Zeit: Die Bronzevase des Privatulus aus archäologischer und philologischer Sicht," in *Der gymnische Agon in der Spätantike*, ed. Andreas Gutsfeld and Stephan Lehmann (Gutenberg: Computus, 2013), 143–50. They date the vase to the sixth century, but Katherine Dunbabin, "Athletes, Acclamations, and Imagery from the End of Antiquity," *Journal of Roman Archaeology* 30 (2017): 159–70, convincingly argues it may be as early as AD 400. On pages 152–4 she discusses the Noheda mosaic from ca. AD 400, the imagery of which is closer to other imperial-age depictions (e.g., victors with garlands, palm branches and metal crowns, trumpeters, victors in musical competitions) but is, given its provenance and date, likewise unlikely to refer to a traditional *agon*. Defeat is not glorified as on the bronze vase, but here too two competitors are identified as unsuccessful on panel E.

46 Roland Barthes, *Mythologies*, trans. Richard Howard and Annette Lavers (New York: Hill and Wang, 2012), 4.

47 Ibid., 9.
48 Cf. John Zilcosky's discussion of the same vase in his chapter in this volume, "Wrestling, or the Art of Disentangling Bodies."
49 Barthes, *Mythologies*, 5–6.
50 Ibid., 10.
51 Fagan, *The Lure of the Arena*, 155–66.
52 See Remijsen, *The End of Greek Athletics in Late Antiquity*, 249–51, for the cooperation of such athletes. For the growing dominance of the circus factions from the fifth century on, see Cameron, *Circus Factions*, 214–22.
53 Barthes, *Mythologies*, 3.

4 Wrestling, or the Art of Disentangling Bodies

JOHN ZILCOSKY

Let us begin with a peculiar question about Plato, one that might seem trivial at first glance: Why did the founder of Western philosophy spend so much time writing about wrestling – literally dozens of times, in texts including *The Republic*, *Phaedrus*, and *Laws*?[1] One explanation is biographical. Plato's teacher, Socrates, engaged regularly in the aristocratic practice of light wrestling with friends and hung out at the Athenian palestras – the wrestling schools or, literally, "sites of wrestling" (*palē*). We find Socrates in gymnasia throughout Plato's dialogues and specifically in palestras in *Charmides*, *Lysis*, and *Symposium*. In the latter, Socrates wrestles for hours "many a time" with Alcibiades.[2] Plato was an even more avid wrestler, at least according to Diogenes. Plato's real name was apparently Aristocles, and "Plato" – meaning "broad" – was his ring name, used by his wrestling coach to describe his shoulders. Plato even wrestled competitively in the elite Pythian and Isthmian games.[3]

But even a quick glance at Plato's writings reveals more than just biographical interest. As Plato knew, wrestling, as both sport and allegory, was vital to Greek culture long before Socrates lived.[4] It was ancient Greece's most popular sport by far and one of the most prevalent rhetorical figures in Greek literature, appearing repeatedly as a symbol for oratorical contests (*logōn agōn*), cunning (*mētis*), sexuality (*erōs*), virtuosity (*aretē*), temporality (the "decisive moment" [*kairos*]), and many other aspects of Greek life.[5] More than this, wrestling was central to the elementary education of Greek boys and to paideia in the broadest sense. As Plato understood, to control wrestling's meaning was to hold great philosophical and cultural sway. Correspondingly, he proposed to instruct all boys in wrestling according to quite particular precepts. As I will argue here, Plato's proposal reached beyond technique toward an attempt to revolutionize existing mythical discourses about the body and, by extension, the soul. With the stakes around wrestling so high, it is not surprising, as I will show in the second half of this chapter, that post-Platonic writers and thinkers continued to contest its cultural, psychological, and philosophical meaning from classical antiquity through to the Middle Ages, Romanticism, and the modern era.

Midway through Plato's *Laws*, a Socrates-like man visiting Crete and known only as "the Athenian Stranger" offers suggestions to a Cretan lawgiver about the ideal state. This state should, he argues, have a strong physical education system, based primarily on two arts: dancing and wrestling. The Athenian focuses most extensively on wrestling – initially, however, describing only what its form should *not* be. It should not be the mythical form revealed in the "devices" (literally, things [*ta*]) concerning wrestling (*kata palēn*) "of Antaeus and Cercyon." Although the Athenian supplies no details about what is wrong with this type of wrestling, he dismisses it, in strongly moral terms, as "idle vainglory." He then describes the wrestling that he *would* permit: "Anything which comes under 'stand-up wrestling,' exercises in the disengaging [disentangling (*exeilēsis*)] of neck, arms, and ribs," which all encourage "spirit and gallant bearing."[6] Why does the Athenian insist on this specific form of wrestling, especially considering that it goes against our – and the Greeks' – normal understanding of wrestling?

As Plutarch's friend Philinus points out, runners aim "to put the maximum amount of space between each other" and boxers "are not allowed by referees to clinch," whereas wrestlers are always "laying hold of each other and embracing each other, – most parts of the contest ... bring them together and mix them up with each other." For Philinus, this is not just one part of wrestling but its defining quality: "wrestling (*palē*) got its name from 'draw near' (*plēsiazein*) and 'be close' (*pelas*)."[7] Why does the Athenian aim, through a strategy of "disentangling," to reverse everything that the Greeks thought they knew about wrestling? And how might this reversal work against a moral failing ("vainglory")?

Historians of ancient sport have either given short shrift to this passage or claimed, like the influential Norman Gardiner, that the Athenian's insistence on "stand-up wrestling" is a technical argument against the "pankration" (pancratium), which combined wrestling with boxing.[8] This argument is cited uncritically in the best sourcebook on ancient wrestling[9] and, in part, in R.G. Bury's commentary to the Loeb edition,[10] even though it is based on three doubtful assertions: that Plato had a prejudice against the pancratium, "expressly exclud[ing]" it from his ideal state; that Plato implicitly was criticizing Antaeus and Cercyon for engaging in leg holds (attributed here solely to the pancratium);

and that leg holds themselves were allowed only in the pancratium, not in wrestling.[11] But Plato's Athenian never excludes the pancratium from the state, rendering it instead – like wrestling and other sports – secondary to military practice.[12] Plato likewise makes no reference to leg holds, and his scholiast (who does so almost 1,500 years later) never connects these to the pancratium.[13] Finally, leg holds, like the other tactics that Gardiner ascribes solely to the pancratium (ground fighting, chokeholds, throwing from one's knee) were also, most likely, part of wrestling proper (*palē*).[14] Given the sparseness of ancient sources, we cannot be certain of the exact differences between wrestling and pancratium, but we can be sure that it is impossible to draw such a clean line between the two.[15]

Even if Gardiner's claim about Plato's severity against leg holds and the pancratium had been true, a focus on this technical argument would be missing the Athenian's point: he wants to codify a form of physical combat, called "wrestling," that should create better, more "gallant" citizens. Acknowledging this ethical imperative, Gardiner claims that Plato prohibits the pancratium because it is brutal, practised by "bullies" who humiliate their opponents and undermine the Greek spirit of "honorable rivalry."[16] But this transposition of a Victorian Eton-esque morality of fair play onto ancient Greece is not borne out in the primary sources. The Greeks, whether wrestlers or pancratiasts or boxers, were not as pure as Gardiner and like-minded early twentieth-century champions of amateurism would have liked.[17] But the question remains: If Plato's Athenian is not distinguishing between wrestling and pancratium, and if he is not defending anachronistically a Victorian ideology of amateurism and fair play, then what precisely is his aim?

To answer this question, let us consider what, if not the pancratium, might make Antaeus's and Cercyon's "devices" or styles ethically objectionable (non-"gallant," "idle," "vain"). Extant texts and images insist that the mythical heroes Antaeus and Cercyon were both great wrestlers – Cercyon even has an eponymous Wrestling Ground – but these sources tell us little about their styles.[18] We obviously see no reference to the pancratium because it was invented, like all rule-based sports, well after this era of mythical giants. Although some sources support the scholiast's claim that Cercyon invented the leg hold, there is little evidence that Antaeus used it.[19] What is more, if Plato had meant something as straightforward as prohibiting a certain hold, he would have stated this. What the classical sources do tell us about Antaeus's and Cercyon's wrestling is at once more simple and more profound, inviting a broader interpretation of style or "device" and exploding purely technical or moral readings of the passage: both Antaeus and

Cercyon generally murdered their opponents while wrestling. As we discover in Apollodorus, Cercyon clasped his opponents and "in wrestling killed them." Antaeus, the Libyan giant, challenged all strangers to wrestling matches, during which he likewise murdered them.[20] In the scholia to the above passage of Plato's *Laws*, we read, of Cercyon, that he "forced passersby to wrestle and killed them."[21]

Seen in this light, we can reconsider the question of what troubles Plato's Athenian, however unconsciously, about Antaeus and Cercyon. The problem is not their wrong style (whether pancratium or leg holds), nor is it their indecorous "bullying." Rather, it is that they embody what lurks behind wrestling and all combat sports regardless of how well regulated they are: rage, violence, and murder.[22] Wrestling as murder indeed runs through the mythical accounts, including those in which Cercyon and Antaeus end up as victims at their own game. They are both killed while wrestling – specifically, with the heroes Theseus and Heracles, respectively. Significant is the fact that these otherwise apparently "noble" heroes also use wrestling as a form of murder, just like the "evil" Cercyon and Antaeus.[23] Especially ironic is Theseus's role. Though he founded the modern rule-based wrestling that Plato's Athenian admires,[24] he nonetheless chooses, after he "out-wrestled" Cercyon, to "kill him."[25]

In the case of Heracles's match with Antaeus, Lucan gives us a sense of what such a wrestling-murder might look like. Heracles wraps his arms around Antaeus and says, "here you shall remain, with your body clasped in my embrace." Heracles then lifts the giant off of his power source on Mother Earth and, holding him there, hugs him till he dies: Heracles "gripped the breast," we read, "that now was stiff with numbing cold" (*Alcides medio tenuit iam pectora pigro stricta gelu*).[26] Apollodorus describes this scene similarly, reporting that Heracles wrapped his arms around Antaeus, "hugged him, lifted him aloft, broke and killed him."[27] The more literal translation is "lifted him aloft with hugs," and it includes Apollodorus's word for the lethal embrace itself, *hamma*, which means something that is tied or bound but also denotes "clinches in wrestling."[28] Specifically the "wrestler's hug," *hamma* is a technical term that recurs in ancient texts about wrestling. And it connects here wrestling, uniquely among sports, to death through hugging.[29]

This death through hugging reveals a second aspect of mythological wrestling that would have disturbed Plato's Athenian: wrestling is a technology that merges two bodies into one. We see this already in pre-Greek texts – for example, in Genesis, where Jacob's wrestling match with the angel ends not with Jacob's famous broken hip but with Jacob hugging the angel for as long as he can, for an entire night. When the angel realizes that he cannot disentangle himself, he cries to Jacob,

"Let me go, for the day is breaking." But Jacob will not comply: "I will not let you go."[30] The Mesopotamian demigods Gilgamesh and Enkidu similarly hug for hours while wrestling until they seem to transform into something extra-human: "they grappled, holding each other ... like bulls locked together."[31] In his versification of this scene, Stephen Mitchell extrapolates from "hold" to "embrace," an embrace that creates a strange amalgamated non-human body of flailing, ownerless limbs: "huge arms gripped huge arms, foreheads crashed like wild bulls, the two men ... grappled each other, limbs intertwined, each huge body straining to break free from the other's embrace."[32]

In the later, Greek accounts, we likewise see wrestlers combining into one body that, like the Gilgamesh bull-body, is no longer human. Odysseus and Telemonian Aias, for example, meld together while wrestling in the *Iliad*: they "grappled each other in the hook of their heavy arms, as when rafters lock, when a renowned architect has fitted them in the roof of a high house." This post-human amalgamation now tears and tugs and sweats until Homer loses track of individual physiques: raw places open up on anonymous bodies and body parts – "ribs," "shoulders" – that become smeared with unidentifiable blood.[33] This fascination with fused bodies persisted into Roman accounts of the Greek myths, as when Ovid describes Heracles and the god Achelous wrestling until they became soldered together: "foot locked with foot, fingers with fingers clenched, brow against brow." Having gained the advantage, Heracles "clung" upon Achelous and "pressed close" upon him. Even when Achelous has metamorphosed himself into a snake and a bull, Heracles still "fixed his vice-like grip" on Achelous and "threw his arms around" him.[34] Examples of this amalgamating body technology are legion in Greek pottery, coins, and sculpture, which usually show the combatants already in contact with each other – not in early match feints. They appear either in the Homerian *systasis* – the frontal "joining together" of bodies at the beginning of a match – or as fully enwrapped, mid-match, in a tangle of appendages.[35] The viewer needs to look twice to distinguish whose limbs are whose (Figures 4.1, 4.2, 4.3, 4.4).

More specifically, ancient Greek art also depicts hugging as a form of murder. Heracles strangles the Nemean lion with a zealous embrace, and he employs expressly the *"hamma,"* the wrestler's hug, to kill Antaeus (Figures 4.5, 4.6). Such intertwinings unto death recall further the ancient statue of Laocoön and his sons. Although this statue does not depict a traditional wrestling match, it tells us much about Greek fantasies of what happens to agonistic bodies. They get entangled, and this entanglement can lead, as in the wrestler's hug, to a murder that is not just any murder.[36] For Laocoön and his sons are not only strangled

Figure 4.1. Wrestlers with referee watching, red-figure kylix, 490–480 BCE.
Bibliotheque nationale de France

Figure 4.2. Wrestling, black-figure amphora, 550–500 BCE. Staatliche
Antikensammlungen und Glyptothek München (photo: Renate Kühling)

Figure 4.3. Wrestling, red-figure psykter, 520–510 BCE. Archaeological Collection, University of Zurich (photo: Frank Tomio)

to death. They are enwrapped with the serpents until their individual body parts become difficult to identify. The human and animal appendages merge into a new, massive, extra-human structure (Figure 4.7).

Possibly inspired by this statue, by Sophocles's lost tragedy about Laocoön, and by ancient wrestling technologies, the second-century AD Greek poet Oppian described an underwater battle between an octopus and an eel as a fight between two "wrestlers." They begin by enwrapping themselves, as in the wrestlers' *hamma*:

> The octopus ... fights under deadly compulsion and twines around her [the eel's] limbs, contriving all manner of twists, now this, now that, with his crooked whips, if haply, embracing her in his nooses ... When the octopus enfolds her, the nimble eel with her slippery limbs easily escapes through his embrace like water. But the octopus twines now round her spotted back, now round her neck, now round her very tail, and anon rushes into the gates of her mouth and the recesses of her jaws. Even as two men skilled in valiant wrestling long time display their might against

Figure 4.4. Wrestling, red-figure krater, 515–510 BCE. Louvre
(photo: RMN-Grand Palais / Art Resource, NY)

each other; already from the limbs of both pours the sweat warm and
abundant and the varied wiles of their art are all abroad and their hands
wave about their bodies; even so the suckers of the octopus, at random
["without order"] plied, are all abroad, and labour in vain wrestling.[37]

The octopus and eel resemble wrestlers because they "embrace" in
battle and then are "twined" and "enfolded" around each other. More
than this, their individual bodies are hard to distinguish, like those of
the wrestlers, whose limbs seem to have lives of their own. We see not
limbs belonging to one or the other person, but simply "the limbs of
both." These undulate wildly ("all abroad" [*plazomenai*]) as if without
proprietors. We likewise see only "their" (not "his" or "her") hands.
And these hands wave aimlessly about "their" bodies – also ownerless.

Figure 4.5. Heracles embracing and killing the Nemean lion, black-figure oenochoe, 520–500 BCE

Figure 4.6. Heracles employing the *hamma* ("wrestler's hug") to kill Antaeus, marble, ca. 200–100 BCE. Commune di Catania – Museo Civico Castello Ursino

These fighting sea creatures, like the wrestlers, mix up limbs "at random," without order (*ou kata kosmon*). Despite the eel's gendering as female and the octopus's as male, the reader must look twice to remember who is who: he "twines around her limbs ... with his crooked whips ... embracing her in his nooses," and he "enfolds her," while she "with her slippery limbs easily escapes through his embrace." As in the epic match between Odysseus and Telemonian Aias, the reader sees one body instead of two individuals. Anonymous parts – limbs, hands, necks, and backs – combine to create a new being.

At this point, the eel begins to ingest the octopus, but because of the jumbled appendages, one cannot immediately distinguish who is eating whom: "Some of his limbs her belly receives, while other parts the sharp teeth still grind in her jaws, others are still quivering and twisting, half consumed, struggling still."[38] The confusion increases in the original Greek, where no article or adjective denotes the owner of the "belly," and the limbs are in the neuter plural. A strict translation would be "the limbs the belly receives." The stomach and teeth are disembodied, and the limbs act as if they were people. Because the participles are in the neuter plural, *the limbs themselves* seem to want to get away (*ekphugein ethelonta*).[39] This grammatical ambiguity heightens the

Figure 4.7. Laocoön and his sons, marble, copy after a Hellenstic original from ca. 200 BCE

uncanny power already present in the image: half-digested limbs still struggle even after the subject (the octopus, we now realize) is dead. This confirms our knowledge from wrestling and explains why Oppian calls these creatures wrestlers: body parts exist independently and take on lives of their own. This eerie separation of bodies from subjects creates new extremes of physical experience that are both brutal and pleasurable. Her/the belly receives his/the limbs, and she bites his "other parts," while still other of his "parts" continue to quiver, even as "he" seems to die. Wrestling heightens here its own mythical body

Figure 4.8. One youth gooses another in the palestra, red-figure kylix, 510–500 BCE. Warsaw National Museum

technology: the orgasmic, dying flesh becomes a mishmash of parts, disconnected from a soul.

Such a *jouissance* through wrestling reminds us of the erotic, naked wrestling culture in ancient Greece, where the palestras were well known as hot spots for sexual encounters. We see this in vase paintings from the fourth and fifth centuries, which depict naked boys flirting with one another and with their teachers (Figures 4.8, 4.9).[40] A telling moment at the outset of Plato's *Lysis* attests to this. Teenage boys draw Socrates into a palestra, where Socrates engages them in a conversation about "handsome boys" and they admire together the body of young Lysis.[41] In *Symposium*, similarly, Alcibiades attempts to seduce Socrates by inviting him to a round of wrestling: "So [Socrates] trained and wrestled with me many a time when no one was there." But Alcibiades's seduction fails: "The same story! I got no further in the affair." Frustrated on the mat, Alcibiades then uses a wrestling metaphor to describe his next move: he makes the "frontal attack" of inviting Socrates to his home.[42]

Figure 4.9. A boy and his sexually aroused teacher fondle each other in the palestra (palestra identified by the boy's athletic bag and the strigil, aryballos, and sponge hanging on the wall), red-figure tondo, ca. 480 BCE. Ashmolean Museum (Oxford)

This metaphor of frontal attack exemplifies wrestling's popularity as an erotic simile. The Greeks spoke wittily of *epiklinopalē*, which sounds like a real wrestling technique but actually means "bed wrestling" or "wrestling while lying down" (*epiklino-palē*).[43] Aristophanes put a fine point on this marriage of wrestling and sex in his 421 BC play, *Peace*, where he equated rough sex with a combination of "wrestl[ing]" (*palē*) and "pancratium": you get your partner/opponent down "on all fours" and then gouge them "with fist and prick alike!"[44] Lucian reinforced this double entendre when humorously describing his own sexual wrestling match with a woman named Palaistra, after the Greek goddess of wrestling. As Michael Poliakoff points out, Lucian's tongue-in-cheek wrestling vocabulary recalls specific sexual positions that were well known to Greek audiences through representations on pottery and trophies (Figures 4.10, 4.11).[45]

Figure 4.10. Erotic scene, black-figure championship trophy, 540 BCE. Staatliche Museen zu Berlin (photo: bpk Bildagentur, Art Resource, NY). Cf. Lucian, *Asin. (The Ass)* 10.17, and Poliakoff, *Studies in the Terminology of the Greek Combat Sports*, 120, 186

Figure 4.11. Erotic scene, red-figure kylix, ca. 470 BCE. Museo Nazionale Tarquiniense. Cf. Lucian, *Asin. (The Ass)* 9.15 ff., and Poliakoff, *Studies in the Terminology of the Greek Combat Sports*, 111–25, 185.

The wrestler's embrace, which mythical wrestlers employed as a murder tool, likewise appears in this sexual context. Straton of Sardis describes sexual penetration as a form of "wrestling" and hugging: you "take your adversary by the middle, and laying him down get astride of him, and shoving forward, fall on him and hold him tight."[46] Lucian's wrestling partner, "Palaistra," equates sex specifically with the wrestler's embrace – the *hamma*. She coquettishly teaches Lucian how to engage her, his "adversary." You must "grapple with" (or "embrace") me,[47] she says, then "grab me by both thighs and put me on my back. Next get on top of me, slip in through my thighs and open me up, keeping your legs poised above me and ... keeping glued to your target." This description of wrestling-sex as an all-encompassing hug continues in the following paragraphs. While "stab[bing]" his adversary in the groin, the wrestler should "lock yourself in close" and "cling round [*hamma*] your opponent by the waist."[48] The wrestler, Lucian, should "embrace me [Palaistra] at the centre of operations [the middle (*mesa*)]" (a pun for genitalia),[49] then "grip me tight, allowing no gap between us" until I am "completely wet" (literally, until "your whole opponent is water" [*hudōr olos esti soi ho antagonistēs*]).[50] Palaistra is giving instructions here for more than wrestling or sex or even wrestling-sex. She is teaching the exciting and dangerous body technology of wrestling, which produces fluids beyond just those of sexual climax. As in the match between the octopus and the eel, wrestling dissolves the borders of the body – causing even human matter to liquefy.

This orgasmic wrestling embrace recalls a famous one in Greek literature: the rape of Thetis by one of mythology's greatest wrestlers, Peleus, the father of Achilles.[51] Among the many rapes in Greek myth, Thetis's is noteworthy because the aggressor (Peleus) ends up taking a beating from his victim and, more important for my purposes, because his method consists simply in holding on to her – never allowing her to disentangle herself, no matter what: "Entwining [her] neck with both his arms," he "held fast" and did "tightly cling" to her while she transformed into fire, water, a serpent, a tiger, and a cuttlefish (*sepia*). As Proteus instructs Peleus: "though she take a hundred lying forms, let her not escape thee, but hold her close, whatever she may be."[52] Peleus does as told. Even though ultimately soaked, scorched, bitten, clawed, and coated in a gluey sepia ink, Peleus does "not let her go."[53] Now "held firmly bound," Thetis realizes that Peleus, the expert wrestler, cannot be shaken. She submits, allowing him to "embrace" her. In so doing, he "attain[s] his desire" and "beg[ets] on her" the warrior Achilles.[54]

This ecstatic wrestler's hug, like Heracles's lethal wrestling embrace, reveals the larger stakes of what initially seemed to be Plato's technical quibble in *Laws* – his call for techniques of "disentanglement" (*exeilēsis*). For we can now see the psychological danger, from Plato's perspective, of the mythical wrestling made notorious by Antaeus and Cercyon. Mythical wrestling merged bodies beyond recognition through sex and death, and as Plato knew, this had not stopped in the post-mythical era: the young men at the palestra still considered wrestling to be foreplay, and just fifty years before Plato's birth, Telemachus of Pharsalia proudly killed his opponent while wrestling at Olympia.[55] The force of Plato's argument rests on the word *exeilēsis*, which he probably garnered initially from Athens's palestras. Although we cannot know the full extent of *exeilēsis's* figurative depth, the Byzantine scholar "Zonaras" testifies that it shifted, beginning already in Classical Greece, from primarily technical to primarily metaphorical meanings. *Exeilēsis* emerged from describing simply "those who free themselves in wrestling" to describing various symbolic forms of disentangling or escaping – also in the psychological sense.[56]

Because of the poor preservation of Hellenistic texts generally, many such metaphorical uses of *exeilēsis* have presumably been lost, and extant examples are rare, but we do still see this in the writings of Marcus Aurelius and other ancient authors. Aurelius re-employed Plato's wrestling term specifically to buttress Plato's theory of the soul (*psyche*): the theory that the *psyche* had its own integrity, as separate from the body. Plato insisted that this separation revealed itself most fully at the point of death, and this is what Aurelius describes: the "gentle slipping away ['disentangling,' *exeilēsis*] of soul [*psyche*] from body."[57] By using Plato's technical term to exemplify a key aspect of Platonic psychology, Aurelius makes explicit what was only implicit in *Laws*. The new disentangled wrestler is a model not just for the more "gallant" citizen but also for the modern *psyche*, which can separate itself from the *soma*. This is what renders the new wrestler pedagogically useful and explains why wrestling, that cornerstone of paideia, is so important to Plato. Boys who learned to disentangle their bodies from other bodies were also learning, through metaphor, to separate their *psyches* – both from their bodies and from the *psyches* of others. They were learning to transcend mythology's old wrestling style and, more important, myth's old form of being. The individual no longer needed to be fully entangled within tragedy's communal chorus.

Because, in Plato's philosophy, the most important part of the tripartite *psyche* is reason (*logos*), it is not surprising that Plato's disentangled wrestler should be a thinking man. Whereas the mythical wrestlers – Antaeus and Cercyon – acted mindlessly, Plato's new wrestler will learn the rules of wrestling set forth in "our code."[58] This tightly governed wrestling shall serve as a model for all sports, as the Athenian announces later in *Laws*: "we shall follow the precedent set by existing authorities on wrestling in their rules for the proper conduct of that sport." In all sports, wrestling's model of rule-based victory will pertain: "We shall ... award the prizes of victory to those who best fulfill the demands of our regulations."[59] Within this rule-based framework, the thinking man will always have the advantage over, say, the rageful Antaeus. Socrates states as much already in Plato's *Alcibiades*, where he uses wrestling as a metaphor for reflection itself: successful wrestlers, he says, must "deliberate" before the match about "with whom they should wrestle close, and with whom only at arm's length, and in what manner."[60] This new, tactical wrestler extends the metaphor of *exeilēsis* in two ways. First, he symbolizes the separation of the modern *psyche*, through *logos*, from its earlier mythical entanglement in choral oneness. Second, he emblematizes social progression: only after this wrestler twists himself free from bodies – both others' and his own – can he become a thinking subject capable of rational decision-making and ethical action. He can now transform the "vainglory" of the murderous, erotic embrace into the "gallantry" of *exeilēsis*.

Long after the death of the philosopher-wrestlers from antiquity – Socrates, Plato, Aristotle – this debate about the psychological and philosophical significance of wrestling continued. Wrestling, like all ancient sports, remained relatively stable (in terms of rules, techniques, and sets of disciplines) into the fourth century AD, at which point it declined; yet it continued to be practised privately and also publicly, often as a circus-like spectacle.[61] Among other sources, a recently discovered bronze vase (ca. 400 AD) hints at these types of over-the-top performances that attracted audiences – precisely through the physical excess that Plato had hoped to banish.[62] In this vase's six scenes, one man repeatedly wrestles, beats, and humiliates another.[63] Scenes one and three explicitly connect wrestling to sex through what seems to be anal intercourse. The inherent violence in this is especially clear in the first scene, where the victim tries to protect his genitals from the attacker's clutching hand. By the second scene, the victim is lying on the ground after being trampled and whipped (Figure 4.12).

A closer look at scenes three and one reveals more than just sex and violence; these scenes point specifically to the pre-Socratic body technology that Plato had censured. The third image shows the victim's right thigh overlapping with the aggressor's such that, at first glance, the aggressor's right knee and lower leg seem to sprout from the victim's thigh. In scene one, more pointedly, the right leg of the aggressor looks as if it could also be the right leg of the victim (Figure 4.13).

Figure 4.12. Privatulus versus Victorinus, bronze vase, ca. 400 AD. Drawn by Willy Remijsen on the basis of photographs by Hartwig Hotter

Figure 4.13. Privatulus versus Victorinus, close-up of scene one (from Figure 4.12)

We eventually see that it belongs to the aggressor but notice that what appears to be the right leg *of the victim* is strangely short and thin. Is it actually an arm? Or, considering its extension from the victim's groin at an impossible angle, a massive crooked penis? Because the right arm of the aggressor is not shown, this renegade leg/arm/penis could also conceivably be *the attacker's* disarranged right arm. However we interpret this fugitive limb, it is out of place, not belonging properly to either man. This recalls the blurring of limbs that we saw in the ancient vases, in *Laocoön and His Sons*, and in Oppian's wrestling sea creatures. A single animal appears with two heads, either four or five arms, and three or four legs.

This confusion is not only physical, but also psychological, as we see from the captions. The victim is called "Victorinus" (the winner), whereas the actual victor is given the pathetic label of "Privatulus" – the little *privatus*, a man without an official function. This mix-up of "Victorinus" and "Privatulus" reveals, as Plato had already implied, the larger stakes of wrestling. We do not know whose identity – whose *psyche* – is whose because we do not know whose limbs are whose. Wrestling is the body technology that threatens the birth of the modern subject metaphorically, through a confusion of flesh.

But the vase engraver, *pace* Plato, finds nothing wrong with this. In fact, his vase reads as a goad against the Platonic praise of subjectivity and virtuous action. The conflation of bodies and subjects is playful, as suggested by the mix-up of "Victorinus" and "Privatulus." Although we could read this name-switching as Plato might – as a further ironic humiliation of the loser – a different reading is more plausible, especially considering the provocative tone of the entire vase. Does the loser actually win? Instead of granting us a moral story about a "bad" aggressor that would, as with the evil Antaeus and Cercyon, teach us to be ethical, the engraver offers a victim who is "Victorinus." Perhaps this victim *likes* what is happening – likes also, as the caption beneath scenes two and three states, to "do this to himself" ("He who did this to himself shouldn't cry" [*qui sibi fecit non ploret*]). The aggressor is now the loser, the pleasure-giver who is ultimately meaningless: a little man with no function.[64]

The engraver overturns also our broader understanding of good and bad. Is the victim now the guilty one, for satisfying his furtive pleasures? And does his satisfaction in losing disgracefully correspond, psychologically, to a secret joy in losing his identity? Might this, *not* his shame, explain Victorinus's covering of his face in scenes three and four? This perverse pleasure takes place in a world free from *logos* and morality, as we see in the final scene, where the victim raises his finger, the typical form of signalling submission to a judge. But no judge is present. No superior being or form of rationality is present to limit this series of self-dissolving excess. Just as Plato the pedagogue had feared, wrestling, when not regulated, threatens the integrity of the *psyche*.

Although wrestling, like all sports, waned during late antiquity and the early Middle Ages, it continued to be practised, and this tension between wrestling as self-immolating excess and as a mode of rational self-realization persisted. Folk wrestling was indeed so popular – and apparently corrupting – that it warranted warnings from the churches. Two different English thirteenth-century texts enjoined clergy to prohibit "wrestling" and "ring-dancing," "especially on church feast-days." This suggests that wrestling was particularly prevalent and, what is more, that it continued to threaten social norms – with the same loss of reason and identity that Plato had feared.[65]

On the other hand, aristocrats viewed wrestling as a salutary model of Platonic subject-creation. Consider Beowulf, the champion of the Geats, who became the first hero in English literature precisely by winning a wrestling match. Significantly, he wins by adhering to Plato's two ideologies: strategic thinking, and disentanglement. Whereas his opponent, the monster Grendel, does not think or plan ahead (has "no thought" of "deferring") and engages in the most extreme form of *entanglement* – he "laid hold" of his opponent, "bit his bone," drank his blood, and, like Oppian's eel, devoured him – Beowulf feigns sleep in order to watch Grendel and *think* about how to fight him.[66] When the battle begins, Beowulf grabs Grendel from as far away as possible, on the wrist. He employs what *Beowulf* scholars have recognized as a wrestler's armlock, likely known to *Beowulf*'s author through representations of wrestling in heroic Germanic literature.[67] Beowulf twists the monster's arm and severs it at the shoulder until he bleeds to death, thus seeming to combine brilliantly, in one move, the Platonic skills of tactical thinking and disentanglement. By deliberating ahead of time, Beowulf wins without getting too close to his opponent; he need not employ the wrestler's hug.

But when Beowulf triumphantly hangs the monster's severed arm in the warrior's hall, we see also residue of that same physical excess that Plato had hoped to banish. The arm that had belonged to one subject now belongs to another. Beowulf's bloodthirsty violence leads to a dismembering and confusion of body parts. Grendel's arm is now Beowulf's. Beowulf indeed becomes a "hero," but only through this ambivalent path of wrestling.[68] His Platonic *exeilēsis* is only partly successful. It cannot completely contain his underlying desires for murder, dismemberment, and the conflation of himself with the monstrous other.[69]

A similar threat of mortal entanglement – now tinged with sexual violence – appears in Beowulf's subsequent wrestling match with Grendel's avenging mother. Grendel's mother overcomes Beowulf's trusty armlock (his "hand-grapple"), then succeeds in wrestling him to the ground. Her next move is telling: she "sat on" him.[70] Her attack with her buttocks recalls the mythical depiction of wrestling as rape: Perseus's violation of Thetis, with the genders now reversed. Beowulf seems certain to die through this combination of sexual suffocation and knife stabs, until God intervenes and allows him to extricate himself. Beowulf now emerges from beneath. He "uprose" and became "erect" – thus disentangling himself again and continuing on his path of heroic individuation.[71] But as in his battle with Grendel, this individuation remains haunted by its opposite. Beowulf is too weak to separate himself (God must help), and more important, his sexual subordination suggests a recurrence of the same illicit desires he had had with Grendel: Beowulf wants both to extricate *and* entangle himself, to break free from Grendel's mother *and* lose himself in her limbs and buttocks.[72]

By the late Middle Ages, this understanding of wrestling as a heroic form of subject formation – however ambivalent – was well-established. Aristocratic families commissioned combat manuals (*Fechtbücher*) from at least the fifteenth century onward. These included Hans Talhoffer's famous 1443–67 series, which featured illustrations of wrestling techniques as well as the first publication of the methods of his predecessor Ott Jud, the wrestling master of the Habsburgs.[73] A few decades later, at the notorious 1520 meeting on the Field of the Cloth of Gold, the English monarch, Henry VIII, challenged the French king, Francis I, to a wrestling match. Francis won, employing his "croc-en-jambe" and then pinning Henry to the ground.[74]

Aware of the psychological and political significance of such entanglements, Albrecht Dürer wrote and illustrated a combat manual in 1512 – drawing what he considered the 120 most important wrestling moves, including Beowulf-like armlocks and other distancing tricks. Like the wrestling images that appeared in the first-ever published work on physical education (ca. 1500), Dürer's manual confirmed the importance of wrestling pedagogy in late medieval Europe.[75] More than this, it reasserted the ancient metaphorical significance of disentanglement. Dürer warns that wrestlers must do whatever it takes to separate themselves from their rivals: you should "push [the opponent] away with your arms" and, to make the opponent himself "shove away," brutally assail him "on his neck by the right ear" (*greife ihn an seinen Hals beim rechten Ohr*) (Figure 4.14).[76] Although Dürer never mentions the potential sexual dangers and thrills of such entanglements, his successors in the Renaissance and the Baroque do – and so return us to the ambivalence in *Beowulf*. Out of many possible examples, consider Michelangelo's *Two Wrestlers* (ca. 1530) and Michael Sweerts's powerfully erotic *Wrestling Match* (1649).[77] The Renaissance and the Baroque also featured compelling re-creations of Heracles's lethal *hamma* against Antaeus, as in works from the German "Little Masters," the Italian Renaissance, and the Spanish Golden Age (Figures 4.15, 4.16, 4.17).

After this early modern period, wrestling, now seen as unrefined and rustic, slipped out of aristocratic practice but remained popular as a folk sport: as Ranggeln in the Habsburg realm, Schwingen in Switzerland, Gouren in northwestern France, and Devon and Cornish

Figure 4.14. "Push him away with your arms," then make him pull farther away by assailing him "on his neck by the right ear," Albrecht Dürer (*Dürers Fechtbuch*, Taf. 20 n. 59 [see my endnote 76]). Heidelberg University Library, *Jahrbuch der Kunsthistorischen Sammlungen des Allerhöchsten Kaiserhauses* vol. 27, Taf. 20 – CC-BY-SA 3.0

Figure 4.15. *Hercules Wrestling Antaeus* (1529), engraving, Heinrich Aldegrever. The British Museum

Figure 4.16. Hercules wrestling Antaeus (ca. 1560–90), marble relief in the style of Bandinelli (artist unknown) (photo: Daniel Katz Ltd.)

Figure 4.17. *Hercules Fighting Antaeus* (1634), Francisco de Zurbaran

wrestling in England. Despite this slip down the social ladder, wrestling continued to fascinate thinkers through its embodiment of the tension between thrilling physical excess and rational disentanglement. Heinrich von Kleist, who would have learned wrestling techniques during his years in the Prussian army, delineates this tension in his 1810 story/essay "Von der Überlegung" ("On Reflection" or "On Thinking Things Over"). Likely drawing on knowledge of Schwingen, featured in the anti-Napoleonic Unspunnen Festival in 1805,[78] and of English folk wrestling, which drew massive crowds in the early nineteenth century,[79] Kleist uses wrestling here to exemplify a point: that thinking is overrated, even dangerous. "If thinking things over – *Überlegung* – comes into play prior to an act, or in the very moment of decision, it seems only to confuse, to obstruct and to repress the power to act."[80] We need only observe wrestlers to discover why:

[The wrestler], having his arms wrapped around his opponent [*da er seinen Gegner umfaßt hält*], simply has no recourse but to act spontaneously, on inspiration; and a man who tried to calculate which muscles he should employ and which limbs he should set in motion in order to win would inevitably be disadvantaged and defeated.

Kleist's narrator combines here not-thinking with, specifically, the willingness to become entangled: to wrap one's arms around – *umfaßt halten* – the other. Only in this way can we thrive, in wrestling and in life: "A man must, like this wrestler, take hold [*umfaßt hält*] of life and feel and sense with a thousand limbs how his opponent twists and turns, resists him, comes at him, evades him and reacts." The successful person, like the successful wrestler, must learn to stop thinking and to embrace – *umfassen* – life.[81]

The subtle key to Kleist's intervention inheres in the word "Überlegung," whose abstract meaning – "thinking things over" – did not exist before Kleist's own eighteenth century; it meant instead, in its Middle High German verb form (*überligen*), to "win" or "be superior to." This meaning itself developed, as the Grimm etymological dictionary tells us, from the "image of the wrestling match."[82] Specifically, *überligen* signified "in wrestling, to come to lie on top."[83] *Überlegung*'s explicit origins in wrestling – of which Kleist likely knew – followed by its abstraction into "thinking" in Kleist's own era, reveals the deeper philosophical stakes of his broadside against reflection. Not only is the wrestler's unthinking activity of lying on top of others at thought's etymological root, so too is his specific form of combat: wrestling, and not, say, boxing or fencing, about which Kleist also wrote.[84] By emphasizing *Überlegung*'s pun in lying on top of, which still exists today, and its now forgotten history in wrestling, Kleist subverts the power of the abstract term. Reflection, he insists, has a long history of people lying on top of other people.

Kleist captures this literalization through a particular instance in the wrestling match: the wrestler, "having his arms wrapped around his opponent, simply has no recourse but to act spontaneously, on inspiration." Kleist's wrestlers always start here, like the wrestlers on the ancient vases: not with pre-contact feints but with two bodies already clasped together. This entwinement is necessary for the wrestler's "inspiration." Wrestling's specific act of entangling – its own form of *Über-legung* – creates here the apparent opposite of abstract "reflection": spontaneous inspiration. On a more general level, the wrestlers' embrace reveals how humanity's primary abstraction – thinking – can never separate itself from the agonistic bodies on which it rests.

In order to overcome the modern bankruptcy of reflection (*Überlegung*), Kleist tells us in his final sentence, we must return to physical *Überlegung*: we must learn to sense and feel the world "with a thousand limbs" (*tausendgliedrig*). Kleist invents this strange neologism – *tausendgliedrig* (implying "with every fibre of our being" but literally "with a thousand limbs") – to remind us of the material roots of *all* abstraction: of thinking *and* the idea of complete commitment while wrestling. He experiments with what would happen if we were to thrust ourselves into the material pasts of our concepts. He envisions a return to the same ancient body technology that drew Plato's ire: the mythical wrestlers merging into one creature with countless limbs, *tausendgliedrig*. Kleist creates a word in order to imagine the unimaginable: heightened pleasure and pain in deindividuated bodies that brutally and ecstatically embrace – *umfassen* – and "feel and sense" each other. This recalls the other meaning of *überlegen*'s Middle High German root, for *überligen* signifies not only "to come to lie on top in wrestling" but also "coitus, to lie with a woman."[85] Through this rapturous intertwining, Kleist challenges Plato's dictum of disentanglement and begins paradoxically – as in the essay's subtitle, "eine Paradoxe" – to think through a radical form of not thinking.

Shortly after Kleist's death in 1811, European folk wrestling began to turn professional, attracting huge crowds from around the world. This culminated, at the end of the century, in the World's Fair in Paris, where Nikola Petroff defeated the long-time world champion, Paul "The Colossus" Pons. Wrestling continued to have great symbolic importance, appearing in the writings of Kafka, Thomas Mann, Broch, and Proust – as in the famous match that causes young Marcel's first orgasm in *À la recherche du temps perdu*. Nietzsche too refers often to wrestling, even using it to deepen his critique of Platonic individualism. In *Twilight of the Idols*, for example, just one sentence before Nietzsche praises Socrates for being "a great erotic [*ein grosser Erotiker*]," he makes a wry reference to Socrates's sexual encounters with boys in the Athenian wrestling schools: Socrates was "fascinating," he claims, because he "introduced a variation [!] into the wrestling match between young men and boys."[86] Just as Plato had used disentangled "stand-up wrestling" as a metaphor for individuation and the ethical life, Nietzsche reminds us of Socrates's perverse "variations" – his penchant for "bed wrestling" (for *epiklinopalē*) with boys – to turn the tables. Nietzsche exposes "disentanglement" as the ideological covering-over – the *Über-legen* – of a Kleistian truth: the mind can never separate itself from the body, just as the *logōn agōn* cannot detach itself from the agon of the flesh.

The nineteenth and early twentieth centuries featured many such sexual wrestling "variations," whether in paintings – Gustave Courbet's *Wrestlers* (1853), Honoré Daumier's *The Wrestlers* (ca. 1855), Frédéric Bazille's *Scène d'été* (1869), Max Slevogt's *Wrestling School* (1908)[87] – or, notoriously, in the novel *Woman in Love* (1920) by the avowed Nietzschean, D.H. Lawrence. The novel's second half features a climactic scene inspired by Lawrence's knowledge of "Japanese wrestling" (introduced to Europe around 1900).[88] Lawrence's two male protagonists strip naked and wrestle. Readers have long noticed the scene's homoeroticism (and how "wrestling is the heterosexually acceptable form of homosexual foreplay")[89] but not how this relies on Lawrence's re-creation of the same ancient body technology that had troubled Plato. The two wrestlers, Lawrence tells us, "drive their white flesh deeper and deeper" into one another "as if they would break into oneness"; they "entwine" and "interfuse" themselves with "the body of the other."[90] The two bodies eventually transform into a single thousand-limbed wrestling creature like the one Kleist had championed, Plato had feared, and Oppian had described pathetically. Lawrence even revives here Oppian's image of the wrestling octopus: a "strange octopus-like knotting and flashing of limbs," an "interlaced knot of violent living," a "physical junction of two bodies clinched into oneness." Out of this outlandish being, two heads uncannily emerge, as in the mythical representations of wrestling. We see, in rotation, "the gleaming ... head" of one man, then the "shadow-like head of the other."[91]

For Lawrence's narrator, this two-headed, thousand-limbed wrestling beast has a vital psychological and philosophical significance. By disappearing into the other's "physical being," the two men become rapturously "mindless at last." They explode the painful dualism of existence by fusing, first, with each other (through "necromantic foreknowledge [of] every motion of the other flesh") and, second, with the world (merging "outside" noises with the beating of their own hearts). According to the narrator, the men have reached a magical pre-subjective state of "not-being," like that of the fencing bear in the story/essay Kleist wrote just days after "Von der Überlegung," "On the Marionette Theater."[92] This new state is blissful but necessarily temporary, sustainable only for the duration of the match. When the wrestling ends, each man is again devastatingly split: separated from the external world, from the other man, and from his own body. Tragically, his "spirit" – Plato's *psyche* – returns to its position beyond his body, which is now

Figure 4.18. Wrestling scene from *Women in Love* (dir. Ken Russell), 1969

just an "unconscious stroke of blood"; the *psyche* observes this body again from the "outside."[93]

Although Lawrence's argument is less sophisticated than Kleist's – ignoring the paradox in thinking about how not to think – it nonetheless gets to the heart of Kleist's experiment: Might the entangled wrestling body grant us, through a return to ancient technologies, a new genealogy of the subject? Might this genealogy allow us to see anew the abject fears that lurked behind the invention of the *psyche* to begin with? And might this body knowledge liberate us? Lawrence's answer seems to be yes. His striking wrestling scene re-creates the ancient *hamma*, which contributed to the censorship controversy around the filming of *Women in Love* (Figure 4.18).[94] And the wrestling scene ends with the protagonists concluding, "One ought to wrestle and strive and be physically close." In mutual silence, they think about what this connotes, what it might mean to *become* wrestlers. But they can only take the first steps along this path: "the wrestling had some deep meaning to them – an unfinished meaning."[95]

In the background of this existentialist, literary wrestling from 1920, so-called "professional" wrestling began to gain its contrapuntal steam, becoming popular after the Second World War and attaining its

Figure 4.19. Chris Masters versus Shawn Michaels, WWE match, Manchester, UK (Nov. 17, 2005)

first golden age in the 1950s through household names like Gorgeous George (USA) and L'Ange Blanc (France). As the literary theorist Roland Barthes remarked already in 1957, professional wrestling (*le catch* in French) created an unheard-of appeal but also generated criticism for being "an ignoble sport." Barthes defends *le catch* by insisting that it is "not a sport" at all but rather a "spectacle," a "wrestled performance of Suffering." It is worth watching as theatre, he argues – as a postmodern inheritor of French classicism ("the sorrows of Arnolphe or Andromaque") and "Greek drama." Like ancient theatre – and unlike "real" wrestling, which Barthes considers tedious – *le catch* represents the thrill of "excess": of "emotion without reserve."[96]

By championing *le catch* as a form of ancient excess, Barthes inadvertently enters the debate about wrestling that first peaked almost 2500 years earlier in Plato's *Laws*. Barthes joins here a long line of anti-Platonic foils: chastising "these ... people" who, like Plato's Athenian, "wax indignant" when noticing unfairness or emotional and physical extravagance. Barthes dismisses such detractors as "sentimental" dupes longing for a "real" wrestling that, with its insistence on fairness and rules, is merely a nostalgic "throwback."[97] But Barthes forgets that this "real" wrestling itself was once a new invention, created as a response to pre-existing mythical forms. And these mythical forms already contained the body technologies of Barthes's beloved *catch*: the pathetic overindulgences, the explosions of rage and sex, the hopeless intertwining of appendages. It is thus more accurate to refer to *le catch* as the "throwback," and Barthes is more correct than he knows when, making a comparison with the theatre, he describes holds from *le catch* – such as the sexual "coupling [*accouplements*] of the wrestlers" – as "ancient postures."[98] These couplings are in fact uncanny replications of the pre-Socratic *hamma*, as seen in many possible examples, including the 2005 match between Chris Masters and Shawn Michaels (Figure 4.19). And all the while the judges look away, like the absent referee on the "Victorinus" vase and the self-interested gods from myth.

Le catch's restaging of the Greek *hamma* explains both its popularity and the backlash against it. It revivifies ancient memories of pleasurable self-dissolution, of being *only* a body – within other bodies. *Le catch* returns us also to the Greek ambivalence about separating ourselves from entanglement. We are back at the crucial moment from the *Laws*. For, as Plato knew, wrestling was not only Greece's most popular sport; it was also the one that, through its mythological excess, most egregiously flouted his plans for a modern *psyche*, a rationalist philosophy, a hermeneutics of the self. Plato's wish to teach boys how to disentangle their bodies was also an attempt to teach them to consider their bodies as separate from themselves – as objects to be observed, categorized, and interpreted. The intertwined bodies of today's wrestlers are celebrated and denigrated because they reveal the persistence of our ancient longings and of our attempts, often failed, to discipline these bodies. We see here again the obscene hugs of death – the ghosts of Antaeus, Cercyon, and Heracles – from which Plato, the champion wrestler, had hoped to untangle us once and for all.

NOTES

Note on references and translations: For all Greek and Latin sources (with the exception of Plato's *Laws* and Homer's *Iliad*), I use the most recent Loeb Classical Library translations, which can be found according to my book/ chapter/line references. In the cases where I emend these translations, I include the original language. I thank Eph Lytle and, especially, Jody Cundy for their help with the Greek texts.

1   The most extensive compendium of ancient wrestling citations lists twenty-two by Plato and acknowledges that this list is not complete. Georg Doblhofer, Werner Petermandl, and Ursula Schachinger, eds., *Ringen: Texte, Übersetzungen, Kommentar* (Vienna: Böhlau, 1998), 272–84 (wrestling citations), vii (incompleteness of list).

2   Plato, *Chrm* 153a; *Lysis* 204a; *Symp.* 217c. On the range of Socrates's visits to gymnasia and palestras, and the importance of wrestling for him, see Heather L. Reid, *Athletics and Philosophy in the Ancient World: Contests of Virtue* (London: Routledge, 2011), 43–4.

3   Diog. Laert. 3.4. See also Apuleius, who claims that Plato competed for the "wrestler's prize" at both the Pythian and Isthmian Games (Apul. *de dogm. Plat.* 1.2.184).

4   Preceding Plato's and Socrates's wrestling experiences and their use of wrestling as a metaphor, the philosopher Protagoras combined competition and rhetoric with the first debate contests (*logōn agōnes*) and wrote about strategies of argument in *The Art of Debating* (*Technē Eristikōn*) and *On Wrestling* (*Peri Palēs*). The latter, Plato says, advocated using tactics from wrestling to defeat rhetorical opponents (*Sophist*, 232e). Protagoras's celebrated work, *Truth*, furthermore bore the alternative title of *Kataballontes*, meaning to "throw over," as in wrestling. See Debra Hawhee, *Bodily Arts: Rhetoric and Athletics in Ancient Greece* (Austin: University of Texas Press, 2004), 28, 34–5; and C.C.W. Taylor and Mi-Kyoung Lee, "The Sophists," *The Stanford Encyclopedia of Philosophy* (Fall 2015 ed.), ed. Edward N. Zalta (http://plato.stanford.edu/archives/fall2015/entries/sophists/).

5   Wrestling was "by far the most popular sport" in ancient Greece, and athletes participated in the life of the palestra the way modern athletes do at sports clubs, spending much of their free time there: H.A. Harris, *Greek Athletes and Athletics* (London: Hutchinson, 1964), 102. For a large but still only partial list of ancient sources that use wrestling metaphorically, see Doblhofer et al., eds., *Ringen*, 379–81. See also Hawhee, *Bodily Arts*, 35–9, 44–6, 54–5, 83–4; and Reid, *Athletics and Philosophy*, 43–55.

6   Plato, *Laws*, trans. A.E. Taylor, in *The Collected Dialogues of Plato* (Princeton: Princeton University Press, 1989), 1368 (7.796a).

7   Plut. *Mor.* 638e–f. Despite Philinus's confidence, the true etymology is unknown.

8   E. Norman Gardiner, "Wrestling," *Journal of Hellenic Studies* 25 (1905): 27–9. Gardiner repeats this argument in *Greek Athletic Sports and Festivals* (London: Macmillan, 1910), 380–1; and *Athletics of the Ancient World* (Oxford: Clarendon Press, 1930), 183–4. See also Ingomar Weiler, who uncritically cites Gardiner's interpretation of this passage (even if Weiler is critical of Gardiner at other points): *Der Agon im Mythos. Zur Einstellung*

der Griechen zum Wettkampf (Darmstadt: Wissenschaftliche Buchge-
sellschaft, 1974), 154n127.

9 Doblhofer et al., eds., *Ringen*, 275.

10 Plato, *Laws* 7.796 (n1).

11 Gardiner, "Wrestling," 27–9, 283; Gardiner later tempers this position – but
only slightly, and only regarding the prohibition of leg holds in wrestling
(*Athletics*, 183–4).

12 Plato, *Laws*, 1399 (8.834a) (on "substitut[ing]" more martial games for traditional wrestling and boxing); see also *Laws*, 1385 (8.814c–d).

13 Plato, *Laws*, 1367–8 (7.796a) (on not mentioning leg holds); Doblhofer et al.,
eds., *Ringen*, 276 (for the scholiast on leg holds). On the dating of the scholia of this section of *Laws* (to the tenth or eleventh century AD), see W.C.
Greene, "The Platonic Scholia," *Transactions of the American Philological Association* 68 (1937): 187.

14 On ground fighting, chokeholds, and falling to one's knee in wrestling (*palē*),
see Michael B. Poliakoff, *Combat Sports in the Ancient World* (New Haven:
Yale University Press, 1987), 24–5, 27–30, 33–4, 50–1; and Stephen G. Miller,
Ancient Greek Athletics (New Haven: Yale University Press, 2004), 47–8.
Despite these rebuttals of Gardiner's position, it has still found wide acceptance in accounts of Greek wrestling (as Poliakoff points out, 170n5). Grant L.
Dunlap, for example, claims in the introduction to the 1970 reprint of Gardiner's *Greek Athletic Sports and Festivals* that "Dr. Gardiner's scholarship was so
careful that subsequent findings altered his conclusions very little."

15 Ingomar Weiler criticizes Werner Rudolph for, like Gardiner, claiming sharper
distinctions between wrestling and pancratium than the sources allow: *Der
Sport bei den Völkern der alten Welt* (Darmstadt: Wissenschaftliche Buchge-
sellschaft, 1981), 171. Poliakoff expands on this point in *Combat Sports* (28–30).

16 Gardiner, "Wrestling," 27.

17 For criticisms of how Gardiner's "Eton"-esque morality distorted accounts
of Greek wrestling for many decades, see David C. Young, *The Olympic Myth
of Greek Amateur Athletics* (Chicago: Ares, 1984), especially chapter 6 ("E.N.
Gardiner, James Thorpe, and Avery Brundage"); Poliakoff, *Combat Sports*,
28–30; and Donald G. Kyle, "E. Norman Gardiner: Historian of Ancient Sport,"
International Journal of the History of Sport 8, no. 1 (1991): 28–55, esp. 38–40.

18 For the "Wrestling Ground of Cercyon," see Paus. 1. 39. 3.

19 The scholiast's claim about Cercyon using leg holds is repeated only once,
by Eusthatius, in the twelfth century AD, but it does appear in several
images. There are no extant descriptions of Antaeus using a leg hold. Gardiner argues that this appears in some images, which is true but inconclu-
sive: many images also show Antaeus fighting Heracles above the waist
(Gardiner, *Greek Athletic Sports*, 380).

20 Apoll. *Epitome* 1.3 (on Cercyon); Apoll. 2.5.11 (on Antaeus).

21 Doblhofer et al., eds., *Ringen*, 276 (my translation).

22 Even if Gardiner's modern, fairness-based criticism of "bullying" makes little sense in the Greek context, one could argue that both Antaeus and Cercyon have – by attacking strangers – violated the sacred Greek obligation of *xenia*. But if Plato had objected to something as straightforward as this, he would have stated it; moreover, such a violation does not relate to his argument for "disentanglement."

23 As Poliakoff points out, our modern concepts of "nobility" and "evil" have little place in the discussion of Greek heroism. Even if some Greek authors did portray Heracles's wrestling match with Antaeus as a "Greek hero clearing the world of evil," others did not shy away from depicting Heracles as engaging in unscrupulous tactics such as beard-pulling and eye-gouging. And Heracles and Theseus certainly both murder, by modern standards, in cold blood. Poliakoff, *Combat Sports*, 54–5.

24 Theseus's new, technique-based style apparently allowed "skill," for the first time, to defeat "size and strength"; Theseus was also pivotal in the establishment of schools that taught "the art of wrestling" (Paus. 1.39.3).

25 Plut. *Thes*. 11.1.

26 Luc. *De Bello Civili* 4.647–53.

27 Apoll. 2.5.11.

28 For the literal translation, see J.G. Frazer's note to Apoll. 2.5.11.

29 On *hamma* as a wrestling technique, see Plutarch's descriptions in *Fabius Maximus* and *Alcibiades* (Plut. *Fab*. 23.2; Plut. *Alc*. 2.2).

30 *Genesis* 32.26 (*The New Oxford Annotated Bible*, www.oxfordbiblicalstudies .com). Greek-language Christian literature in late antiquity similarly made use of wrestling as a metaphor for the struggles of faith. Basilius of Seleuca, for example, describes Jesus's temptation by the devil explicitly as "wrestling" (*palē*) (Doblhofer et al., eds., *Ringen*, 381).

31 *The Epic of Gilgamesh*, trans. N.K. Sandars (London: Penguin, 1972), 69.

32 *Gilgamesh: A New English Version* (New York: Free Press, 2004), 89.

33 Homer, *The Iliad*, trans. Richard Lattimore (Chicago: University of Chicago Press, 1951), 469–70 (23.700–37).

34 Ovid, *Met*. 9.42–84.

35 Both Gardiner and Miller refer to Odysseus and Aias's locked-rafter position as a prime example of *systasis*. Gardiner, "Wrestling," 264; Miller, *Ancient Greek Athletics*, 47.

36 See Nigel Spivey, *Enduring Creation: Art, Pain, and Fortitude* (Berkeley: University of California Press, 2001), 25.

37 Oppian, *Halieutica* 2.265–83. Hawhee uses this scene to discuss wrestling's privileged relation, in Greek culture, to cunning (*mētis*), specifically to what she calls "bodily intelligence" or "somatic cunning" (*Bodily Arts*, 44–6, 54–5). For an earlier treatment of the *mētis* of the wrestling octopus in

this passage, see Marcel Detienne and Jean-Pierre Vernant, *Cunning Intelligence in Greek Culture and Society*, trans. Janet Lloyd (Atlantic Highlands: Humanities Press, 1978), 28–43.

38 Oppian, *Halieutica* 2.284–8.

39 I am grateful to Jody Cundy for pointing out the ambiguity of the Greek.

40 On homosexuality in the palestras and attempts to curb it, see Miller, *Ancient Greek Athletics*, 189–93; and Thomas F. Scanlon, *Eros and Greek Athletics* (Oxford: Oxford University Press, 2002), 213–15.

41 Plato, *Lysis* 203a–211a ("handsome boys," 206a).

42 Plato, *Symp.* 217c. I use "frontal attack" from Michael Joyce's translation (in *Collected Dialogues*) instead of W.R.M. Lamb's "charge full tilt" (the Loeb Library version) because the former hews slightly closer to Alcibiades's extension of the wrestling/sex metaphor: *epitheteion einai tōi andri*, literally "one [I] must set upon the man" – as in the contemporary "make a move on." On sex and wrestling in *Symposium* and the Socratic dialogues (*Lysis* and *Charmides*), see Scanlon, *Eros and Greek Athletics*, 216–18; and Allen Guttmann, *The Erotic in Sports* (New York: Columbia University Press, 1996), 19–21.

43 Martial and Aurelius Victor both use this Greek term – *epiklinopalē* – within their Latin texts (Mart. 14.201; Aur. Victor 11.5). According to Suetonius, the Roman emperor Domitian liked to joke using a Latinized version (*clinopale*) (Suet. *Dom.* 22). See Doblhofer et al., eds., *Ringen*, 380; and Scanlon, *Eros and Greek Athletics*, 216. On the Roman usage of the Greek term, see Andrew Dalby, *Empire of Pleasures: Luxury and Indulgence in the Roman World* (London: Routledge, 2000), 123.

44 Aristoph., *Pax* 896–9.

45 Lucian, *Asin.* (*The Ass*) 8–11. Michael B. Poliakoff, *Studies in the Terminology of the Greek Combat Sports* (Königstein: Anton Hain, 1982), 101–27, 185–8 (images).

46 Strato, *Greek Anthology* 12.206.

47 The Greek here for "embrace" is *symplekou*.

48 *Hamma* is a noun here (*hamma kat' ixuos dēsas*), so the literal translation would be more like "binding clinch [*hamma*] down from the waist."

49 The Greek is *ekheis ta mesa*: literally, "you hold the middle (parts)." On the sexual pun, see Doblhofer et al., eds., *Ringen*, 173n7.

50 Lucian, *Asin.* (*The Ass*) 9–10.

51 On Peleus's many wrestling exploits beyond this wrestling rape of Thetis, see Dio Chrys. 37.14; Hyg. *Fab.* 273.10; Paus. 5.17.10; Philostr. *Gym.* 3; and Apollod. 3.9.2 (the latter is his only recorded defeat, to the virgin huntress, Atalanta). See also Doblhofer et al., eds., *Ringen*, 408.

52 Ovid, *Met.* 11.238–40, 253–4. For another description of this scene, see Apollod. 3.13.5. For the various sources describing Thetis's

transformations into what J.G. Frazer catalogues as "fire, water, wind, a tree, a bird, a tiger, a lion, a serpent, and a cuttle-fish," see Frazer's explanatory note in Apollodorus, *The Library*, 2:67–8n6.

53 Apollod. 3.13.5. The only Greek author directly suggesting Peleus's injuries is Pausanias ("Peleus is taking hold of her, and from the hand of Thetis a snake is darting at Peleus"); Robert Graves logically infers Peleus's injuries from what would be expected from wrestling a creature shifting its form from fire, to water, to serpent, to tiger, to a cuttlefish (Paus. 5.18.5; Graves, *The Greek Myths*, 2 vol. [New York: Penguin, 1960], 1:271).

54 Ovid, *Met.* 11.261–5.

55 Telemachus's wrestling-murder gave him the status of a hero, like Heracles: Nigel Nicholson, *The Poetics of Victory in the Greek West* (Oxford: Oxford University Press, 2016), 28.

56 Zonaras identifies this shift within *exeilēsis* as occurring primarily in Alexandria. From [Zonaras]: "Ἐξειλῆσαι. The Alexandrians use this in the sense of 'to escape.' Their use seems to be metaphorical from those who free themselves in wrestling. For in Book 7 of the Laws Plato says the following about wrestling: 'Anything which comes under "stand-up wrestling," exercises in the disengaging [disentangling (*exeilēseōs*, ἐξειλήσεως)] of neck, arms, and ribs ...'" Cited in F. Dübner, *Platonis opera quae feruntur omnia*, ed. J.G. Baiter, J.K. Orelli, and A.W. Winckelmann (Zurich: Meyer & Zeller, 1839), 985 (trans. Eph Lytle). This lexicon referred to as "Zonaras," compiled in the first half of the thirteenth century (but not written by Zonaras, who died earlier), does not specify which "Alexandrians" are meant, but it is likely Alexandrian scholars from the Hellenistic period onward.

57 M. Aur. *Med.* 10.36. Related ancient uses include the soul escaping or disengaging (*exeilēsan*, ἐξείλησαν) from peril when battling evil (the "spiritual aspects of wickedness" [*pros ta peumatika tēs ponērias*]) (Pseudo-Macarius, *Sermones 64* [collectio B], Homily 50.4.12 [trans. Jody Cundy]) and a description of Odysseus escaping or freeing himself (*exeilēsas*) from the Sirens (Dictys, Jacoby [*FGrH*] 49, F1a: 282). In Adorno and Horkheimer's reading (*Dialectic of Enlightenment*), the latter signifies the giving over of pleasure for rationality and, with this, the birth of modern subjectivity.

58 Plato, *Laws*, 1368 (7:796b).

59 Plato, *Laws*, 1399 (8:834a).

60 Plato, *Alcib.* 1:107e. Plato's authorship of *Alcibiades* has of course been contested, but recent scholars have made a strong case for its authenticity. See Nicholas Denyer, Introduction to Plato, *Alcibiades* (Cambridge: Cambridge University Press, 2001): 14–26.

61 On the recent historiographic shift arguing for the relative stability of ancient sports from the sixth century BC into the fourth century AD, see Sofie Remijsen, *The End of Greek Athletics in Late Antiquity* (Cambridge: Cambridge University Press, 2015), 3–14; and her article in this volume

("The Fading Allure of Greek Athletics"). On the general shift toward athletics as spectacle in late antiquity, see her *End of Greek Athletics*, 321–42. On
the end of classical wrestling (marked by the paving of the palestras in the
fourth century AD) and the transformation of wrestling into a spectacle,
again see her *End of Greek Athletics* (260–1, 147–50, 336–40); and "Fading
Allure."

62 Dietrich Klose and Thomas Klein initially dated this vase to the sixth century AD, but K.M.D. Dunbabin persuasively argues that it should be dated
closer to 400. Klose and Klein, "Werbung für den Wettkampf in spätantiker
Zeit: Die Bronzevase des Privatulus aus archäologischer und philologischer Sicht," in *Der gymnische Agon in der Spätantike*, ed. Andreas Gutsfeld
and Stephan Lehmann (Gutenberg: Computus, 2013), 143–50; Dunbabin,
"Athletes, Acclamations, and Imagery from the End of Antiquity," *Journal
of Roman Archaeology* 30 (2017): 151–74.

63 Klose and Klein claim that the aggressor in scene two differs from the
aggressor in the others. Although this is possible, it is impossible to distinguish with certainty: "Werbung für den Wettkampf in spätantiker Zeit,"
144.

64 I thus disagree with Klose and Klein, who miss the irony in "Privatulus,"
seeing instead an aptronym describing the man's "lack of professionalism," and also with Remijsen, who sees, in the victim's naming, only
further humiliation. In general, Remijsen views this vase as an allegory for
the tragic end of wrestling's "moral" aspect instead of as an exploration
of the sadistic qualities always just beneath wrestling's surface. Klose and
Klein, "Werbung für den Wettkampf in spätantiker Zeit," 143; Remijsen,
"Fading Allure." See also Remijsen, *The End of Greek Athletics*, 339–40.

65 Gerald W. Morton and George M. O'Brien, *From Wrestling to Rasslin:
Ancient Sport to American Spectacle* (Bowling Green: Bowling Green State
University Popular Press, 1985), 15.

66 *Beowulf*, trans. Lesslie Hall (Boston: Heath, 1892), 27.

67 Calvin S. Brown, Jr., "Beowulf's Arm-Lock," *PMLA* 55, no. 3 (September
1940): 621–7, esp. 626.

68 *Beowulf*, 29.

69 On Beowulf's similarities with the monsters he battles, see Fred Robinson's
classic *Beowulf and the Appositive Style* (Knoxville: University of Tennessee
Press, 1985), and, more pointedly, Alexander Bruce's "Evil Twins?: The Role
of the Monsters in *Beowulf*," *Medieval Forum* 6 (January 2007).

70 *Beowulf*, 52, 53. Fred Robinson argues that the Old English, *ofsittan*, traditionally translated "sit on," is more properly rendered as "set upon." But
Robinson admits that the "central meaning of the simplex *sittan*" remains
"to sit," and Edward Risden claims that, despite Robinson's argument
for "set upon," we must remember the general punning sense of humour
of *Beowulf*'s author: the "punning suggestion of 'sat on' remains, with its

incongruous sexual undertones." Dana Oswald insists furthermore that specific aspects of the fight – the dramatic reversal to Beowulf's erect status at the end and Grendel's Mother's use of a short blade (a *seaxe*) – only make sense if Grendel's Mother is, in some way, on top of Beowulf. See Robinson, "Did Grendel's Mother Sit on Beowulf?" in *From Anglo-Saxon to Early Middle English*, ed. Malcolm Godden, Douglas Gray, and Terry Hoad (Oxford: Oxford University Press, 1994), 7, 3; Risden, "Heroic Humour in *Beowulf*," in *Humour in Anglo-Saxon Literature*, ed. Jonathan Wilcox (Cambridge: D.S. Brewer, 2000), 77; and Oswald, *Monsters, Gender, and Sexuality in Medieval English Literature* (Cambridge: D.S. Brewer, 2010), 95.

71 *Beowulf*, 53.

72 On the un-heroic, sexually emasculating nature of Beowulf's "victory" over Grendel's Mother, see Oswald, *Monsters, Gender, and Sexuality in Medieval English Literature*, 91–101.

73 A facsimile of Talhoffer's 1443 *Fechtbuch*, including the techniques of Ott Jud, is available at wiktenauer.com/wiki/Talhoffer_Fechtbuch (MS_Chart.A.558). Karl Wassmannsdorff published an amalgamation of Jud's methods (mostly their post-Talhoffer version in the Codex Wallenstein), in *Die Ringkunst des Deutschen Mittelalters mit 119 Ringerpaaren von Albrecht Dürer*, ed. Wassmannsdorff (Leipzig: Verlag Briber, 1870), 139–56. On the history of wrestling as depicted in the *Fechtbücher* of the Middle Ages, see Wassmannsdorff's introduction, i–xxii. On the history of the medieval *Fechtbücher* in general, see Heidemarie Bodemer: *Das Fechtbuch*. Diss. Stuttgart, 2008 (on the chronology and details of the various manuals, see 83–202).

74 Jules Michelet, *Histoire de France au seizième siècle, VIII, Réform* (Paris: Chamerot, 1857), 163. See the similar account in *Mémoires du maréchal de Florange dit le juene adventureux* (Paris: Renouard, 1913), 1:272.

75 On the wrestling images published around 1500 (strikingly early in the history of printing), see Carl Diem, *Weltgeschichte des Sports* (Stuttgart: Cotta, 1971), 1:540. See also 509–10, 541–6.

76 Dürer's *Fechtbuch* is reproduced by Friedrich Dörnhöffer in *Albrecht Dürers Fechtbuch* (Vienna: Tempsky, 1910). The quotation accompanies a wrestling image that Dürer inexplicably drew twice, perhaps speaking to its importance (nos. 7 [Tafel 3] and 59 [Tafel 20]). The transcribed caption is in Dörnhöffer, lxii (for the repeated image, with slight variations and perhaps a different hand, see p. lxviii [for a discussion of the handwriting, see iv–v]). As Dörnhöffer points out, Dürer seems to have copied most of his images and captions from the earlier, ca. 1470, anonymous combat manual, the Codex Wallerstein (ix–xiv). Like the images mentioned in the previous note, this manual and similar ones attest to the importance of wrestling in the late Middle Ages.

77 See Guttmann, *The Erotic in Sports*, 45–7.

78 On the politics of Unspunnen, see Rudolf Gallati and Christoph Wyss, *Unspunnen – Die Geschichte der Alphirtenfeste* (Interlaken: Schlaefli, 1993), 9–14.

79 Devon and Cornish wrestling matches regularly drew crowds in the thousands in the early nineteenth century, culminating in the 1827 match between the Devonshire and Cornish champions, in front of approximately 17,000 fans, as reported in the 1827 *Sporting Magazine* (see "Devonshire Wrestlers," in S. Baring-Gould, *Devonshire Characters and Strange Events* [London: J. Lane, 1908]), 520–3). Kleist likely knew of such English folk wrestling, not just because of its massive popularity but also because he had just published, two weeks before "Von der Überlegung," a similar account of a well-attended English boxing match.

80 Heinrich von Kleist, "Von der Überlegung," in *Sämtliche Werke und Briefe*, 4 vols., ed. Helmut Sembdner (Munich: Hanser, 1982), 3:337. I consulted the English translations by Philip B. Miller ("On Thinking Things Over") and David Constantine ("Reflection"), and I made emendations where necessary.

81 Kleist, "Von der Überlegung," 337–8.

82 *Deutsches Wörterbuch von Jakob und Wilhelm Grimm*, vol. 23, col. 398, http://woerterbuchnetz.de/DWB/ ("aus der vorstellung des ringkampfes entnommen").

83 *Trübners Deutsches Wörterbuch*, 8 vols. (1939–56), 7:195 ("beim Ringen oben zu liegen kommen"). A similar etymology appears in *Duden: Das große Wörterbuch der deutschen Sprache*, 3rd ed., 10 vols. (1981), 6:2657.

84 For Kleist's descriptions of boxing and fencing, where, unlike wrestling, physical distance is maintained, see his "Anecdote" about "two English boxers" and his "On the Marionette Theater," respectively. For the relation between the latter and "Von der Überlegung," see John Zilcosky, "'Von der Überlegung': Of Wrestling and (Not) Thinking," *Canadian Review of Comparative Literature* 41 (2014): 19–20, 23–4.

85 *Deutsches Wörterbuch von Jakob und Wilhelm Grimm*, vol. 23, col. 398, http://woerterbuchnetz.de/DWB/ ("coire, eine Frau beschlafen").

86 Nietzsche, *Götzen-Dämmerung*, in *Kritische Studienausgabe*, 15 vols., ed. Giogio Colli and Mazzino Montinari (Berlin: de Gruyter, 1988), 6:71 (my translation).

87 On the eroticization of wrestling in the visual art of the nineteenth and early twentieth centuries, see Margaret Walters, *The Nude Male: A New Perspective* (New York: Paddington, 1978), 238; and Guttmann, *The Erotic in Sports*, 63–4.

88 In 1899–1901, E.W. Barton-Wright, who learned judo and jujitsu in Japan, wrote a series of popular articles on so-called Japanese wrestling, notably his two-part "The New Art of Self-Defence: How a Man May Defend

Himself Against Every Form of Attack," in *Pearson's Magazine* 7 (1899): 268–75, 402–10. For the post–First World War German context, see Sarah Panzer, "Importing a German *Kampfsport*: the Reception of Japanese Martial Arts in Interwar Germany," in this volume. Franz Kafka's protagonist, Karl Rossmann, suffered a chokehold already before the war from a girl who knew "jiu-jitsu" (in chapter 3 of *The Man Who Disappeared* [1911–12]). On Kafka and jujitsu, see Wolf Kittler's article in this volume, "A Well-Trained Community: Gymnastics for the German Nation."

89 The quotation (in a different context from *Women in Love*) issues from Gregory Wood, cited in Brian Pronger, *The Arena of Masculinity* (New York: St Martin's Press, 1990), 184. On the homoeroticism of this scene in *Woman in Love*, see Guttmann, *The Erotic in Sports*, 142–3. For a continuation of Lawrence's trajectory, consider the 1973 photographs of wrestlers by Leni Riefenstahl (*The Last of the Nuba*).

90 D.H. Lawrence, *Women in Love* (New York: Penguin, 1984), 262.

91 Ibid., 263.

92 Ibid., 262, 263.

93 Ibid., 264.

94 Louis K. Greiff, *D.H. Lawrence: Fifty Years on Film* (Carbondale: Southern Illinois University Press, 2001), 76–7; and "Banned Movies: The Films That Vexed the Censor," *BBC Magazine*, 29 September 2011.

95 Lawrence, *Women in Love*, 265.

96 Roland Barthes, "The World of Wrestling," in *Mythologies* (New York: Hill and Wang, 1972 [1957]), 15.

97 Ibid., 15, 23.

98 Ibid., 21.

5 The Allure and Ethics of Ancient Aesthetics: Hellenism in the Modern Olympic Movement[*]

CHARLES STOCKING

When considering the social significance of sport, both ancient and modern, one might consider the categories of "allure" and "ethics" to be oppositional. But for Pierre de Coubertin, the self-proclaimed "founder" of the modern Olympic movement, the allure and the ethics of sport were inseparable, or at least, he wanted to make them as such.[1] In many respects, it was de Coubertin's appeal to the ancient Greek tradition that served this very purpose. But in place of "allure and ethics," de Coubertin offered the related categories of "beauty and reverence." Thus in a 1908 article titled "Why I Revived the Olympic Games," de Coubertin explains his motivation as follows: "Anyone who studies the ancient Games will perceive that their deep significance was due to two principle elements: beauty and reverence. If the modern Games are to exercise the influence I desire for them they must in turn show beauty and reverence – a beauty and reverence infinitely surpassing anything hitherto realized in the most important athletic contests of our day."[2]

Among modern sports historians, there has been significant research on de Coubertin's philosophy of beauty and its relationship to contemporary European philosophical thought.[3] Surprisingly, however, there has been almost no research on the relationship between de Coubertin's aesthetics and the ancient athletic tradition, despite his insistence on their close connection. When we dig deeper into de Coubertin's copious writings on Hellenism, however, it becomes clear that he did have considerable familiarity with ancient aesthetic theory. At first glance, he seems to make use of ancient aesthetics in a distinctly modernist capacity. In particular, he presents an aesthetic imperative that functions as a type of mimetic reversal, where the physical body of the athlete is to be viewed as an imitation of ancient sculpture. As such, de Coubertin's work can be seen as part of a long intellectual tradition dating back to Johann Joachim Winckelmann. At the same time, however, a closer analysis of our ancient evidence regarding the body and sculpture suggests that this very same mimetic reversal was also a common discursive strategy even in antiquity, especially in the work of Galen and Philostratus during the Roman Imperial period. Thus, while de Coubertin's own motives for Olympic revival may be historically and ideologically grounded in the intellectual traditions of modern Europe, his aesthetics may also be viewed as part of a much broader historical discourse on art, athletics, and embodiment, a discourse that was present in antiquity and that has continued even up to the present. It is this discourse on embodied Hellenism, a nostalgic appeal to the aesthetics of an athletic past, in both antiquity and modernity, that has so often given the allure of sport an ethical quality. But as I hope to demonstrate in this chapter, it was that very effort to join the allure and ethics of sport together through Hellenism that has generated its own ethical problems throughout history.

It should first be noted that de Coubertin was not simply inspired by the ancient athletic tradition in general terms. Rather, he sought to transpose a very specific idea from ancient art onto the modern Olympics, namely, the concept of *eurythmia*. For de Coubertin, *eurythmia* was synonymous with Hellenism. In a lecture from 1929, he made the following proclamation: "It was Hellenism's immortal glory to have conceived of the codification of the pursuit of balance, and to make of it a formula for social greatness. Here in Olympia we stand on the ruins of the first capital of the kingdom of eurythmy, for eurythmy is not merely applicable in the field of art. There is also the eurythmy of life."[4]

Eurythmia, however, was by no means a straightforward or universally recognized concept. In a four-part article series that appeared in the German newspaper *BZ am Mittag* in 1936, just before the Berlin Olympics, de Coubertin explained his own views on this ancient aesthetic concept:

> Proper proportion is the sister of order. They are siblings, intended to grow up together. I use the term "proportion" but that is not the word I want. The term that springs to mind is "eurythmia." In this regard, however, we the French and the Germans do not see eye-to-eye very well. The Germans believe that the concept of rhythm predominates in the Greek term. In French, we focus more attention on the first syllable. It evokes the idea of the beautiful, the perfect. Everything that is properly proportioned is eurythmic. It was Hellenism, above all else, that advocated measure and proper proportion, co-creators of beauty, grace, and strength. We

must return to these Greek concepts to offset the appalling ugliness of the industrial age through which we have just lived.[5]

In the late nineteenth and early twentieth centuries, the very concept of *eurythmia* was a significant point of debate among philologists and art historians.[6] It is not clear whether de Coubertin was aware of these debates among specialists, but such debates did have significant implications outside of academia. In suggesting the notion of "movement" for German *eurythmia*, de Coubertin may have been referring to Rudolph Steiner's creation of an expressive dance form also identified as "eurythmy." First established in 1912, Steiner's eurythmy was a central aspect of the larger occult movement in Germany known as Anthroposophy, and it served as a major component in the development of the Waldorf schools.[7] Steiner's eurythmy can be viewed as an outgrowth of the tradition in German gymnastics and Friedrich Jahn's *Turnen* movement, which was founded early in the nineteenth century and experienced a revival in the late nineteenth and early twentieth centuries, primarily because the stated purpose of *Turnen* was to unify and militarize the German *Volk* through coordinated athletic activity.[8] Hence, when he refers specifically to the eurythmy of dance or to German gymnastic training more generally, de Coubertin's emphasis on the "French" versus "German" view of *eurythmia* may reflect his attempt to de-emphasize the militaristic implications of athletic training, which would have been a prominent feature of German *Körperkultur*.[9] In contrast to what he qualifies as a "German" perspective, however, he seems to insist that French *eurythmia* has a more presentational artistic significance – a significance that reflects engagement with ancient usage of the term.

The *locus classicus* for the term *eurythmia* is Vitruvius's *De Architectura*, where Vitruvius explains the relationship between the five principles of architecture: *ordinatio, eurythmia, symmetria, decorum,* and *oikonomia*. Given that de Coubertin mentions both "order" and "proportion" in relation to *eurythmia*, it is most likely that he had Vitruvius in mind in his championing of *eurythmia*. Vitruvius explains *eurythmia* as follows: "Eurythmia is a pleasing appearance and a fitting aspect in compositions of its parts. This is achieved when the parts of a work have a height suitable to their width, a width suitable to their length, in short, when all the parts respond to each other in proportion" (Vitruvius 1.2.3).[10] Vitruvius then connects the concept of *eurythmia* to *symmetria* through explicit comparison with the human body: "As in the human body, the quality of *eurythmia* is a proportionality between the forearm, the foot, the palm, the finger, and other small details, so too in the finished details of a building" (Vitruvius 1.2.4). Despite Leonardo da Vinci's own attempts to demonstrate the validity of Vitruvius's claims for human proportionality in his famous "Vitruvian Man," it was most likely not the biological body *per se* that was a source of inspiration for Vitruvius but rather the work of the Classical Greek sculptor Polyclitus, who was best known for his theory of *symmetria*.[11]

One of our best accounts of Polyclitan *symmetria* comes from Galen and his work *On the Doctrines of Hippocrates and Plato*.[12] In discussing the Stoic philosopher Chrysippus, Galen shows an implicit link between art and philosophy in the notion of proportion: "He [Chrysippus] thinks that beauty lies not in in the proportion of elements but in the proportion of the parts of the body: of finger obviously to finger, of all the fingers to palm and wrist, of these to the forearm, of the forearm to upper arm and of all to all, as it has been written in the Canon of Polyclitus" (Galen, *De placitis Hippocratis et Platonis*, 5.3.15).

We no longer have the *Canon*, but this has not prevented scholars from attempting to reconstruct Polyclitus's theory based on the multiple Roman copies of his famous work, the *Doryphorus*.[13] Setting aside that there are many contrasting interpretations of the *Doryphorus*, most scholars agree that Polyclitus's notion of proportion represents a direct departure from "natural" representation of the physical body.[14] The ancient reception of Polyclitus, and of Greek sculpture in general, would seem to support such a conclusion. For instance, Isocrates claimed, "No one can make the nature of his body resemble those that are shaped and carved" (Isocrates 9.75).[15] And regarding Polyclitus, Quintilian stated, "For he (Polyclitus) added *decor* to the human form beyond what is real" (Quintilian 12.10.8).[16] It would appear that Polyclitus did not simply seek to imitate the physical body. Rather, Polyclitan *symmetria* may have had a more mathematical and perhaps even philosophical basis.[17] A key philosophical feature of Polyclitan sculpture is thought to be the principle of "perfection," defined in Greek as "*to eu*." In a passage from Philo Mechanicus, the Greek engineer from the third century BCE, for instance, we are told: "[Polyclitus] said that perfection [*to eu*] comes about just barely through many numbers" (Philo Mech. *Belopoeic* 4.1.49). Andrew Stewart has linked this claim with the larger philosophical discourse on *to eu*.[18] In particular, he offers a quotation from Diogenes of Laertius, who makes similar claims for Socrates and Zeno: "[Zeno] used to say that perfection comes about *para mikron*, but that it is by no means small. Others say that Socrates said this" (Diog. Laert. 7.26).[19] Here we find the same notion of perfection, *to eu*, coming about *para mikron*, attributed to philosopher and sculptor alike.[20]

In these several ancient textual sources on *eurythmia* and the related concept of *symmetria*, we find further parallels with de Coubertin's own vision of Hellenism. De Coubertin makes use of the terms "order," "proportion," and "*eurythmia*," all of which are associated with Vitruvius, who in turn relies on Polyclitus; in addition, he gives pride of place to the abstract notion of beauty as a moral and ethical imperative. The same moral associations can also be found regarding Polyclitan sculpture and its philosophical implications. De Coubertin himself emphasized the *eu-* in *eurythmia* as an invocation of "the beautiful, the perfect" (as quoted in Müller, *Olympism*, 202), and it is precisely the notion of *to eu* that the ancient evidence associates with Polyclitan perfection. Thus, it would seem that de Coubertin's own vision of Hellenism was informed by a distinctly *sculptural* ancient aesthetic.

This sculptural aesthetic also seems consistent with de Coubertin's view of the modern athlete. Throughout his writings, we are presented with a mimetic reversal, where sculpture does not stand as an imitation of the athlete; rather, the athlete is viewed as an imitation of sculpture. In 1927, de Coubertin gave the following account of an athlete who had just competed at an athletics meet held at the Panathenaic Stadium in Athens: "The student, full of the joy of living, his body suffused with the voluptuous glow that comes only from healthy tiredness induced by sport, and fired with youthful hope and ambition, seemed, with his fixed stare, to be imploring Minerva and paying her homage. He was like a sculpture representing neo-Olympism, the symbol of the future victories awaiting Hellenism – still so very much alive, and eternally adapted to human circumstances."[21] And again, in discussing "beauty" as the motivation for the modern Olympics and for sport more generally, he claims: "Sport must be seen as *producing beauty* and as an *opportunity for beauty*. It produces beauty because it creates the athlete, *who is a living sculpture*. It is an opportunity for beauty through the architecture, the spectacles, and celebrations which it brings about."[22] In this last quote, it would seem that de Coubertin is seeking to create a symbiotic relationship between architecture and athlete by reconfiguring the living athlete as sculpture. According to Vitruvian (and Polyclitan) principles of proportionality, the beauty of sculpture applies equally to the biological body and to man-made structures.

Ultimately, de Coubertin's view of the "body as sculpture" may be considered part of a larger effort to make the modern Olympic movement not just a global event, but a religion. In a talk titled "The Philosophic Foundation of Modern Olympism," de Coubertin made the following claim: "The primary, fundamental characteristic of ancient Olympism, and of modern Olympism as well, is that it is a religion.

By chiseling his body through exercise as a sculptor does a statue, the ancient athlete "honored the gods." In doing likewise, the modern athlete honors his country, his race, and his flag."[23] Note the metaphor employed by de Coubertin to describe ancient athletics – to "chisel" the body, like a sculpture being dedicated to the gods. It is not entirely clear from our ancient evidence whether athletic practice at that time had the same type of aesthetic motivation.[24] But for de Coubertin, this aesthetic *religio athletae* had a distinctly modern purpose, as a form of *political* religion with explicit national and racial implications, "to honor country, race, and flag." Like his earlier exposition on *eurythmia*, de Coubertin's statements on *religio athletae* were made in 1935, just prior to the infamous Berlin "Nazi Olympics" of 1936.[25] And perhaps the most visually striking demonstration of de Coubertin's own argument for the body as "living sculpture" can be found in Leni Riefenstahl's documentary of the Berlin Olympics, *Olympia*, where the Lancellotti Discobolus is transformed into the German decathlete Erwin Huber.[26] The correspondence between Riefenstahl's documentary and de Coubertin's own writings on athletic aesthetics reveals just how dangerously close de Coubertin came to promoting the problematic ethics of "body fascism" in his insistence on Hellenism.[27] When he gave his earlier aesthetic imperative of *eurythmia* in the newspaper *BZ am Mittag* before the Berlin Olympics, it had a very specific purpose, namely, to explain what he thought was required "in order for a handsome athletic race to flourish."[28] In other words, Coubertin's praise of the allure of athletics had deeply problematic ethical implications.

De Coubertin sought to distance himself from this German perspective in his account of ancient *eurythmia*; even so, his promotion of the sculpted athletic body may ultimately be viewed as part of a long tradition in Germanic philosophy and aesthetics dating back at least to Johann Joachim Winckelmann.[29] Like de Coubertin, Winckelmann had insisted that the superiority of the ancient Greeks was based on the body as a product of physical exercise, and in his first major work, *Reflections on the Imitation of Greek Works in Painting and Sculpture* (1755), he singled out the games at Olympia as the primary social motivation for such training.[30] In addition, Winckelmann saw ancient sculpture as the best evidence for the Greeks' physical superiority. Thus concerning the training that would have taken place at Olympia, Winckelmann states: "These exercises gave the bodies of the Greeks the strong and many contours which the masters then imparted to their statues without any exaggeration or excess."[31] Here, Winckelmann may be making use of a passage from Lucian, which describes how statues at Olympia were not allowed to be larger than the athletes and points out that judges at Olympia conducted an "examination," *exetasis*, of the statues in order to ensure that "not one of them go beyond the truth," μηδὲ εἷς ὑπερβάληται τὴν ἀλήθειαν (Lucian *Pro Imaginibus* 11).[32] This supposed exactness in the victor statues at Olympia is quite contrary to the view of sculpture as *supra verum*. In order to move beyond this apparent contradiction in the views on ancient sculpture as either realistic or hyper-realistic, Winckelmann creates a historical narrative on the development of Greek art. He thus explains that at a later stage, "[t]hese frequent opportunities to observe nature prompted Greek artists to go still further. They began to form certain general ideas of the beauty of individual parts of the body as well as of the whole – ideas which were to rise above nature itself; their model was an ideal nature originating in the mind alone."[33] Thus, Winckelmann is thought to be the first modern to give expression to the paradox of the "classical ideal." As we can see from this particular quote, such an ideal is located to a large extent in the notion of bodily proportion in ancient sculpture.[34]

We find similar rhetoric to Winckelmann's in the writings of Wilhelm von Humboldt.[35] Like Winckelmann, von Humboldt gave pride of place to the Greek body: "The value which the Greeks placed on a free developed [*ausgebildeten*] body stands out for all the nations."[36] According to von Humboldt, this bodily value was conveyed in antiquity in two forms – the worship of heroes and the Olympic Games, both of which testified to what he considered the "sensual idealistic nature of the Greeks."[37] And like Winckelmann, he understood this physical ideal of the Greeks primarily in terms of art, such that "[l]ife can be considered like an art [*Kunst*] and that in life, character can be considered like a work of art [*Kunstwerk*]."[38] James Porter has termed this tradition of art, embodiment, and classicism *Body-Bildung*, where the physical body itself is treated as an aesthetic object.[39] Such a notion points to how, historically, the allure and ethics of Greek sport were never understood in opposition to each other. Of course, one obvious result of this historical discourse on art and embodiment was the development of the subculture of bodybuilding proper at the turn of the twentieth century, which began with figures such as Eugen Sandow striking poses in direct imitation of ancient Greco-Roman sculpture.[40] The analysis of de Coubertin's own views on Hellenism and sculpture presented here, however, indicates that the modern Olympic movement is just as much a product of the intellectual tradition of *Body-Bildung*.

Thus, not only was de Coubertin's promotion of Hellenism engaged in ancient aesthetic theory, but it also appears that he made use of ancient aesthetics in the context of a distinctly modernist nostalgia to re-embody the ancient Greek past by way of sculpture. Yet if we turn once again to our ancient sources on the relationship between body and sculpture, it becomes evident that the ancients may have been engaged in a similar project of *Body-Bildung*. This seems to be especially true for Galen, one of our best sources for testimony on Polyclitus.[41] When we excavate Galen's text for mentions of Polyclitus, we find that Polyclitus's theory of *symmetria* of the limbs of the body was part of a larger theory of "health" as it related to the elements of the body.[42] Thus, in the *Doctrines of Hippocrates and Plato*, after explaining what exactly *symmetria* means in the passage quoted above, Galen continues: "For having taught us all the *symmetria* of the body in his writing [τῷ συγγράμματι τὰς συμμετρίας τοῦ σώματος], Polyclitus confirmed his account in action through the creation [δημιουργήσας] of a statue based on his prescription, which he also called the Canon. The beauty of the body then exists in the *symmetria* of the parts of the body according to all doctors and philosophers, and health of the elements, whichever there are at any point, is *symmetria* between them" (Galen, *De Placitis Hippocratis et Platonis*, 5.3.16–17).

Here I would call special attention to the verb Galen employs to demonstrate how Polyclitus put his theory into practice. The verb he uses for creating the statue is *dêmiourgeô*. This of course is a standard verb referring to the work of a craftsman, but Galen also uses the term *demiourgos* to refer specifically to the work of nature, *physis* as an act of craftsmanship.[43] Thus in his programmatic text, the *Ars Medica*, Galen explains that "[n]ature is the craftsman of all things, and the doctor is the servant [ἁπάντων δ' αὐτῶν ἡ μὲν φύσις ἐστὶ δημιουργὸς, ὁ δ' ἰατρὸς ὑπηρέτης]" (*Ars Medica* 1.378.9). Galen goes into the greatest detail on nature as craftsman in one of his earlier works, *On the Function of the Parts*, where he presents the human body as a product of provident creation through reason and design. In that work, he also explicitly links the work of nature with Polyclitus. He exclaims:

Here is something to wonder at in these men who say that nature has no skill, namely, that they praise sculptors for making the parts on the right side precisely like those on the left but fail to praise Nature, who in addition to making the parts equal also supplies them with actions and more than this with usefulness that is taught to the animal right at the beginning, as soon as it is born. Or is it right to admire Polyclitus for the symmetry of the parts in his statue called the Canon and yet necessary to deprive Nature not only of praise but of all skill – Nature, who exhibits the symmetry of the parts both on the outside, as sculptors do, and also deep below the surface? Or was it not Polyclitus himself who was the imitator, at least in what he was able to imitate? (Galen *De Usu Partium* 4.351–352K)

Thus instead of viewing Polyclitan sculpture as somehow *supra verum* (as Quintilian had claimed), or as "beyond nature" (as Winckelmann had later insisted), Galen understands the embodied *symmetria* found in sculpture as the supreme and prescriptive expression of Nature, thereby uniting the generally opposed categories of *physis* and *technê*.[44]

Galen thought it quite possible for human bodies to be similar to Polyclitan sculpture, just not *all* human bodies. He described how the right balance in the environment and climate affects the balance of the body. Thus in his work *On the Preservation of Health*, he states: "For nobody can grow up well-mixed or faultless in nature in the immoderately extreme climates, as reason teaches and experience proves ... But the best body, about which we are now speaking, is like the Canon of Polyclitus, and many similar bodies are seen in our land, which also has a temperate climate, but among the Kelts, Scythians, Egyptians, or Arabians, one would never dream of seeing such a body" (Galen, *De Sanitate Tuenda* 6.126K).

Galen's emphasis on climate and environment for the production of beautiful bodies makes for a striking parallel with the writings of figures such as Winckelmann and von Humboldt.[45] These racially and culturally motivated connections between the body, sculpture, and cultural/ethnic groups render Galen's comments a prime exemplar for an ancient form of "body fascism."[46] Immediately after making this claim regarding where the most Polyclitan-like bodies can be found, Galen notes that the central part of Italy has the most moderate climate and also the climate most similar to Greece, which Galen describes as the "fatherland of Hippocrates" (Galen, *De Sanitate Tuenda*, 6.127K). Galen may be referring to Hippocrates because arguments regarding the effect of climate on the body were most likely first articulated in Hippocratic writings.[47] At the same time, Galen's periphrasis for Greece as "the fatherland of Hippocrates" provides additional insight into how and why Galen would turn to Polyclitus. Polyclitan *symmetria* underscores Galen's own philosophy of *physis*; furthermore, his allusion to Polyclitus is apparently motivated by a desire to appeal to the classical Hellenic heritage as a mode of cultural authority, in much the same way that Galen makes use of Hippocrates. Thus, just as de Coubertin employed the metaphor of ancient athletic sculpture in order to re-embody a lost ancient Greek past, so Galen makes use of Polyclitan sculpture for a similar purpose in the context of the Roman Imperial period. Through the critical gaze of the doctor, whose purpose is to realign the "balance of the body" – a gaze that is partly informed by Polyclitan *symmetria* – the Roman Imperial doctor becomes the agent by which the classical past is brought physically into the present.

As a final point, we may note that like medicine, ancient athletics itself in the Roman Imperial period was engaged in this very same effort to re-embody the past through an appeal to ancient Greek sculpture. One of our best albeit largely understudied texts on athletics from the ancient world is Philostratus's *Gymnasticus*, written sometime in the third century CE.[48] Where Galen was extremely critical of ancient athletic practice, Philostratus's *Gymnasticus* is largely aimed at demonstrating how *gymnastikê* does constitute a legitimate form of both *technê* and *sophia*.[49] Just as the medical doctor's skills in diagnosis and prognosis were conditioned by Polyclitan *symmetria*, so Philostratus argues that the critical gaze of the athletic coach, the *gymnastês*, should operate in the very same fashion: "The nature of the parts of the body is to be observed in the following manner, as in sculpture: that the ankle correspond with the wrist, the forearm with the shin, and the arm matches with the thigh and the buttocks with the shoulder, the back be seen in relation to the stomach, and that the chest project similar to the area below the hip, and the head, as the benchmark of the whole, be commensurable with all of these" (Philostratus, *Gymnasticus* 25).[50] In the first place, we should note that Philostratus's version of *symmetria* is not quite the same as that of Polyclitus, since Polyclitus's theory suggests that each part of the body be measured against its neighbouring part and according to the whole, whereas Philostratus here proposes commensurability between top and bottom, back and front. Philostratus prescribes this manner of viewing and examining the body of the athlete in order to elevate the status of the coach above that of the "Judges of Greece," the *Hellanodikai*, who also subjected the athlete to their own critical gaze in determining an athlete's status and qualification for participation in the contests.[51]

We should note that this is not the only occasion in the *Gymnasticus* where the body is viewed on analogy with sculpture. Philostratus too describes the ideal body of the wrestler, and explains: "The proper wrestler is tall rather than proportional, but let him be put together like the well-proportioned [man], neither long necked, nor with a neck yoked to his shoulders. For the latter is suitable [προσφυὲς], but for those familiar with the statues of Heracles, [the body with a neck yoked to the shoulders] appears more similar to one punished rather than trained. How much more pleasing and god-like are the noble statues that do not have short necks" (Philostratus *Gymnasticus* 35).

It is important to note that Philostratus dedicates more time in the *Gymnasticus* to describing the wrestler's body than that of any other type of athlete. As John Zilcosky has noted in his chapter in this volume, "Wrestling, or the Art of Disentangling Bodies," wrestling had pride of place as the pre-eminent athletic event of antiquity, and a large part of the ancient (and modern) fascination with wrestling rests in the fact that the entanglement of bodies leads to critical questions about subjectivity and individuality.[52] The *Gymnasticus*, I believe, follows very much in line with this broader philosophic concern with wrestling, individuality, and identity.[53] Yet Philostratus does not engage in the issue of entanglement of bodies *per se*; instead, he treats the wrestler's body as an individual subject. This focus on the wrestler as individual subject comes through in his focus on the single body rather than on the activity of wrestling. For in *Gymnasticus*, Philostratus specifically argues against functionality – that is, what is naturally suitable (προσφυὲς) to the act of wrestling – in favour of the aesthetics of athletic sculpture (35).[54] In his 1908 commentary, Julius Jüthner noted that the "punished" Heracles type is most likely the extremely hypertrophied Farnese Heracles from the Baths of Caracalla, who would have been considered punished because of his labours and servitude to Eurystheus and Hera.[55] And Zahra Newby has noted that athletic sculpture such as the Farnese would have had a mimetic function at the Baths of Caracalla. She explains that "[w]hile the mosaics in the palaestra suggest that the bathers could see themselves in these figures of athletic prowess, Heracles too acts as an athletic role model, the brawniest and burliest of them all."[56] But what is so striking in the *Gymnasticus* is that Philostratus declares the Farnese-type Heracles statue to be a *bad* role model for ancient athletes. In this regard Philostratus is adding a level of refinement to the argument for *Body-Bildung* by specifying and classifying which types of Greco-Roman sculpture are the best to imitate. That is to say, according to Philostratus, athletes in the Roman Imperial period should imitate classical *symmetria* rather than Hellenistic hypertrophy. Of course it was precisely this Hellenistic hypertrophy, and the Farnese in particular, that gave rise to modern bodybuilding, starting with Eugen Sandow.[57] In Philostratus's *Gymnasticus*, however, we do not have a blanket prescription for the imitation of ancient sculpture. Rather, Philostratus offers a type of sociology of muscle – too much muscle signifies punishment and/or slavery, whereas a symmetrical build demonstrates classical "freedom," *eleutheria*.[58] Thus, where Galen made use of Polyclitan sculpture to demonstrate how nature herself was an artist, Philostratus proposes that the athletic coach serve as a type of "critic of nature," *phuseôs kritês* (*Gymnasticus*, 25). When Philostratus describes how the athlete should be viewed in relation to sculpture, he seems to suggest that being a "judge of nature" is equivalent to becoming a type of art critic for the physical body. In this regard, the critical gaze of the coach competes with that of the doctor, and like the doctor, the athletic coach is also able to bring to bear his entire knowledge of the Hellenic heritage on a single body.[59]

Overall then, when we examine the aesthetic allure on which de Coubertin based his notion of Hellenism, a notion that served in many ways as the ostensible *raison d'être* for the revitalization of the Olympic Games, we find a considerable degree of historical depth to his discursive strategies and implicit ideology. While de Coubertin's use of aesthetics can be seen as symptomatic of a modern or even pre-postmodern nostalgia, we might more appropriately term this nostalgia post-Hellenic.[60] This post-Hellenic nostalgia presents us with a desire to re-embody the ancient Greek past through an appeal to the beauty of Greek figural representation, and it was just as present in the Roman Imperial period as it was at the turn of the twentieth century. What we have then is a type of *mise en abyme* for a discourse on aesthetics, athletics, and Hellenism. From the initial sketch provided here, we see that this discourse on the body and sculpture, though especially strong in the modern Olympic movement, can be traced back to the early modern era in Europe. But it need not stop there. As we have seen from the work of Galen and Philostratus, the same discourse on sculpture, the body, and imitation was already present in antiquity.[61] At the same time, we should note how such a discourse is put to very different purposes in different historical and ideological contexts. Galen and Philostratus employed the same strategy for different ends, just as Winckelmann and de Coubertin had very different ends in mind in their promotion of *Body-Bildung* as a type of moral imperative. In each case, however, we see an effort to join the physical with the philosophical, to bring together allure and ethics, although the ethics in each respective time period were always highly problematic.

And of course, the present era is participating in this very same discourse. Most recently the connections among aesthetics, athletics, and Hellenism have been invoked by Hans Ulrich Gumbrecht in *In Praise of Athletic Beauty* (2006). In that work, Gumbrecht seeks to carve out an intellectual space where one can freely praise athletics, with praise understood as the "determination to see and to value athletic beauty as an embodiment of a culture's highest values."[62] Like many before him, Gumbrecht appeals to the Greek tradition as a window onto this mode of praise.[63] Yet it is important to note that Gumbrecht also seeks to avoid the ideological and ethical dangers implicated in post-Hellenic discourse; he does so be focusing on "presence" and a Kantian concept of beauty.[64] The result, for Gumbrecht, is that sports are imbued with a type of embodied immanence, where special attention is given to human movement and time-suspended events. This effect of kinaesthetic presence effectively removes sport from the realm of social meaning, power relations, and politics more generally.[65] To be sure, there are many who would argue that Gumbrecht's own focus on "beauty" reproduces the strategies of the fascist ideologues of the 1930s.[66] Gumbrecht himself is certainly aware of the dangers in his project, and he even anticipated those accusations when he mentioned how often the 1936 Olympics had been invoked "to make a slam dunk case for sports as a tool of political manipulation."[67] So the question remains, is it possible to appreciate and even praise the beauty of sport in a way that is free from the force of earlier ideological discourse? Can we appreciate the allure of sport without concern about the ethics of doing so? And from a historical perspective, is there a way to praise the beauty of athletics without reference to Hellenism?

A critical step in that direction is Gumbrecht's own distinction between the kinaesthetic beauty of movement and the aesthetic appeal of the "sculpted" body. Regarding the modern metaphor of the "sculpted body," Gumbrecht draws a connection between the ancient Greek *gymnasion* and the modern-day workout studio.[68] According to Gumbrecht, those engaged in training at the gym are less focused on kinaesthetics and more focused on body transformation.[69] Rather than losing itself in both movement and the moment, the self becomes the object of attention, constrained by time and intentionality. Hence in contrast to the "presence" created by the sporting event, the one who goes to the gym in order to "sculpt" the body is a self-referential "athlete and spectator simultaneously."[70] In this regard, Gumbrecht makes an important and critical distinction between the sporting event and the long tradition that blended Hellenism, athletics, and figural representation as described in this chapter. Indeed, de Coubertin's arguments for the athlete as "living sculpture" collapse the categories of kinaesthetic beauty and the philosophical/ethical implications of body sculpting as *Selbstbildung*. As I have argued, the reception of Greek sculpture is what caused those two categories to be collapsed. On the one hand, the unique ways in which Greek sculpture itself may capture movement may create a type of kinaesthetic empathy in the viewer, perhaps not very different from the experience of the modern spectator at a sporting event.[71] On the other hand, as we have seen, there is also a long tradition that equates the perfection of Greek sculpture with moral and ethical perfection. The collapsing of these two categories is perfectly captured in the history of debates on that ancient aesthetic term "eurythmia," which served as the foundation for de Coubertin's own efforts to revive the Olympics. Of course, even Gumbrecht's transcendental approach cannot help but appeal to the ancient Greek tradition. But in place of ancient aesthetic terminology, Gumbrecht appeals to the notions of *aretē* and *agōn* and the ways in which "excellence" and "competition" become occasions for producing and experiencing kinaesthetic beauty.[72] And here too Gumbrecht is fully aware of the historical implications of his philosophical project. Concerning these two terms, Gumbrecht states: "It is hard to tell how much their present-day use was shaped by the nineteenth-century waves of Philhellenic enthusiasm."[73]

The fact remains that the history of discourse on Greek athletics and aesthetics from antiquity to the present has made appeals to Hellenism virtually unavoidable. One might therefore be surprised to learn that Pierre de Coubertin, one of the most ardent promoters of Hellenism in the twentieth century, at first resisted making any appeal whatsoever to the ancient Greeks as the means for combining the allure and the ethics of sport. In 1888, after visiting William Penny Brookes and observing Brookes's own effort to revive the ancient Olympics in England, de Coubertin praised him for his promotion of athletic education, but also commented: "There was no need to invoke memories of Greece."[74] Clearly, in the short time between that statement and the first IOC Olympics of 1896, de Coubertin had changed his mind. Later, in a 1908 article titled "The Philhellene's Duty," he declared: "From now on let us let Hellenism do as it pleases."[75] Yet we can be certain that Hellenism has not done as it pleases, and never will.

As I have argued, albeit in brief terms, Hellenism has been appealed to as a type of eternal signifier of transcendent allure and has been equated with concepts such as "beauty" and "nature" throughout Western history. But none of these concepts, neither "Hellenism," nor "beauty," nor "nature," exist in a historical and ethical vacuum. In response to de Coubertin's notion of the "Philhellene's duty," we might insist that it is the *Hellenist*'s duty to increase our historical awareness of the ancient Greek tradition, in both ancient and modern contexts. Perhaps we cannot prevent the abuse of Hellenism, but we can promote a greater degree of historical consciousness and conscientiousness when confronted with that eternal effort to return to the Greeks.

NOTES

* Special thanks are owed to James Porter, Andrew Stewart, and Paul
  Christesen, who kindly commented on earlier versions of this chapter.
  I am especially grateful to John Zilcosky, Sepp Gumbrecht, and all the participants at the Allure and Ethics conference for their excellent feedback,
  and I am especially indebted to Marlo Burks for her diligence and patience
  in the editing process.

1 On de Coubertin's own positioning in the Olympic movement, see David
  Young, *The Modern Olympics: A Struggle for Revival* (Baltimore: Johns Hopkins
  University Press, 1996); and Young, *A Brief History of the Olympic Games*
  (Malden: Blackwell, 2004), 150–7.

2 Norbert Müller, *Olympism: Select Writings of Pierre de Coubertin* (Lausanne:
  International Olympic Committee, 2000), 545.

3 See, among others, Jean Durry, "Pierre de Coubertin: Sport and
  Aesthetics," *Olympic Review* 225: 390–6; Douglas A. Brown, "Pierre de
  Coubertin's Olympic Exploration of Modernism 1894–1914," *Research
  Quarterly for Exercise and Sport* 67, no. 2 (1996): 121–35; Jeffrey O. Seagrave
  and Dikaia Chatziefstathiou, "Pierre de Coubertin's Ideology of Beauty
  from the Perspective of the History of Ideas," in *Pathways: Critiques and
  Discourse in Olympic Research*, ed. B. Barney et al. (London: International
  Centre for Olympic Research, University of Western Ontario, 2008), 31–43.

4 Müller, *Olympism*, 567.

5 Ibid., 202.

6 For the history of debates on eurythmia at the turn of the twentieth
  century, see Jerome Jordan Pollitt, *The Ancient View of Greek Art: Criticism,
  History, and Terminology* (New Haven: Yale University Press, 1974), 174–7,
  222–5.

7 On Steiner and the occult in Germany, see Helmut Zander, *Anthroposophie
  in Deutschland* (Göttingen: Vandenhoeck und Ruprecht, 2007); Heiner
  Ullrich, *Rudolf Steiner*, trans. Janet Duke and Daniel Balestrini (London:
  Continuum, 2008); and Peter Staudenmeier, *Between Occultism and Nazism*
  (Leiden: Brill, 2014). On ancient eurythmia related to movement and
  dance, see, for instance, Plato, *Laws* 7.795e.

8 Steiner's Eurythmy and Anthroposophy had many affinities with the
  Nazi *Volksgemeinschaft*, although the relationship with National Socialism
  was politically complex, on which see Staudenmeier, *Occultism*, 146–78.
  For a historical overview of the relationship between German dance and
  gymnastic training, see also Marion Kant, "The Moving Body and the Will
  to Culture," *European Review* 19, no. 4 (2011): 579–94. On Friedrich Jahn's
  Turnen movement and the political implications of German gymnastics,
  see Wolf Kittler's piece in this volume: "A Well Trained Community:

Gymnastics for the German Nation." See also Allen Guttmann, *Games and Empires: Modern Sports and Cultural Imperialism* (New York: Columbia University Press, 1994), 143–5; Cornelia Kessler, Hans-Joachim Bartmuss, and Eberhard Kunze, *Friedrich Ludwig Jahn und die Gesellschaften der Turner* (Halle: Landesheimatbund Sachsen-Anhalt, 2004); and Paul Christesen, *Sport and Democracy in the Ancient and Modern Worlds* (Cambridge: Cambridge University Press, 2012), 220–3.

9 Just as Pierre de Coubertin sought to distinguish between French and German perspectives through language, so Jahn had made a similar effort with *Turnen*. As Kittler notes in his chapter in this volume, Jahn created a language for *Turnen* that was intended to have no similarity with any other language, especially the French language. As Jahn states: "To French is to falsify, to emasculate the Ur-force, to poison the language source, to hamper the possibility of further language formation, and total language meaninglessness": Jahn, *Turnkunst* XXII, translation from Kittler, "A Well Trained Community."

10 Translations are mine unless otherwise stated.

11 See Pollitt, *The Ancient View*, 14–23.

12 See J.E. Raven, "Polyclitus and Pythagoreanism," *Classical Quarterly* (1951): 147–52; Pollitt, *The Ancient View*, 14–15; Andrew Stewart, "The Canon of Polykleitos," *Journal of Hellenic Studies* 98 (1978): 122–31, esp. 125; Nigel Spivey, *Understanding Greek Sculpture* (Cambridge: Cambridge University Press, 1996), 40; Andrew Stewart, *Art, Desire, and the Body in Ancient Greece* (Cambridge: Cambridge University Press, 1997), 93; and Michael Squire, *The Art of the Body: Antiquity and Its Legacy* (New York: I.B. Tauris, 2011), 8.

13 For the *Doryphorus* and its relation to the Canon of Polyclitus, see Hanna Philipp, "Zu Polyklets Schrift," and Ernst Berger, "Zum Kanon des Polyklet," in *Polyket: Der Bildhauer der griechischen Klassik: Ausstellung im Liebieghaus Museum alter Plastik, Frankfurt am Main*, ed. Herbert Beck, Peter C. Bol, and Maraike Bückling (Mainz am Rhein: von Zabern, 1990), 156–84; and the collection of essays in Warren G. Moon, ed., *Polykleitos, the Doryphoros, and Tradition* (Madison: University of Wisconsin Press, 1995).

14 See, for instance, Spivey, *Understanding Greek Sculpture*, 39–43; Stewart, *Art, Desire, and the Body*, 93–96; Richard Neer, *The Emergence of the Classical Style in Greek Sculpture* (Chicago: University of Chicago Press, 2010), 152; Robin Osborne, *History Written on the Classical Body* (Cambridge: Cambridge University Press, 2011), 44; and Squire, *The Art of the Body*, 57.

15 See James I. Porter, *The Origins of Aesthetic Thought in Ancient Greece* (Cambridge: Cambridge University Press, 2010), 416–20, on evidence for idealism and visual experience in Classical Greece.

16 In the ancient discourses of art and rhetoric, *decor* comes to mean
    "appropriateness," on which see Ellen Perry, *The Aesthetics of Emulation
    in the Visual Arts of Rome* (Cambridge: Cambridge University Press, 2005),
    31, who suggests that *decor* "provides the essential theoretical justification
    for visual formulae."

17 There is a long history of scholarship connecting Polyclitus with Pythag-
    orean philosophy, on which see Hermann Diels, *Antike Technik* (Leipzig:
    Teubner, 1914), 15; Raven, "Polyclitus and Pythagoreanism"; Pollitt, *The
    Ancient View*, 17–22; Stewart, "The Canon of Polykleitos," 127; Gregory
    Vincent Leftwich, *Ancient Conceptions of the Body and the Canon of Polyklei-
    tos* (Princeton: Princeton University Press, 1987), 32–41; Andrew Stewart,
    "Nuggets: Mining the Text Again," *American Journal of Archaeology* 102,
    no. 2 (1998): 271–82; and Deborah Tarn Steiner, *Images in Mind: Statues
    in Archaic and Classical Greek Literature and Thought* (Princeton: Princeton
    University Press, 2001), 40–1. For more recent arguments against direct
    connection between Polyclitus and Pythagoras, see Carl Huffman,
    "Polyclète et les Présocratiques," in *Qu'est-ce que la Philosophie Présocra-
    tique?*, ed. André Laks and Claire Louguet (Paris: Presses Université
    Septentrion, 2002), 303–27; and Andrew Stewart, *Classical Greece and the
    Birth of Western Art* (Cambridge: Cambridge University Press, 2008),
    146n10.

18 Stewart, "Nuggets," 273–5.

19 The other major source Stewart discusses is Diog. Laert. 2.32, which
    presents similar phrasing.

20 See Stewart, "Nuggets," 102. Stewart,*Classical Greece*, 146n10, now con-
    curs with Huffman in "Polyclète et les Présocratiques," who has argued
    against any explicit connection between Pythagoreanism and Polyclitus.
    Yet Huffman's point does not vitiate the force of Stewart's original obser-
    vation – namely,that Polyclitus and Pythagoras were both participating in
    what would have been a common discourse of measurement.

21 Müller, *Olympism*, 512.

22 Pierre de Coubertin, *Pédagogie sportive* (Paris: Librairie Philosophique
    J. VRIN, 1972), 146.

23 Müller, *Olympism*, 580.

24 In *History Written on the Classical Body*, Osborne criticizes modern schol-
    ars for applying modern notions of physical culture to the ancient world;
    thus he claims that "[a] fantasy world is conjured up by mixing together
    elements of textual depictions of the ancient with the categories promoted
    in textual description of the modern world" (29). Regardless of how valid
    or not Osborne's criticism is for Classical scholars, such criticism could
    certainly apply to de Coubertin's references to antiquity.

25 On the Berlin Olympics as the "Nazi Olympics," see especially Richard
    D. Mandell, *The Nazi Olympics* (Urbana: University of Illinois Press, 1987);
    Susan D. Bachrach, *The Nazi Olympics: Berlin 1936* (Boston: Little, Brown,
    2000); and Arndt Krüger and William J. Murray, *The Nazi Olympics: Sport,
    Politics, and Appeasement in the 1930s* (Urbana: University of Illinois Press,
    2003).
26 The Discobolus has its own complex history in the modern Olympics.
    See Squire, *Art of the Body*, 20–3; and Ian Jenkins, *The Discobolus. British
    Museum Objects in Focus* (London: British Museum Press, 2012), esp. 53–63.
    For the early history of European traffic in the copies of Myron's Discobo-
    lus, see V. Coltman, *Classical Sculpture and the Culture of Collecting in Britain
    Since 1760* (Oxford: Oxford University Press, 2014), 96–100.
27 In *Understanding Greek Sculpture*, Spivey defines "body fascism" as "[t]he
    imposition of norms for acceptable or successful bodies brought about by
    a great commercial exposure to paragons of ideal proportions" (39). Again,
    Osborne specifically criticizes Spivey for anachronism in applying the
    concept of "body fascism" to the ancient world (*History Written on the Clas-
    sical Body*, 30). But perhaps the notion of "body fascism" could be applied
    more appropriately to the role of idealized Greek sculpture and athletics
    in 1930s Germany. For criticism of Riefenstahl's *Olympia* as a mode of
    Nazi propaganda through the use of a fascist aesthetic, see most famously
    Susan Sontag's essay "Fascinating Fascism," *New York Review of Books* 22,
    no. 1 (1975). For a more subtle interpretation of Riefenstahl's *Olympia*, see
    Michael Mackenzie, "From Athens to Berlin: The 1936 Olympics and Leni
    Riefenstahl's *Olympia*," *Critical Inquiry* 29, no. 2 (2003): 302–6. Mackenzie
    suggests that Riefenstahl's documentary reflects a conservative and racial
    political ideology of the body associated with the Expressive Dance move-
    ment of the 1910s and 1920s rather than operating as a pure expression of
    the political ideology of National Socialism.
28 Müller, *Olympism*, 202. On de Coubertin's own complex relationship with
    Germany especially during the Berlin Olympics, see W.J. Murray, "France,
    Coubertin, and the Nazi Olympics," *Olympika* 1, no. 1 (1992): 46–69; and
    T. Alkemeyer, *Körper, Kult und Politik* (Frankfurt am Main: Campus Ver-
    lag, 1996). The relationship between ancient Greek athletics and "body
    fascism" can also be seen as a tenet of nineteenth-century French ideology
    going back to the figure Arthur de Gobineau, on which see Athena S.
    Leoussi, *Nationalism and Classicism: The Classical Body as National Symbol in
    Nineteenth-Century England and France* (New York: St Martin's, 1998), 16–19.
29 A full explication of Winckelmann's theory of art and the body is well be-
    yond the scope of this chapter, and the bibliography on this topic is grow-
    ing rapidly. See Josef Chytry, *The Aesthetic State: A Quest in Modern German
    Thought* (Berkeley: University of California Press, 1989), 11–37; Ian Jenkins,

Archaeologists and Aesthetes in the Sculpture Galleries of the British Museum 1800–1939 (London: British Museum Publications, 1992), 19–24; Alex Potts, *Flesh and the Ideal* (New Haven: Yale University Press, 1994); James Porter, "Introduction," in *Constructions of the Classical Body*, ed. James Porter (Ann Arbor: University of Michigan Press, 1999), esp. 16n12; Edouard Pommier, *Winckelmann: inventeur de l'histoire de l'art* (Paris: Gallimard, 2003); Porter, "What Is Classical about Classical Antiquity?," in *Classical Pasts*, ed. Porter (Princeton: Princeton University Press, 2006), 1–65; M. Marvin, *Language of the Muses* (Los Angeles: Getty Publications, 2008), 103–19; Louis Ruprecht, *Winckelmann and the Vatican's First Profane Museum* (New York: Palgrave Macmillan, 2011); Delia Tzortzaki, "Myth and the Ideal in 20th C. Exhibitions of Classical Art," in *A Companion to Greek Art* (Malden: Wiley-Blackwell, 2012), 667–82; John Harry North, *Winckelmann's Philosophy of Art* (Newcastle upon Tyne: Cambridge Scholars, 2012); Elizabeth Prettejohn, *The Modernity of Ancient Sculpture* (London: I.B. Tauris, 2012); and Katherine Harloe, *Winckelmann and the Invention of Antiquity* (Oxford: Oxford University Press, 2013).

30 J. J. Winckelmann, *Reflections on the Imitation of Greek Works in Painting and Sculpture*, trans. Elfriede Heyer and Roger C. Norton (La Salle: Open Court, 1987), 7.

31 Ibid., 7.

32 *Carmina Epigraphica Graeca* 394, our earliest inscription of an Olympic victor statue, states that the statue is equal in "size and thickness" to the actual athlete. See Joachim Ebert, *Griechische Epigramme auf Sieger an gymnischen und hippischen Agonen* (Berlin: Akademie-Verlag, 1972), 251–4; Deborah Tarn Steiner, "Moving Images: Victor Statues in Art and Epinician Song," *Classical Antiquity* 17, no. 1 (1998): 123–50, esp. 125; and Leslie Kurke, "The Economy of Kudos," in *Cultural Poetics in Archaic Greece*, ed. Carol Dougherty and Leslie Kurke (New York: Oxford University Press, 1998), 131–63, esp. 141–2.

33 Winckelmann, *Reflections on the Imitation of Greek Works*, 15.

34 Porter, "What Is Classical," 40–3. On Winckelmann's treatment of proportionality, see J. J. Winckelmann, *History of Ancient Art*, vols. 1 and 2, trans. Alexander Gode (New York: F. Unger, 1968), 261–9; and A.A. Donohue, "Winckelmann's History of Art and Polyclitus," in Moon, ed., *Polykleitos, the Doryphoros, and Tradition*, 327–53, esp. 338–44.

35 On von Humboldt and the Classical ideal, see J. Porter, *Nietzsche and the Philology of the Future* (Stanford: Stanford University Press, 2000), 186–91.

36 W. von Humboldt, *Werke in fünf Bänden*, ed. Andreas Fliner and KlausGiel (Darmstadt: 1960–81), 2:49. My translation.

37 Ibid., 2:49.

38 Ibid., 2:66.

39 James Porter, "Foucault's Antiquity," in *Classics and the Uses of Reception*, ed. Charles Martindale and Richard F. Thomas (Malden: Blackwell, 2006), 175–9.

40 On Greco-Roman Sculpture and the history of modern bodybuilding, see Kenneth R. Dutton, *The Perfectible Body* (New York: Continuum, 1995); Michael Anton Budd, *The Sculpture Machine* (New York: NYU Press, 1997); Budd, "Herculean Muscle! The Classicizing Rhetoric of Bodybuilding," *Arion* 4, no. 3 (1997): 54–5, reprinted in Porter, ed., *Constructions of the Classical Body*, 355–79; Jan Todd, "The History of Cardinal Farnese's Weary Heracles," *Iron Game History* 9, no. 1 (2005): 29; Bryan E. Burns, "Classicizing Bodies in the Male Photographic Tradition," in *A Companion to Classical Reception*, ed. L. Hardwick and C. Stray (Malden: Blackwell, 2006), 441–5; and Charles H. Stocking, "Greek Ideal as Hyperreal" *Arion* 21, no. 3 (2014): 45–74.

41 Polyclitus is mentioned fourteen times in the texts of Galen.

42 Galen is particularly interested in constructing "health" as its own unique *technê* of the body, on which see Galen, *Thrasybulus* K5.860–4, *De Sanitate Tuenda* K6.1. For Galen's theory of elements and their balance, see R.J. Hankinson, "Galen and the Best of All Possible Worlds," *Classical Quarterly* 39, no. 1 (1989): 206–27, esp. 210–23.

43 On Galen's Demiurge, especially regarding its relationship to Aristotle, Plato, and Stoicism, see Friedrich Solmsen, "Nature as Craftsman in Greek Thought," *Journal of the History of Ideas* 24 (1963): 473–96; Hankinson, "Galen and the Best of All Possible Worlds," 218–19; Franjo Kovačić, *Der Begriff der Physis bei Galen vor dem Hintergrund seiner Vorgänger* (Stuttgart: Steiner Verlag, 2001), 210–53; Michael Frede, "Galen's Theology," in *Galien et la philosophie, Fondation Hardt Entretiens sur l'Antiquité Classique*, ed. J. Barnes and J. Jouanna (Vandoeuvres-Geneva: Fondation Hardt, 2003), 73–126, esp. 105–26; Rebecca Flemming, "Demiurge and Emperor in Galen's World of Knowledge," in *Galen and the World of Knowledge*, ed. C. Gill, T. Whitmarsh, and J. Wilkins (Cambridge: Cambridge University Press, 2009), 59–84; and Susan P. Mattern, *Prince of Medicine: Galen in the Roman Empire* (New York: Oxford University Press, 2013), 168–71. For the specifically artistic implications of *physis* as a *demiourgos* in Galen, see Kovačić, "Die Natur als Künstler und Baumeister bei Galen," *Traditio* 58 (2001): 1–57.

44 On the history of *physis* and *technê* in medical discourse, see H. von Staden, "*Physis* and *Technê* in Greek Medicine," in *The Artificial and the Natural: An Evolving Polarity*, ed. B. Bensaude-Vincent and W.R. Newman (Cambridge, MA: MIT Press, 2007).

45 See Winckelmann, *Reflections on the Imitation of Greek Works*, 7: "The first development of the Greeks was influenced by a mild and clear sky; but the

practice of physical exercises from an early age gave this development its noble forms." Similarly, on the connection between "bodily strength" and the "Greek climate," see von Humboldt, *Werke in fünf Bänden*, 2:13.

46 See n27 above for the debate on ancient versus modern "body fascism." Osborne's comments on the anachronism of Spivey's "body fascism" are specifically applied to the Classical period.

47 See J. Jouanna, *Hippocrates* (Baltimore: Johns Hopkins University Press, 1999), 231–2.

48 Until the last decade, the *Gymnasticus* was generally dismissed as a "sophistic" text, but significant research has been done to demonstrate that we should take the *Gymnasticus* seriously. See J. König, *Athletics and Literature in the Roman Empire* (Cambridge: Cambridge University Press, 2005); Jason König, *Philostratus, Gymnasticus*. *Loeb Classical Library* 521 (Cambridge, MA: Harvard University Press, 2014); Onno van Nijf, "Athletics, *Andreia*, and the *Askesis* – Culture in the Roman East," in *Andreia: Studies in Manliness and Courage in Classical Antiquity*, ed. Ralph M. Rosen and Ineke Sluiter (Leiden: Brill, 2003), 263–6; Onno van Nijf, "Athletics and Paideia: Festivals and Physical Education in the World of the Second Sophistic," in *Paideia: The World of the Second Sophistic*, ed. Barbara Borg (Berlin: Walter de Gruyter, 2004), 203–28; Zahra Newby, *Greek Athletics in the Roman World: Victory and Virtue* (Oxford: Oxford University Press, 2005); and Charles H. Stocking, "The Use and Abuse of Training 'Science' in Philostratus' *Gymnasticus*," *Classical Antiquity* 35, no. 1 (2016): 86–125.

49 For Galen's criticism of athletics, see especially the *Protrepticus* and *Thrasybulus*, and König, *Athletics and Literature*, 274–300. On Philostratus's arguments for *gymnastikê* as a form of *sophia*, see König, *Athletics and Literature*, 315–16; König, "Training Athletes," 260–1; and Stocking, "The Use and Abuse of Training 'Science.'" For the general instability of categories of knowledge in the Imperial period, see Jason König and Tim Whitmarsh, "Ordering Knowledge," in *Ordering Knowledge in the Roman Empire*, ed. König and Whitmarsh (Cambridge: Cambridge University Press, 2007), esp. 24–7.

50 Translations are my own, unless indicated otherwise. As a basis for the translations I am using the Greek text of Philostratus's *Gymnasticus* from König's 2014 Loeb edition.

51 See Philostratus, *Gymnasticus* 25 as well as *Gymnasticus* 18, where Philostratus also asserts, "Let the coach have some [authority] even over the Hellanodikai in Olympia [ἐχέτω δή τι ὑπὲρ τὸν Ἑλλανοδίκην ὁ γυμναστὴς ἐν Ὀλυμπίᾳ]." On Philostratus's treatment of the coach as a "moral guardian of Hellenism" and its relationship to Philostratus's own self-positioning, see König, *Athletics and Literature*, 331.

52 So concerning Plato's philosophic treatment of wrestling, Zilcosky comments: "Because modern man has twisted himself free – like a wrestler – both from other subjects and from his own body, he can be capable of individual decision-making and of moral action" (in this volume, "Wrestling, or the Art of Disentangling Bodies").

53 Thus, for instance, according to Philostratus, the "first" and "best" generation of athletes includes the mythic wrestlers Peleus, Heracles, and Theseus (*Gymnasticus* 1), mythic figures also discussed by Plato (on which see Zilcosky in this volume). For Philostratus's treatment of these three mythic figures within a type of moral genealogy of athletes, see Stocking, "Ages of Athletes," *Classics@13: Greek Poetry and Sport*, ed. Thomas Scanlon (Cambridge, MA: Center for Hellenic Studies, 2015), http://chs.harvard.edu/CHS/article/display/6050.

54 A similar argument for form over function is made regarding the wrestler's chest and back at *Gymnasticus*, 35.

55 Julius Jüthner, *Philostratos über Gymnastik* (Leipzig: Teubner, 1909), 253. On the significance of the Farnese to the Severan emperors and to Caracalla especially, see Janet DeLaine, *The Baths of Caracalla in Rome*, JRA Suppl. no. 25 (Portsmouth, RI, 1997), 80–1. That Philostratus would be referring explicitly to the Farnese from the Baths of Caracalla seems historically possible, given Philostratus's close association with the Severans and dating of the *Gymnasticus* to around the time of the Baths of Caracalla, on which see Newby, *Greek Athletics in the Roman World*, 67–76. For Philostratus's involvement with the Severan dynasty, see Tim Whitmarsh, "Prose Literature and the Severan Dynasty," in *Severan Culture*, ed. Simon Swain, Stephen J. Harrison, and Jas Elsner (Cambridge: Cambridge University Press, 2007), 29–51, esp. 31–4; For athletics and the Severan emperors more generally, see König, "Greek Athletics in the Severan Period," 139–40.

56 Newby, *Greek Athletics in the Roman World*, 74.

57 On the unique role of the Farnese Heracles in the history of European physical culture, see Todd, "The History of Cardinal Farnese's Weary Heracles."

58 For a similar association between Classical art and "freedom" in the work of Winckelmann, see Chytry, *The Aesthetic State*, 23–33. For muscularity associated with slavery in a modern context, see Ronald L. Jackson, *Scripting the Black Masculine Body: Identity, Discourse, and Racial Politics in Popular Media* (Albany: SUNY Press, 2006), 79.

59 On the act of vision, *skepsis*, as a critical activity that connects and contrasts the coach and the doctor in both Galen and Philostratus, see König, *Athletics and Literature*, 272–3, 333–4.

60 For further development of the notion of "post-Hellenic nostalgia," see Stocking "Greek Ideal as Hyperreal," *Arion* 21, no. 3 (2014): 45–74.

61 This discourse, which presents a mimetic reversal between body and sculpture, can perhaps be traced back even to the Archaic and Classical periods, although the analogy is far less explicit. For instance, Pindar calls the athletic trainer the "the maker/craftsman [tektôn] for athletes" (Nemean 5.49), employing terms generally used for craftsman, on which see Leslie Kurke, The Traffic in Praise (Ithaca: Cornell University Press, 1991), 192–4; Deborah Tarn Steiner, Images in Mind (Princeton: Princeton University Press, 2001) 263–4; and Nigel Nicholson, Aristocracy and Athletics in Archaic and Classical Greece (Cambridge: Cambridge University Press, 2005), 176–80. See also Kurke, "Imagining Chorality: Wonder, Plato's Puppets, and Moving Statues," in Performance and Culture in Plato's Laws, ed. Anastasia-Erasmia Peponi (Cambridge: Cambridge University Press, 2013), 123–70, esp. 146–70, where Kurke demonstrates how the term for sculpture, agalmata, is applied to those engaged in choral dance in Archaic and Classical Greece.

62 Gumbrecht, In Praise of Athletic Beauty (Stanford: Stanford University Press, 2006), 24.

63 See ibid., 21–4, 57–8, 69–73, 91–9, 231.

64 Ibid., 37–84. An exposition of Gumbrecht's theory of presence and his use of Kant is beyond the scope of this chapter. For Gumbrecht's philosophical project on presence, see also In 1926: Living at the Edge of Time (Cambridge, MA: Harvard University Press, 1997); The Powers of Philology: Dynamics of Textual Scholarship (Chicago: University of Illinois Press, 2003); and The Production of Presence: What Meaning Cannot Convey (Stanford: Stanford University Press, 2004). On the intellectual influences for Gumbrecht's treatment of beauty and athletics, see Christopher Young, "Kantian kin(a) esthetic," Sport in History 28, no. 1 (2008): 5–25; and A. Regier, "Judgment and Experience in the Language of Confessional Sports," Sport in History 28, no. 1 (2008): 26–38.

65 See especially Gumbrecht, In Praise of Athletic Beauty, 57–84.

66 See especially Hayden White, "The Place and Value of College Sports: 2 Views: They Have Betrayed Their Educational Purpose," in Chronicle of Higher Education 52, no. 42 (2006); and Simon Martin, "In Praise of Fascist Beauty?," Sport in History 28, no. 1 (2008): 64–82.

67 Gumbrecht, In Praise of Athletic Beauty, 26. It is hoped that the mention of the Berlin Olympics in this chapter is viewed as more than simply another attempt at such a "slam dunk."

68 Ibid., 153–7. But see Osborne, History Written on the Classical Body, 27–44, on the problems with comparisons between Classical Greek and modern "gym culture." As I have argued in this article, the "sculpted body" metaphor certainly appears in the Roman Imperial period, but it is not entirely clear if it occurs in the Classical era. Further research is required to see if the same notion dates back to the earlier periods of Greek history.

69 In discussing two separate modes of body transformation through physical training, Gumbrecht makes a striking comparison between Arnold Schwarzenegger and Judith Butler, on which see Gumbrecht, *In Praise of Athletic Beauty*, 154–7.

70 Ibid., 157.

71 On the kinaesthetics of ancient Greek sculpture such as the Artemision Zeus and Myron's Discobolus and connections to an immanent sense of beauty or wonder, see Neer, *The Emergence of the Classical Style*, 71–91. On the notion of "kinaesthetic empathy" among spectators in physical performances, see, for instance, Susan Leigh Foster, *Choreagraphing Empathy: Kinaesthesia in Performance* (New York: Routledge, 2011), esp. 6–15.

72 Gumbrecht, *In Praise of Athletic Beauty*, 69–73.

73 Ibid., 70.

74 Young, *A Brief History of the Olympic Games*, 151. De Coubertin's initial resistance to Hellenism also seems to go against a long history of French classicism dating back at least to the French Revolution, and there was also a significant discourse on the "ancient Greek body" and French nationalism in the nineteenth century, on which see Leoussi, *Nationalism and Classicism*, 180–99.

75 Müller, *Olympism*, 250.

PART IV

Modern Europe

6 Attractive or Repugnant? Foot Races in Eighteenth-Century Germany and Britain

REBEKKA VON MALLINCKRODT

Introduction

In the *Nicomachean Ethics*, Aristotle writes: "Other traits generally attributed to the great-souled man are a slow gait, a deep voice, and a deliberate utterance; to speak in shrill tones and walk fast denotes an excitable and nervous temperament, which does not belong to one who cares for few things and thinks nothing great."[1] As Dilwyn Knox has argued in a now classic essay, this statement locates Aristotle in a tradition that valued restrained physical movement as an expression of magnanimity and dignity and that associated haste and violent movement with a lack of self-control and mastery over worldly affairs.[2] This ideal was conveyed to the European elites via the *Nicomachean Ethics*, which was well received in the late-medieval and early-modern period, and through numerous books on etiquette up to the nineteenth century.[3] Even in the same century, we find witnesses from the period who characterize fast or long-distance running as mindless. In this vein, a contemporary of Mensen Ernst (1799–1843), who was then the most famous long-distance runner on the European continent, wrote in 1842: "This racing through the world is reminiscent of the restless rush of the animals, from whom certain parts of the brain are taken, so that now, the eternal drive of movement no longer finds equilibrium or hold."[4] The perception of running as an aesthetic activity and an achievement is thus neither self-evident nor timeless. In examining the shifting social perspectives on running, we witness a particularly striking example of how the allure and ethics of the sport come up against each other, both in practice and in viewing:

As early as the seventeenth century, public races attracted hundreds or even thousands of spectators.[5] A great deal of money was bet on the outcomes of these races, which increased the excitement even further. Both indirect participation – by attending and placing bets – and direct participation – by running in the races – allowed for what Norbert Elias has described as the "controlled decontrolling of emotions," that is, a "[temporal and local] relaxation of the control ordinarily exercised over the emotions."[6] It is difficult to find sources that indicate how these races were emotionally perceived; even so, the high number of spectators alone points to their appeal.

Yet the running races of the early modern era were not necessarily held as tests of performance, the way they are in modern sport. Especially in Britain in the seventeenth and eighteenth centuries, a preference developed for bizarre competitions among small children, pregnant women, old men, and corpulent or disabled people, that is, people who lacked the right qualities for rapid and agile running.[7] In other European countries, foot races between prostitutes or between Jews represented a form of humiliation. This late-medieval tradition persisted in some places until the eighteenth century.[8] In Rome, Jews were chased along the Corso until 1668, when they were allowed to buy themselves out of the race by paying an annual sum of 300 écus.[9] The tenuous association between these races and genuine sporting competitions was underscored by the custom of forcing the runners to eat beforehand. The races were thus deliberately burlesque and ridiculous. Despite repeated prohibitions, the spectators pelted the runners with water, rotten fruit, stones, and other things. In Padua, prostitute races were still being held in 1668; in Breslau, such races were organized until at least 1686; and in Lucerne, they were held until the French Revolution.[10] Finally, there was a popular tradition of running races, and an instrumental use of long-distance runners for errands, which made active involvement of the elites – as sportsmen or runners – in these events in the public sphere problematic.

All of these aspects demonstrate that in the early modern period, races were viewed with ambivalence. At issue was not only appropriate behaviour and an individual's rank and reputation, but also the relationship between classes and estates. In the eighteenth century, the question of whether people should be instrumentalized in this way for service or pleasure was the subject of increasingly heated discussions. By the end of the eighteenth century, elite perceptions of running races in Great Britain and the Holy Roman Empire of the German Nation had apparently diverged to such an extent that Johann Wilhelm von Archenholz (1743–1812), who regularly reported from Great Britain to his contemporaries in Germany, described the following scene with astonishment:

Colonel Cosmo Gordon, of the well-known noble family, had the sans-culottic idea of exhibiting himself publicly as a runner. He had claimed

that in less than an hour he would run a distance of five English miles ...
on the Uxbridge Road, near London, and for that purpose had entered
a handsome bet in March, which had soon become known and had inspired many other bets, and drew a number of people on horseback and in
post-chaises to look at the leaps of the noble runner. He took only 56 minutes to complete the operation, and thus won the bet, the sum of which
was, however, given to an endowment for the widows and children of
soldiers who had fallen during the war, in order to mitigate the lowness
of the scene.[11]

Apparently, Archenholz did not find the colonel's behaviour proper. In
this, he was not alone: Heinrich von Watzdorf (1753–1826) was similarly
surprised by the fact that, during his journey to England in 1784, respected
adults of rank took part in cricket matches without embarrassment.[12]
This chapter takes this finding as a starting point for examining through
a comparative lens the social contexts and appraisals of running races in
the eighteenth-century Holy Roman Empire and in Great Britain. Was
Cosmo Gordon's behaviour "sansculottic" only in German eyes or was
it so from a British perspective as well? What connotations did the races
have in terms of social status and honour and with regard to ideas about
gender- and age-appropriate behaviour? And what exactly was problematic: the competition, the running, the fact that these races were held
in public, the betting, or the possible economic gain?

Running Races in the Holy Roman Empire of the Eighteenth Century

As in other countries on the European continent, there was a tradition
of foot races in the Holy Roman Empire long before the eighteenth century. From the fifteenth century on, running races for men and women
were regularly organized as a side attraction at shooting festivals, at
fairs, and at carnival time.[13] As the example of the Augsburg Shooting
Festivals of 1470 and 1509 shows, members of the aristocratic and civic
elites also participated in these races.[14] With the advent of standing ar-
mies, however, the importance of marksmen, and thus also of shooting
festivals as contexts for such races, declined; in the eighteenth century,
such festivals were held less regularly or not at all, and when they were
held, they were less splendid than before.[15] Yet in the same century,
we find more and more evidence of races either between women or
between girls,[16] who had already been competing at the shooting festivals, albeit far less frequently than men. At the "scarlet race" in Munich,
before the actual horse race, for which the prize was twelve lengths of

scarlet cloth, there were sack, satchel, and stilt races, and in addition, a race of "strong mayden[s]" with water buckets, although a poem written about the occasion in 1780 places the girls' race within the burlesque tradition of fun, while the horse race had the seriousness of a sporting competition.[17] In Hallein, unmarried young women ran in races to compete for unprocessed cloth,[18] and Krünitz's *Oekonomische Encyklopädie* from 1795 reports on an annual race between shepherdesses: "In Bretten, a town of the Electoral Palatinate, every year on St. Laurence day, a race of all the shepherd girls takes place in the most celebratory manner, attracting a great many people. The prize is mutton and certain articles of clothing, for which all the shepherdesses compete in light attire."[19] Even if there were practical reasons for wearing the light clothing, the erotic component of the shepherdesses' race could not be overlooked, and tellingly, here, it was the *unmarried* masters' daughters and sons (of the shepherds, who were once regarded as dishonourable) who competed – just like the unmarried young women in Hallein.[20] This is particularly interesting from a gender-historical perspective, as it demonstrates not only male voyeurism but also the active participation of women and girls in sporting events, which is often assumed to have first emerged around the turn of the last century. Still, this tradition has generally been ignored from a sports-historical perspective, because these races did not lead to rules or a differentiation of roles, to the founding of clubs or competitions beyond the regional level, or to the keeping of records, all of which are essential criteria in Allen Guttmann's now classic, though disputed, definition of modern sport, which views the various pre-modern sporting activities only as archaic forerunners.[21] These foot races, which were held in the context of fairs, also reveal why it was not socially desirable for a noble man like Archenholz to participate in such an event in the eighteenth century – it was not only because of the passionate, fast, and sweaty movement, which clearly violated early modern ideals, but also because of the rank and gender of the runners.

It was also because running of any kind – be it fast or for long distances – was the task and duty of servants. In the eighteenth century, runners were a highly specialized and comparatively well-paid group of servants.[22] Although the postal system was replacing these messengers as it expanded, the smaller German cities that were not located on the routes served by postal riders were dependent on running footmen until the nineteenth century.[23] Most of these messengers were in the service of the nobility and wealthy citizens as couriers or so-called forerunners, whose task it was to scout the route for a carriage ride, illuminate the street with torches at night, beat a path through the crowd in a city, and announce the guests' arrival at the destination.[24] Above all, these relatively expensive runners were status symbols for their masters, which is why they were dressed in particularly lavish clothing. This kind of forerunner was described in 1737 in Zedler's Lexicon as follows: "Runner, estafier, is a kind of steward on foot, who must run beside his master's chariot or horse with the same speed. To make them more suited to this purpose, they wear shoes without heels, light clothing made in a particular way, and bear a long stick in their hands. For running, they are trained from youth onwards through certain exercises in lead shoes, which are increased in weight from time to time, but not by cutting out the spleen, as was erroneously believed."[25] Gerhard Ulrich Anton Vieth describes the job profile of a runner in 1795: "From a trained runner, one expects that he should run as fast as a horse in a trot; and endure this for long periods."[26] Due to the conditioning, speed, and technique required, running evolved into a skilled occupation.[27] In Vienna, where there were a great many runners,[28] apprentices had to complete a journeyman's examination in running. A young man had to complete a "free-run" to Mariabrunn and back (about 18 kilometres) in an hour and twelve minutes in order to be recognized by the guild-like runners' association.[29] In the eighteenth century, the imperial city witnessed an annual competition between these runners, who represented the various noble houses they served. The president of the Viennese police, however, advised in 1795 that the races be abolished because of the danger they posed to the participants and the audience, and the "unpleasant mood which was noticed because of this"; in Krünitz's *Oekonomischer Encyklopädie* the following lines were printed in the same year: "[T]he bets between the masters, as well as between the runners themselves, with regard to the greater nimbleness and agility in running of one over another, must not go unpunished, because too much is inflicted upon one's nature, and it should not easily be allowed to a wealthy citizen to put horses and men in one class, and use them in order to present to the world in full sweat an insentient weakling."[30] Thus, the use of runners and the organizing of races between them by members of the aristocracy were increasingly criticized as "slavish" and "against human nature" in the late eighteenth century.

The Viennese police president and the author of the article "Läufer" in Krünitz's *Oekonomischer Encyklopädie* expressed not only moral concerns but also medical ones. Reading dietary tracts from the Holy Roman Empire of the eighteenth century, one gets the impression that running was a lethal activity.[31] In 1701, Engelbertus Andreas Otto warned of dehydration and the weakening of the body through running, which would lead not only to headaches but also to haemorrhage and pneumonia.[32] In 1738, Gottfried Samuel Bäumler assumed that running would heat and circulate the blood too much.[33] Overly vigorous movement was injurious to health, so according to Bäumler, one should exercise only to the point of blushing, not to sweating. Two editions of Johann Christian Reil's *Diätetischer Hausarzt*, published in 1787 and 1812, show that such ideas lasted until the early nineteenth century: "But both do harm, too much as well as too vigorous walking. Messengers and express men suffer rheumatic pains in their legs, stiff knees, and trembling feet from their occupation. Running, if it is continued too long, is harmful to anyone, especially to an unaccustomed person ... After a meal, it ruins the digestion, running in the wind can lead to a stitch in the side and pneumonia."[34] Friedrich Ludwig Jahn, known as Turnvater Jahn due to his role as the founder of gymnastics, had to appease his worried contemporaries in 1816: "In the beginning, one should only run with the wind, not against the wind,"[35] and one should do this "on cool, windless days." This explains why running – despite its military usefulness – did not play a central role in his patriotic exercises.[36]

Although the ideal of moderation had been handed down from antiquity, Greek and Roman physicians were not as critical of running as their colleagues in the eighteenth century.[37] One can only assume at this point that social concerns lurked behind the medical ones, because running messengers were regularly referred to as a group from whom one could decipher the negative effects of running. If the mere act of running was considered injurious to health, we can assume that foot races, which were not mentioned, would certainly have been as well.

These contexts illustrate why running was much more difficult to establish in the Holy Roman Empire than other sports. Although it was a part of the "Dessauer Pentathlon" and was one of the physical exercises of the philanthropic schools founded in Dessau and Schnepfenthal,[38] the texts of enlightened school reformers clearly show that there was greater resistance to running than to other disciplines. Contemporaries argued that running was indecorous for adolescents and adult men, as well as dangerous, for it could cause tuberculosis.[39] Of course, departing from traditional customs was a common strategy among Enlightenment authors seeking to legitimize themselves as reformers and does not, in itself, allow us to draw any conclusions about actual practice; even so, it is striking that the arguments against running were more numerous and elaborate.[40] GutsMuths recommended to educators: "he [the teacher] compels nothing, he does not stimulate with anything, he instead holds back";[41] but regardless, he diligently recorded his pupils' best performances, presented them to the public with pride, and organized annual athletic competitions between 1776 and 1799 for the birthday of Princess Louise von Brandenburg-Schwedt, including running races for men and for women.[42] Thus, the philanthropists contributed to the spread of the races, to a certain extent even beyond their schools, as male and female youths from the surrounding areas took part in the Dessau Pentathlon. Nevertheless, one certainly could not speak in the Holy Roman Empire of a "rage for pedestrian exercises," as a British writer recorded in England.[43] Although it is necessary to take into account the different research possibilities for eighteenth-century British and German newspapers, it hardly seems coincidental that the 1748 entry under "Wett-Rennen [running races]" in Zedler's Lexicon includes races between both horses and humans in its definition but only provides contemporary examples of horseracing.[44] Vieth's statement of 1795 makes it entirely clear how long the Aristotelian ideal of restrained mobility persisted: "For us, boyhood is the only short period during which men practise in running; our young men already walk with a slow gait, and a man could not dare to use his legs to run without looking ridiculous."[45]

Foot Races in Eighteenth-Century Great Britain

The initial situation in Great Britain was similar to that of the Holy Roman Empire: here too, foot races were held long before the eighteenth century, in the context of folk festivals. Running races were also part of the Cotswold Olympic Games, rural games that were held in Gloucestershire between 1612 and 1852, with an interruption at the time of the Civil War and the establishment of the Commonwealth.[46] In 1779, however, Samuel Rudder reported in his *New History of Gloucestershire*: "[W]e hear but little on the Coteswolds [*sic*] of his worthy friend Mr. Dover, since whose time the diversions have also much declined, for want of so good a patron."[47]

In Great Britain, women and girls often ran in races too. According to Peter Radford, in the eighteenth century, women and girls – who ran in "smock races," named after the item of clothing they could win – were even more likely to compete with one another than boys and men were. "In an analysis of 50 such events, less than one-third had running events for men or boys, but nearly 80 per cent had running events for women or girls. Viewed as a folk-event, running races seem, therefore, to have been largely a woman's affair."[48] The German examples were thus in no way unique. One custom that was particular to Britain was the holding of races at weddings in the north of England,[49] as described, for example, in the *English Chronicle* in 1790: "The wedding was attended with the usual divertissments, a horse and a foot race, a bull baiting, wrestling &c. ... The whole concluded with dancing."[50] Additionally, in England, people raced to win not just aprons but also hats, fabric, legs of mutton, tea, or money. The light clothing worn by the female runners was sometimes criticized. Still, the vast majority of participants were women from the locality, and they were not members of marginal groups, whose participation in such races would have been a form of degradation. British newspapers did not usually report on these events, which were held as part of annual fairs and church festivals.[51] Perhaps this limited publicity was intended to preserve the honour of the girls and women.[52] But it is also an indication that gender-specific distinctions were made between those who were considered important enough to be reported on in a newspaper and those who were not.

By contrast, daily newspapers reported on foot races held in the context of other sporting events, such as cricket matches or horse races; they described commercial races that were increasingly organized by innkeepers in urban areas and races between two or three named persons.[53] The announcements in newspapers were intended to attract spectators; they also allowed interested individuals to place bets in advance, whether they attended or not. For the same reason, the races' results were reported afterwards. These short reports provided information on who won and, with increasing frequency, on what the distance was to the next-placed runner (which may have been of interest for subsequent bets). As we can see by comparing three samples from the Burney Collection from 1700–20, 1740–60, and 1780–90 as well as the Eighteenth Century Journals database,[54] the number of journalistic reports increased, as did their scope; and at least in the samples, they exclusively pertained to men.[55]

In a rare case that does not come from within the sample, there is a report of a race between two women in 1725. The sensationalism and erotic appeal is evident: "Vast numbers of the lower class of Gentry attended on that Occasion, expecting that they would have run in puris naturalibus; but that was over-ruled, and they were clad in white Waistcoats and Drawers, but without Shoes or Stockings."[56] A race of this kind, in which the participants wore only their underwear, certainly showed more of the female body than men typically saw on the street; nevertheless, one cannot assume that the race participants were all women of easy virtue. In this vein, French traveller Abbé Le Blanc reported on the participants in a competition of this kind in the middle of the eighteenth century: "They are commonly strong robust country girls, who run with surprising swiftness."[57] Since the women were also weighed – as were the jockeys – and differences in stature were counteracted by weights, the focus was apparently not just on erotic but also on sporting aspects.[58]

Clothing was at times an issue for male runners too, because occasionally, race participants had eschewed all clothing for reasons of aerodynamics and ease. This was noted with shock, and led to brief arrests, and to the introduction of explicit rules: "that the Ladies may not be put out of Countenance they are to run decently Dress'd."[59] This did not, however, result in the decline of such races, nor did it detract from their reputation.[60]

On the contrary, the spectrum of social origins among the participants broadened during the eighteenth century, laying the basis for different developments in Great Britain and in the Holy Roman Empire: whereas in the first sample, the active participants in the British contests were all running footmen, by the middle of the century, the name of the master had been replaced by a surname or a surname followed by the geographical origin; this means that the race participants were probably no longer running footmen.[61] The newspapers now listed nicknames that suggested a certain degree of fame, such as Joseph Brown "commonly called the rabbit lad"[62] or "the flying weaver,"[63] or they included characterizations implying comparisons beyond the regional level, such as: "They are said to be the two best runners in England."[64]

When eighteenth-century newspaper reports did provide information on participants' occupations (which was increasingly the case), they listed jobs including – beside running footmen – tanners, farm workers, grooms, coachmen, tailors, hairdressers, platers, frame-work-knitters and weavers, gamekeepers, calico printers, and shoemakers.[65] Thus, the runners still primarily came from the lower classes, but the races had lost their social sting, because they were no longer exclusively organized by masters among their servants. The advertising of prize money and opening of the races to all interested competitors[66] meant that the races primarily attracted those who were looking for economic gain; yet the compulsory aspect, and the servants' dependence on their masters' benevolence, had not disappeared. In 1675, this was still evident in the fact that footmen were registered for races by their masters.[67] In 1721, the Welsh Ambassador at Belsize even organized a race exclusively for running footmen. By the end of the seventeenth century, we find the first runners who were independently able to make their own bets and make money on their own behalf, even though most of them were still running on behalf of their masters. "Professional runners" who could make a living by participating in races only appeared in the course of the eighteenth century. Because of this development it was no longer objectionable to put man and beast on an equal footing, as was criticized in the German sources, and to organize contests between people in the context of horseraces and even on horseracing courses, thereby securing an even greater audience.[68]

As early as the seventeenth century, Samuel Pepys was noting down the names of individual aristocratic runners in his diaries.[69] The full names of aristocratic competitors appeared in the daily press only at the end of the eighteenth century. Before that time, reports about aristocratic races were anonymized,[70] an indication that even in Great Britain, foot races were compatible with aristocratic values only to a limited extent. By contrast, in 1789 the *English Chronicle or Universal Evening Post* named and reported on the participants in a race in Kensington Gardens between Lord Paget[71] and the barrister Mr Humphreys for a 20-guinea stake.[72] The sum was comparatively small – although it was still twice as much as the maximum 10-pound stake allowed by the Statute of Anne, which, apparently, nobody observed[73] – and it was probably this feature that should set it apart from other contests.[74] A year later, in 1790, Lord Paget, Lord Barrymore,[75] and two other runners were apparently less concerned, and raced one another for 100 guineas.[76] Barrymore had a dubious reputation as an enthusiastic gambler and bon vivant. It was he, among others, who opened up running as a sport for the British elite, whose members were being named more regularly as active participants in athletics. In this respect, the aforementioned Cosmo Gordon belonged to a small but expanding group of upper-class men at the end of the eighteenth century who wanted not only to bet on races but also to run in them. Still, such participation could not at all be taken for granted at the beginning of the nineteenth century, a fact that is underscored by the British sports historian Joseph Strutt in 1801. Strutt took a positive view of running, yet he drew a distinction between hunting, hawking, and horse racing, which he described as "rural exercises practised by persons of rank," and running, which he categorized as "rural exercises generally practised." He commented: "In the present day foot-races are not much encouraged by persons of fortune, and seldom happen but for the purpose of betting, and the racers are generally paid for their performance ... Two centuries back running was thought to be an exercise by no means derogatory to the rank of nobility."[77]

The sports historiographical literature has repeatedly referred to the importance of betting, and hence of bourgeois and aristocratic sponsors, for the development of sport in England in the seventeenth and eighteenth centuries. Betting made it possible to offer prize money; it also led to the establishment of rules.[78] The bizarre races mentioned earlier in this chapter sought to attract the largest possible crowds by varying the challenge.[79] The size of the bets heightened the tension regarding the race's outcome, because now the spectators too had something to lose. But this alone cannot explain why members of the British bourgeoisie and aristocracy increasingly took part in races themselves – after all, people in Vienna also bet on the outcome of the races between running footmen. A re-valuation was only possible when races were opened to other occupational groups and thus lost their character as a form of pleasure staged by masters, who instrumentalized their running footmen for the purpose. For instance, Captain Allardyce Barclay, a wealthy landowner and one of the most famous British long-distance runners at the beginning of the nineteenth century, was certainly not dependent on the proceeds from his bets; he is thus a perfect example of the opening of the sport to all social classes.[80]

When they began to assess running in more positive terms in their medical tracts, British physicians were merely catching up with their contemporaries in the press. Like their German colleagues, British physicians favoured moderate forms of movement and were initially cautious about recommending overexertion in any form.[81] But in the last quarter of the eighteenth century, increasing experience with running races was reflected in more positive health assessments: in the press, emphasis was placed on the ease with which victors passed the finish line. Physicians adopted this new view: while William Buchan argued both for and against racing in the same text,[82] Sir John Sinclair wrote at the beginning of the nineteenth century: "On the whole, in regard to quantity, I am much inclined to think, that excess of exercise is not so dangerous, as some physicians are apt to imagine."[83]

Conclusion

Comparing the development of foot races, we can see that their spread and evaluation took different courses in the Holy Roman Empire of the German Nation and Great Britain. In both countries, foot races started out as popular contests of running servants and the lower classes; then in Great Britain, opening the competitions to other occupational groups and subsequently to different social classes removed the social sting – no longer was running a degrading entertainment for the pleasure of the rich and noble. This in turn influenced nineteenth-century developments as well as medical views on the topic.

On the continent, the occupation of the forerunner was abolished in France after the French Revolution as a consequence of Enlightenment criticism of running footmen.[84] In Vienna, however, this fashion persisted until the mid-nineteenth century; in 1822, the so-called *Lauferfest* (runners' festival) was moved to the Prater, which increased its popularity even more.[85] Criticism grew yet again in the period preceding the March 1848 revolution. In *Neuen komischen Briefen des Hans Jörgels von Gumpoldskirchen* in 1840, the author writes in a satirical manner, but still with serious criticism: "I think of the horseracing and the foot races in the Prater as nothing but torture for horse and man. Even though the runners are only from the *ordinary* class of people and the horses are all *noble*, it cannot be that man and horse are ranked equally." [86] After the 1848 revolution, the servants' foot race – which had been held the previous year and was still regarded as medically harmful[87] – and indeed the profession of the forerunner itself, seemed an overly dangerous and provocative marker of aristocratic rule. Consequently, the former runners, if they were not dismissed, were reassigned to work as valets or stable boys.[88] Runners, who found themselves unemployed again after being replaced by the postal service, began looking for new opportunities to earn their livelihood as independent *artistic runners* by exhibiting their skills at fairs. This fashion began in the 1820s and reached its peak between 1840 and 1850. This development apparently occurred independently of similar processes in Great Britain, for in 1827, one could read in Krünitz's *Encyklopädie* under the entry "Schnellläufer" (speed runners): "Recently, high-speed running has also been practised as an art, and such artists who can move their legs quickly enough, so that they can pass a good German mile and more in 45 minutes, travel all over Europe to show their art, and thus earn a living. Until now, it is the Germans and the French who practise this art."[89] Since the audience was still familiar with forerunners and running messengers,[90] these performances had to be made more spectacular in order to arouse the interest of spectators. Thus, the participants not only ran very quickly but also – as in Great Britain – backwards, in chains, in harnesses, on stilts, and in waltz step.[91] Once again, running appeared in the context of markets and fairs as a form of entertainment for the lower classes and was thus not socially desirable; this was all the more true as fun races continued to be organized at folk festivals.[92]

This tradition, along with a commercialization of the races, existed in equal measure in Great Britain. But in the same period, unlike in the Holy Roman Empire, modern athletics developed within British public schools and colleges. This transition from commercial pedestrianism to track and field was by no means smooth. According to Dennis Brailsford, the upper classes first withdrew from the sport, which was especially susceptible to manipulation, before modern athletics emerged in the second half of the nineteenth century and established an amateur ethos in opposition to professional running.[93] After the 1840s, elite schools and colleges in Great Britain began to compete with one another, and the first athletics clubs emerged in the middle of the century. Amateur clauses, of the kind formulated by the London Athletics Club in 1866, prohibited the admission and participation of professional athletes in competitions. These clauses were directed against the aforementioned artistic and speed runners, or generally against athletes who relied on prize money.[94] The social upgrading of foot races, accompanied by a simultaneous erection of barriers to the lower classes, led to the establishment of the first athletics clubs in Germany. These clubs, such as the Hamburg Sport Club in Bahrenfeld near Altona, adopted English practices. In the magazine *Daheim* in 1882, the races it held were described in clear opposition to the commercial practices of professional runners: "As far as we know, there is currently only one club in the German Reich that is concerned with athletic sports, the *Hamburger Sportklub*, and this has only existed for about two years, after a certain distrust of all such endeavours had at first confronted it with strong opposition ... Fifty-four gentlemen now devote themselves to athleticism ... excluding all professional sportsmen, completely abstaining from the awarding of monetary prizes in their races ... and granting the victors only honorary gifts as a souvenir and a reminder of the happy hours they have spent in their circle of like-minded comrades."[95]

In contrast to what one might first presume, running was thus an untypical case in the development of sports, both in Great Britain and on the continent. Because there were no material prerequisites, running was not a suitable way to express status and hence did not attract elites to the same extent as hunting or horseback riding. At the same time, at least on the continent, running still carried the stigma of service owing to its (partly) instrumental character, which – like foot races as part of folk festivals – had a lasting negative effect and delayed its spread. In this aspect it was comparable to rowing, which was originally also practised for pragmatic reasons of transport and not for sporting ones. Thus, for example, *jeu de paume*, the predecessor of modern tennis, had spread across Europe since the late Middle Ages and was being played enthusiastically by nobles and burghers, but also by craftsmen and students, men and women,[96] whereas running did not begin to bloom until the eighteenth century, when most other sports were stagnating.[97] In Britain, the opening of races to all professional groups removed the discipline's social sting, and moreover, the closure of the sport to the lower classes as a result of the rules regarding amateurism led to the lasting growth of athletics among the elites. This fiction of disinterested sporting competition free from social tensions cleared a pathway for people to experience the fascination of sport without moral condemnation.

Translated by Roisin Cronin

NOTES

1 Aristotle, *The Nicomachean Ethics*, trans. H. Rackham, Loeb Classical Library (Cambridge, MA: Harvard University Press, 1975), 225 (IV iii 34; 1125a 13–15), quoted after Dilwyn Knox, "On Immobility," in *Begetting Images: Studies in the Art and Science of Symbol Production*, ed. Mary B. Campbell and Mark Rollins (New York: Peter Lang, 1989), 71–87, here 73.
2 Ibid., 72f., 79.
3 Kirsten O. Frieling, "Haltung bewahren: Der Körper im Spiegel frühneuzeitlicher Schriften über Umgangsformen," in *Bewegtes Leben. Körpertechniken in der Frühen Neuzeit*, ed. Rebekka von Mallinckrodt, exhibition catalog Herzog August Library Wolfenbüttel (Wiesbaden: Harrassowitz, 2008), 39–59, 260–9.
4 *Allgemeine Theaterzeitung*, Vienna 1842, n.p., quoted after Stephan Oettermann, *Läufer und Vorläufer. Zu einer Kulturgeschichte des Laufsports* (Frankfurt am Main: Syndikat, 1984), 101.
5 Maria Kloeren, *Sport und Rekord. Kultursoziologische Untersuchungen zum England des 16. bis 18. Jahrhunderts*, Reprint PhD 1935 (Münster: Lit, 1985), 238, 253f.
6 See Roger Chartier, "Sports, or The Controlled Decontrolling of Emotions," in *On the Edge of the Cliff: History, Language, and Practices*, ed. Roger Chartier (Baltimore: Johns Hopkins University Press, 1997), 132–43, here 139. Chartier for the most part describes Norbert Elias's and Eric Dunning's positions.
7 Earl R. Anderson, "Footnotes More Pedestrian than Sublime: A Historical Background for the Foot-Races in *Evelina* and *Humphrey Clinker*," *Eighteenth Century Studies* 14, no. 1 (1980): 56–68, here 56, 58, 66f.; Allen Guttmann, *Sports: The First Five Millennia* (Amherst: University of Massachusetts Press, 2004), 72; Guttmann, *Women's Sports: A History* (New York: Columbia University Press, 1991), 73; Oettermann, *Läufer und Vorläufer*, 119; and Kloeren, *Sport und Rekord*, 240, 250–2, 261.
8 Ilaria Taddei, "Les rituels de dérision entre les villes toscanes (XIIIe-XIVe siècles)," in *La dérision au Moyen Âge. De la pratique sociale au rituel politique*, ed. Élisabeth Crouzet-Pavan and Jacques Verger (Paris: Presses de l'Université Paris-Sorbonne, 2007), 175–89; Andrea Sommerlechner,

"Die ludi agonis et testatie – Das Fest der Kommune Rom im Mittelalter," in *Römische Historische Mitteilungen*, ed. Richard Bösel and Otto Kresten (Vienna: Verlag der Österreichischen Akademie der Wissenschaften, 1999), 339–70; Deanna Shemek, *Ladies Errant: Wayward Women and Social Order in Early Modern Italy* (Durham: Duke University Press, 1998), 17–44.

9   This and the following Martine Boiteux, "Les Juifs dans le Carnaval de la Rome moderne, XVe–XVIIIe Siècles," *Mélanges de l'Ecole française de Rome. Moyen-Age, Temps modernes* 88, 2 (1976): 745–87, here 748, 751, 753, 756.

10   Richard C. Trexler, "Correre la terra: Collective Insults in the Late Middle Ages," *Mélanges de l'Ecole française de Rome. Moyen-Age, Temps modernes* 96, 2 (1984): 845–902, here 886; [Daniel Gomolky], *Des kurtzgefaßten Innbegriffs Der vornehmsten Merckwürdigkeiten Von der Kayser und Königl. Stadt Breßlau in Schlesien Dritter Theil/ Worinnen von einigen Solennitäten/ Ceremonien/ Gebräuchen und Gewohnheiten der Stadt Breßlau gehandelt wird. Durch einen Liebhaber Breßlauischer und Schlesischer Geschichten, Nebst beygefügten Kupffern* (Breslau: Hilsen, 1733), 183f.

11   Johann Wilhelm von Archenholz, *Annalen der Brittischen Geschichte des Jahres 1793. Als eine Fortsetzung des Werks England und Italien*, vol. 11 (Hamburg: Cotta, 1795), 368f. This probably refers to a walking competition that expressly prohibited running, as the best English runners in the late eighteenth and early nineteenth centuries ran the same route in half the time. See *Pedestrianism; or an Account of the Performances of celebrated Pedestrians during the last and present century; with a full narrative of Captain Barclay's public and private matches; and an Essay on Training*. By the author of the History of Aberdeeen [Walter Thom] (Aberdeen: D. Chalmers & co., 1813), 45, 72–4, 96f., 99.

12   Paul Langford, *Englishness Identified: Manners and Character 1650–1850* (Oxford: Oxford University Press, 2000), 45; Heinrich Maximilian Friedrich von Watzdorf, *Briefe zur Charakteristik von England gehörig: geschrieben auf e. Reise im Jahre 1784* (Leipzig: Verlag der Dykischen Buchhandlung, 1786), 205f.: "As often as I saw it, I always found various men among the players who appeared to be quite close to fifty years of age; I heard they were married, had grown-up children, and enjoyed great respect. Here, then, is a striking difference between our customs and those of this country. Think of any man of our acquaintance who is of this age, and I would wager he would consider it quite against the character of a respectable man, especially one who holds a public office – a title, to run after a ball in his waistcoat before the eyes of several hundred spectators – this is only for school boys! – it is probable that the people here are no less respectable than us, and yet they do so. It is a national pastime!"

13   Guttmann, *Sports*, 60f.; Guttmann, *Women's Sports*, 62–5; Oettermann, *Läufer und Vorläufer*, 123.

14 "Chronik des Hector Mülich 1348–1487," in *Die Chroniken der deutschen Städte vom 14. bis 16. Jahrhundert*, here vol. 22, Augsburg vol. 3, published by the Historical Commission at the Royal Academy of Sciences (Leipzig: Hirzel, 1892), 1–274, here 233; "Die Chronik von Clemens Sender von der ältesten Zeit der Stadt bis zum Jahre 1536," in *Die Chroniken der deutschen Städte vom 14. bis 16. Jahrhundert*, here vol. 23, Augsburg vol. 4, published by the Historical Commission at the Royal Academy of Sciences (Leipzig: Hirzel, 1894), 1–404, here 124, 126 and ibid, footnote 1.

15 Klaus Zieschang, *Vom Schützenfest zum Turnfest. Die Entstehung des Deutschen Turnfestes unter besonderer Berücksichtigung der Einflüsse von F.L. Jahn* (PhD diss., Julius Maximilian University of Würzburg, 1973), 88–94.

16 See, for example, Guillaume Depping, *Die Körperkraft und Geschicklichkeit des Menschen. Historische Darstellung der Leibesübungen bei den alten und neueren Völkern*, trans. Robert Springer, 2nd ed. (Minden: Bruns, 1881), 137: "In some parts of Germany races are also held between the women. One of the best known races takes place at the St. Bartholomew Day at Markt-Gröningen in the Kingdom of Württemberg." Oettermann, *Läufer und Vorläufer*, 127: "Das jährliche Belzlaufen dreier alter Weiber im Gostenhof zu Nürnberg," engraving from the eighteenth century.

17 *Das uralte Pferd- oder Scharlachrennen, von einem löblichen Magistrat der churft. Haupt- und Residenzstadt München gegeben zur Zeit der Jakobimesse.* 1 August 1780, n.p. here [2f.].

18 Joseph Kyselak, *Skizzen einer Fußreise durch Oesterreich, Steiermark, Kärnthen, Salzburg, Berchtesgaden, Tirol und Baiern nach Wien [...] unternommen im Jahr 1825*, vol. 1 (Vienna: Pichler, 1829), 145f.

19 Johann Georg Krünitz, *Oekonomische Encyklopädie, oder allgemeines System der Staats- Stadt- Haus- u. Landwirthschaft, in alphabetischer Ordnung*, 242 vols. (Berlin: Pauli, 1773–1858), here vol. 66 (1795), art. "Laufen," 69f.

20 Siegmund Friedrich Gehres, *Bretten's Kleine Chronik welche zugleich umständliche Nachrichten von Melanchton und seiner Familie enthält. Ein Beitrag zur Kunde teutscher Städte und Sitten als Seitenstük zu Pforzheim's kleiner Chronik* (Eßlingen: Lochner, 1805), 33.

21 Allen Guttmann, *From Ritual to Record: The Nature of Modern Sports* (original ed. 1978; New York: Columbia University Press, 2004). The modernization thesis is upheld by Guttmann to the present day: Guttmann, *Sports: The First Five Millennia*, 68–76; Guttmann, "Afterword. From Ritual to Record: A Retrospective Critique," in Guttmann, *From Ritual to Record*, 163–74.

22 Halgard Kuhn has reconstructed the biographies of two runners, who were working at the court of the Electorate of Trier between 1755 and 1812, from the records of the deceased Hans Wolfgang Kuhn. Runners belonged to the category of so-called liveried court servants, who constituted a

social group of their own. In the hierarchy, runners were behind personal lackeys and haiduks, but their wages were considerably higher: Halgard Kuhn, "Die Läufer Bartholomäus und Valentin Treine am Kurtrierischen Hof zur Regierungszeit der Kurfürsten-Erzbischöfe Johann Philipp von Walderdorf und Clemens Wenzeslaus von Sachsen," *Jahrbuch für westdeutsche Landesgeschichte* 23 (1997): 403–47, here 411, 413. Barbara Purrucker also reports that the two runners in the employ of the Princely Bishop of Hildesheim received twice the lackeys' wages in 1763: Purrucker, "Läufer – eine Dienersparte im 18. Jahrhundert," *Waffen- und Kostümkunde* 1 (1999): 1–28, here 14.

23 Wolfgang Behringer, *Im Zeichen des Merkur. Reichspost und Kommunikationsrevolution in der Frühen Neuzeit* (Göttingen: Vandenhoeck & Ruprecht, 2003); Oettermann, *Läufer und Vorläufer*, 17, 22, 24.

24 Ibid., 31, 35; Purrucker, "Läufer," 1.

25 Johann Heinrich Zedler, *Grosses vollständiges Universallexicon Aller Wissenschafften und Künste*, 64 vols. and 4 supplementary vols. (Halle & Leipzig: Zedler, 1731–54), here vol. 16 (1737), art. "Läuffer," col. 208. See also Krünitz, *Oekonomische Encyklopädie*, vol. 66 (1795), art. "Läufer," 80–93, here 80: "The runners, trained runners, artistic runners, runners by trade, are specially dressed servants who run before the carriage or horse of their master."

26 Gerhard Ulrich Anton Vieth, *Versuch einer Encyklopädie der Leibesübungen*, 3 vols. (Berlin: Hartmann, 1794–1818), here vol. 2 (1795), 193f. See also ibid., 194: "In general, great endurance with moderate speed is more to be esteemed than great speed without endurance ... There are runners who make it incredibly far with regard to both aspects, running 15, even 20 miles in a day, and from early in the morning to the late evening they run almost without interruption."

27 Oettermann, *Läufer und Vorläufer*, 36; Purrucker, "Läufer," 3.

28 See, for example, Johann Pezzl, *Skizze von Wien. Ein Kultur- und Sittenbild aus der josefinischen Zeit*, ed. Gustav Gugitz and Anton Schlossar (Graz: Leykam, 1923), 203: "Runners are plentiful. They are mainly used to deliver letters and news in the city and run with a torch in front of the carriage at night."

29 This and the following: Oettermann, *Läufer und Vorläufer*, 51; "Zur Geschichte der Wiener Laufer," *Wiener Neujahrs-Almanach* 4 (1898): 163–73, here 165 (quotation), 167.

30 This and the following: Krünitz, *Oekonomische Encyklopädie*, art. "Läufer," 87f.

31 For more information on this subject, see Rebekka von Mallinckrodt, "Beschleunigung in der Sattelzeit? – Sportliche, medizinische und soziale Perspektiven auf den Wettlauf um 1800," in *Frühe Neue Zeiten. Zeitwissen*

zwischen Reformation und Revolution, ed. Achim Landwehr (Bielefeld: Transcript, 2012), 83–104.

32 Friedrich Hoffmann / Engelbertus Andreas Otto, *De motu optima corporis medicina* (PhD Diss, med. University of Halle, 1701), 21f., § XXX.

33 This and the following: Gottfried Samuel Bäumler, *Präservirender Artzt, oder Gründliche Anweisung wie sich der Mensch/ mit Verleihung Göttlicher Gnade / durch eine ordentliche Diät / bey guter Gesundheit erhalten / und folglich zu einem hohen und geruhigen Alter gelangen könne* (Straßburg: Dulßecker, 1738), 449f., 451, 456.

34 Johann Christian Reil, *Diaetetischer Hausarzt für meine Landsleute*, 2 vols. (Aurich: Borgeest, 1785–1787), here vol. 2, 252. See also Reil, *Diätetischer Hausarzt, oder höchst wichtige Anleitung zu einer naturgemäßen Gesundheitspflege*, 2nd ed. (Vienna: Doll, 1812), 190 with identical formulations, only with altered orthography.

35 This and the following: Friedrich Ludwig Jahn and Ernst Eiselen, *Die Deutsche Turnkunst zur Einrichtung der Turnplätze* (Berlin: self-published, 1816), 7 and 9.

36 For the relation of sports to patriotism, see Kittler in this volume.

37 See examples of positive evaluations of running in the ancient world in Krünitz, *Oekonomische Encyklopädie*, art. "Laufen," 54f.

38 Johann Christoph Friedrich GutsMuths, *Gymnastik für die Jugend. Enthaltend eine praktische Anweisung zu Leibesübungen. Ein Beytrag zur nöthigsten Verbesserung der körperlichen Erziehung von GutsMuths, Erzieher zu Schnepfenthal* (Schnepfenthal: Verlag der Buchhandlung der Erziehungsanstalt, 1793), 252–64.

39 GutsMuths, *Gymnastik für die Jugend*, 252f.: "It is very striking that we seemingly do all we can to make our youths unlearn how to run. The first physical treatment appears to seek to destroy this skill entirely: later, the boy is often not even allowed to indicate that he would like to run: we forbid him to do so as it is a bad habit, and when he is more adult, a fine tone gets entirely in the way and prevents him from getting through. Medical prejudices and our own comfort add to this, and never let us acquire a skill that is so necessary and harmless to everyone. – We may get tuberculosis from running, but it is hardly ever the running that is to blame, but only ourselves if we must run without ever practising." See also ibid., 261. He recommends, however, only running on cool days in autumn and winter.

40 For this reason, Friedrich Ludwig Jahn still had to explain in 1816 that "running ... done with caution, was a very curative exercise especially for chest and lung": Jahn and Eiselen, *Die Deutsche Turnkunst*, 7.

41 This and the following: GutsMuths, *Gymnastik für die Jugend*, 260.

42 This and the following: Wolfgang Behringer, *Kulturgeschichte des Sports* (München: Beck, 2012), 250; Peter F. Radford, "The Olympic Games in the

Long Eighteenth Century," *Journal for Eighteenth Century Studies* 35, no. 2 (2012): 161–84, here 176.

43 *The Craftsman; or Say's Weekly Journal*, 19 July 1788, quoted after Peter F. Radford, "Escaping the Philippedes Connection: Death, Injury and Illness in 18th Century Sport in Britain," in *Sport et santé dans l'histoire*, ed. Thierry Terret (Sankt Augustin: Academia, 1999), 87–100, here 90.

44 Zedler, *Grosses vollständiges Universallexicon*, vol. 55 (1748), art. "Wett-Rennen," col. 1085–98.

45 Vieth, *Versuch einer Encyklopädie*, vol. 2, 191f.

46 Behringer, *Kulturgeschichte des Sports*, 248.

47 Samuel Rudder, *A new history of Gloucestershire* (Cirencester: Samuel Rudder, 1779), 25.

48 Peter Radford, "Women's Foot Races in the 18th and 19th Centuries. A Popular and Widespread Practice," *Canadian Journal of History of Sport* 25, no. 1 (1994): 50–61, here 56.

49 Joseph Strutt, *The Sports and Pastimes of the People of England* (1801), a new edition, much enlarged and corrected by J. Charles Cox (London: Methuen & co., [1903]), 67.

50 *English Chronicle or Universal Evening Post* (London), 28 August 1790–31 August 1790. See also *Felix Farley's Bristol Journal* (Bristol), 17 January 1789.

51 In the Burney Collection, there are only two hits for the search term "smock race" from 1745 and 1768. The Burney Collection contains digitized English newspapers and pamphlets (a total of 1,270 titles) from the seventeenth and eighteenth centuries from the collection of the clergyman Charles Burney (1757–1817), http://www.bl.uk/reshelp/findhelprestype/news/newspdigproj/burney/index.html.

52 Radford, "Women's Foot Races," 52.

53 Dennis Brailsford, *A Taste for Diversions: Sport in Georgian England* (Cambridge: Lutterworth Press, 1999), 29; Dennis Brailsford, *British Sport: A Social History* (Cambridge: Lutterworth Press, 1992), 68; David Day, "An 'Art and a Science': Eighteenth-Century Sports Training," in *Sports and Physical Exercise in Early Modern Culture: New Perspectives on the History of Sports and Motion*, ed. Rebekka von Mallinckrodt and Angela Schattner (London: Routledge, 2016), 125–44, here 125; Radford, "Women's Foot Races," 50f., 53. See also Kloeren, *Sport und Rekord*, 263.

54 On the Burney Collection, see n51. The Eighteenth Century Journals database contains more than 150 popular journals of the eighteenth century, published in the UK, in the full text. I was able to access ECJ I and II (http://www.18thcjournals.amdigital.co.uk).

55 See, for example, *Flying Post or The Post Master* (London), 14 December 1700–17 December 1700: "This Day [7 December] a Foot-Race was run at Leith for 30 Guinea's, by three Foot-men, belonging to the Earl of Mar and

London and the Lord Rae." *Weekly Journal or Saturday's Post* (London), 18 April 1719: "Last Friday 7 Night the Foot Race spoken of in our last, was Ran at New Market, between Mawbone, the Duke of Wharton's Running Footman, and Groves, the Lord Castelmaine's and the former was head above two miles." *Weekly Journal or Saturday's Post* (London), 26 December 1719: "The same Day [Monday] it was expected that two Running Foot-men, one as 'tis said, belonging to the Duke of Chandois, the other to the Earl of Essex, would have set for a Foot Race." *Applebee's Original Weekly Journal* (London), 24 September 1720: "On Monday last the famous Foot-Race between the Duke of Wharton's Running Footman, named Groves, and another of Mr. Diston's, named Phillips, was run at Woodstock in Oxfordshire."

56 *The Weekly Journal or Saturday's Post*, 23 October 1725; quoted after Kloeren, *Sport und Rekord*, 265.

57 Jean Bernard Le Blanc, *Letters on the English and French Nations*, translated from the French, 2 vols. (Dublin: Richard James, 1747), 2:76; quoted after Kloeren, *Sport und Rekord*, 264. Le Blanc stayed in England in 1737–47.

58 Kloeren, *Sport und Rekord*, 264.

59 *Read's Journal*, 9 September 1721, quoted after Kloeren, *Sport und Rekord*, 258. See also ibid., 239.

60 Brailsford, *A Taste for Diversions*, 66f.

61 *Whitehall Evening Post or London Intelligencer* (London), 21 October 1749–24 October 1749: "Yesterday in the Afternoon the Foot-Race in the Artillery Ground for 50 Guineas aside, between James Marsden a Derbyshire man, and Stephen Morris, of London was run." *Read's Weekly Journal Or British Gazetteer* (London), 13 October 1753: "Monday, the foot race in the artillery ground for 20l. between a Taner of the borough and one Fitch, a Worcestershire man, was run one heat four miles." In some cases, aristocratic patrons are named, but this seems to have been the exception – probably because running, unlike other, more costly sports, did not require any great outlay of money or complex equipment. *London Evening Post* (London), 30 August 1750–1 September 1750: "Foot Race. On Monday next, the 3d Instant, Jacob Millner, the Staffordshire young man, who beat Stell, the Mile Match, runs against Joseph Brown, a young man, who is back'ed by the Gentlemen of Kent and Sussex, for one hundred guineas a side."

62 *Whitehall Evening Post or London Intelligencer* (London), 12 June 1755–14 June 1755.

63 *General Evening Post* (London), 15 October 1789–17 October 1789. See also "the Uxbridge Boy" (*Lloyd's Evening Post and British Chronicle* (London), 5 September 1757–7 September 1757); "the noted Hitton" (*Public Advertiser* (London), 4 July 1783).

64 *World and Fashionable Advertiser* (London), 8 October 1787. See also "Smith is supposed to be one of the swiftest runners in the kingdom of his age, which is forty-two." *Morning Post and Daily Advertiser* (London), 27 July 1786.

65 *Read's Weekly Journal Or British Gazetteer* (London), 13 October 1753; *Whitehall Evening Post (1770)* (London), 30 August 1785–1 September 1785; ibid., 1 September 1785–3 September 1785; ibid., 2 May 1786–4 May 1786; *Morning Herald* (London), 25 May 1786; *Public Advertiser* (London), 10 April 1789; *Argus* (London), 11 March 1790; *English Chronicle or Universal Evening Post* (London), 14 September 1790–16 September 1790; *London Chronicle* (London), 28 June 1787–30 June 1787; ibid., 30 October 1787–1 November 1787; *General Evening Post* (London), 15 October 1789–17 October 1789; *World and Fashionable Advertiser* (London), 8 October 1787.

66 *London Evening Post* (London), 2 October 1750–4 October 1750: "Foot Race in the artillery ground, London ... Those that intend to run for this purse must give in their names to Mr. Smith tomorrow, by two o'clock at farthest, and deposite half a guinea, which shall be return'd to those that start."

67 This and the following: Kloeren, *Sport und Rekord*, 202, 245, 252, 258.

68 *London Evening Post* (London), 15 July 1742–17 July 1742: Hereford Races; *St. James's Chronicle or the British Evening Post* (London), 1 May 1788–3 May 1788: Epsom Races; *St. James's Chronicle or the British Evening Post* (London), 15 October 1789–17 October 1789: Newmarket.

69 Strutt, *The Sports and Pastimes of the People of England (1903)*, 65f.

70 See, for example, *Mist's Journal*, 15 April 1721: "Last Tuesday the Lord D-k-h- and the Earl of E---x walked to Richmond-Green for a Wager of 200 guineas; which was won by the Earl of E---x." (quoted after Kloeren, *Sport und Rekord*, 259).

71 It is not possible to unambiguously identify the person. It was probably Henry William Paget (formerly Bayly), first marquess of Anglesey, army officer and politician, who was born in 1768 in London and named Lord Paget from 1784 on (Anglesey [*sic*], "Paget, Henry William, first marquess of Anglesey (1768–1854)," *Oxford Dictionary of National Biography* (Oxford: Oxford University Press, 2004); online ed., January 2008, http://www.oxforddnb.com.460264923.erf.sbb.spk-berlin.de/view/article/21112.

72 *English Chronicle or Universal Evening Post* (London), 29 December 1789–31 December 1789; *Argus* (London), 30 December 1789.

73 Apparently, this rule was only of practical relevance if a court case arose. Complainants could not collect more than 10 pounds of money owed from betting: "a bill of exchange, which was cut down by the Statute of Anne to 10 l. – every thing above that sum was ilegale, and could be recovered in a court of justice": *Evening Mail* (London), 6 July 1792–9 July 1792.

According to Brailsford, this law was "a dead letter virtually from the start": Brailsford, *British Sport*, 49.

74 See *St. James's Chronicle or the British Evening Post* (London), 27 July 1790–29 July 1790: 60 guineas; *Gazetteer and New Daily Advertiser* (London), 13 September 1790: 50 guineas.

75 This was probably "Barry, Richard, seventh earl of Barrymore (1769–1793), rake and actor." Richard Davenport-Hines, "Barry, Richard, seventh earl of Barrymore (1769–1793)," *Oxford Dictionary of National Biography* (Oxford: Oxford University Press, 2004); online ed., May 2006, http://www.oxforddnb.com.460264923.erf.sbb.spk-berlin.de/view/article/65302.

76 *London Chronicle* (London), 30 October 1790–2 November 1790.

77 Joseph Strutt, *Glig-Gamena Angel-Deod. Or The Sports and Pastimes of the People of England* (London: T. Bensley, 1801), 61.

78 Contemporaries like Joseph Strutt were already aware of this connection: *The Sports and Pastimes of the People of England* (1801), 60f. In the articles of the time, this is evident through the demarcation of racetrack boundaries with strings: *Morning Post and Daily Advertiser* (London), 27 July 1786), or in discussions of proper behaviour: Is it permissible to cut the track or to lean into a bend? *Morning Herald* (London), 25 May 1786.

79 Strutt, *The Sports and Pastimes of the People of England* (1903), 66. See also examples in Kloeren, *Sport und Rekord*, 265–9.

80 Brailsford, *British Sport*, 77. See also Peter Radford, *The Celebrated Captain Barclay: Sport, Money and Fame in Regency Britain* (London: Headline, 2001).

81 This and the following: Radford, "Escaping the Philippides Connection," 87, 89, 93f.

82 William Buchan, *Domestic Medicine. Or, a Treatise on the Prevention and Cure of Disease* (London: A. Strahan, 1803), 38, 79f.; quoted after Radford, "Escaping the Philippides Connection," 94.

83 John Sinclair, *The Code of Health and Longevity*, 4 vols. (Edinburgh: Arch. Constable & Co., 1807), vol. 1, 676f.; quoted after Radford, "Escaping the Philippides Connection," 95.

84 Oettermann, *Läufer und Vorläufer*, 44.

85 "Zur Geschichte der Wiener Laufer," 163.

86 Joseph Alois Gleich, *Neue komische Briefe des Hans-Jörgels von Gumpoldskirchen an seinen Schwager Maxel in Feselau und dessen Gespräche über verschiedene Tagsbegebenheiten in Wien* (Vienna: Bauer and Dirnböck 1833–40), here vol. 8 (1840), 21; quoted after Oettermann, *Läufer und Vorläufer*, 69f.

87 "Zur Geschichte der Wiener Laufer," 170–3.

88 This and the following: Herbert Bauch and Michael Birkmann, "*... die sich für Geld sehen lassen ...*" *Über die Anfänge der Schnell- und Kunstläufe im 19.*

Jahrhundert (Marburg: Jonas, 1996); Oettermann, *Läufer und Vorläufer*, 74, 79f.

89 Krünitz, *Oekonomische Encyklopädie*, vol. 147 (1827), art. "Schnellläufer," 431.

90 According to Depping (*Die Körperkraft und Geschicklichkeit des Menschen*, 133), the King of Saxony had runners until at least 1845.

91 Oettermann, *Läufer und Vorläufer*, 82f., 87–90.

92 See, for example, Johann Evangelist Fürst, *Bauernzeitung aus Frauendorf* 4 (1822): 369: "In Landau, in the Rhine region, the following folk festival was held on the 13th of October 1822, for the glorification of the name-day of His Majesty, our most gracious king: 1) Horseraces. 2) Battle between two knights in armour according to old German custom. 3) Tilting at the ring 4) Bird shooting with hunting guns. 5) Funny entertainments. An egg-and-spoon race 6) Running races 7) Sack races 8) Wheelbarrow races 9) Race of young people blindfolded. 10) Race with full water pails etc."

93 Brailsford, *British Sport*, 73.

94 Tony Collins, "Pedestrianism," in *Encyclopedia of Traditional British Rural Sports*, ed. Tony Collins et al. (London: Routledge, 2005), 203f., here 204; Guttmann, *Sports: The First Five Millennia*, 98.

95 Hermann Vogt, "Athletik," in *Daheim* 35 (1882): 1st Supp.; quoted after Oettermann, *Läufer und Vorläufer*, 158.

96 Wolfgang Behringer, "The Invention of Sports: Early Modern Ball Games," in *Sports and Physical Exercise in Early Modern Culture*, ed. von Mallinckrodt and Schattner, 21–48. For many other examples of early modern sporting culture, including those outside of England, see the introduction and essays in *Sports and Physical Exercise* as well as John McClelland and Brian Merrilees, eds., *Sport and Culture in Early Modern Europe* (Toronto: Centre for Reformation and Renaissance Studies, 2009).

97 Brailsford, *A Taste for Diversions*, 29f.

7 A Well-Trained Community: Gymnastics for the German Nation

WOLF KITTLER

Turnen in the Twentieth Century

Asked to contribute to a book on the allure and ethics of sports, I cannot but start with a personal anecdote, my first lesson in gymnastics at the age of thirteen. I grew up in a tiny village in the German Democratic Republic. Two cars: my uncle's – the butcher's – 1927 Ford, and the country doctor's prewar VW. No tractors, only horses and oxen. The schoolhouse: the manor of the Lord, who had died in the Battle of Berlin. Sports: mostly soccer, dodge ball, some running in summer, and skiing in winter; best of all, however, was the occasional small-bore rifle shooting.

Turned into a reluctant refugee by my parents' decision to leave the GDR for the Federal Republic of Germany, I was introduced to gymnastics – or to use two German terms, *Turnen*, or *Leibesübungen* (bodily exercises) – in the fall of 1957. It must have been on a Tuesday or Thursday afternoon that my classmates led me to a hall the likes of which I had never seen before, a hall that should not be particularly new to anyone in the so-called civilized world today but that, I have to admit, still sent a chill down my spine when I discovered a picture of it on the Internet, as I was thinking about the topic of this volume.

After some preparatory exercises, the teacher initiated a ritual that was remarkably similar to the one described in the opening paragraph of Rainer Maria Rilke's story "Die Turnstunde" ("The PE Lesson"):

> In the military school at Saint Severin. Sports hall. The class stands in clear ticking blouses, arranged in two rows, under the big gas candelabra. The PE teacher, a young officer with a hard brown face and snarky eyes, has ordered artistic gymnastics and is now arranging the gym teams. "First

'Riege,' or team, single bar, second team double bar, third team vaulting horse, fourth party climbing. Dismissed!" And, on their colophony insulated shoes, the boys quickly disperse. Some are lingering in the middle of the hall, hesitantly, unwillingly, as it were. It is the fourth team, the ones who are bad at sports, and the ones who are not having fun at the apparatuses, and already tired from the twenty knee bends and a bit confused and breathless.[1]

Riege, English "team" or "squad," was a word I had never heard before. I was assigned to *Riege* no. 1, which meant that my group, just like the first team in Rilke's story, had to set up the single bars, a contraption that, needless to say, was as foreign to me as all the other objects in the hall. Once we were finished, the teacher told me to step up to it and perform what he called a *Felgaufschwung* followed by an *Abschwung vorwärts*. Since I had no idea what these words meant, he ordered one of the boys from the first team, whom he called the *Vorturner*, that is, the model or chief gymnast, to demonstrate the sequence of these two exercises to me. I tried to do it myself, failed, tried again, failed again, and, for the rest of my high school days, ended up in *Riege* no. 4, the group of those who always try to linger in the middle of the hall hoping that the teacher – distracted by the marvellous performances of the jocks – will forget that they exist, in short, those for whom Jahn coined the term: *turnscheu*,[2] that is, the students shy about doing PE.

To make a long story short, I had been introduced to a strange and completely new universe: a new vocabulary, new apparatuses, new movements, and unexpected contortions required of my body. Little did I know that almost everything that was said and done in this hall was the invention of one charismatic teacher and his students at a specific moment in time, the years between 1810 and 1816, in a specific place, the Hasenheide in Berlin, and assembled and systematized in an encyclopaedic volume, *Die Deutsche Turnkunst zur Einrichtung der Turnplätze*, by Friedrich Ludwig Jahn and Ernst Eiselen, published in 1816. An English translation, titled *A Treatise on Gymnasticks*, was published by Simeon Butler in 1828.[3]

The sequence of moves I had been asked to perform is ranked as no. 13, out of 32, on Jahn's list of increasingly difficult exercises to be practised on the single bar,[4] hence, perhaps a bit much for the bloody beginner I was at the time. Following the order established by the young PE teacher in Rilke's story, here are reproductions of the four different apparatuses mentioned in his speech, taken from the plates of Jahn's book:

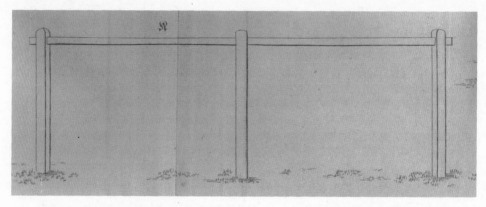

Figure 7.1. *Reck*, or Single Bar

The German word *Reck* is a neologism for a new kind of device, which Jahn borrowed from Low German *Reck* or *Rick*, and which denotes a bar used to hang up laundry or for chickens to roost.

Figure 7.2. *Barren*, or Double Bars

The term *Barren* is a neologism of Jahn's making as well.

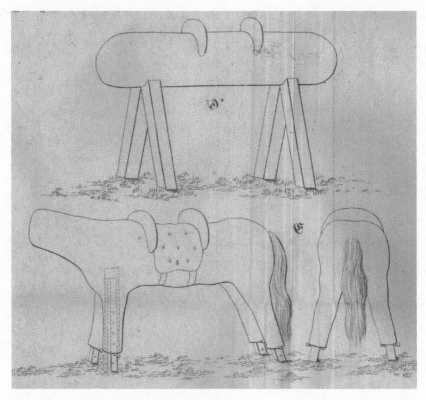

Figure 7.3. *Schwingel Pferd*, or pommel horse

Das Bockspringen, "leapfrog," is according to Jahn "the jump over a standing man." It is a specific kind of what he calls "swinging."[5]

Figure 7.4. *Klettern*, or climbing

This is the original of the ropes and ladders that are regular pieces of equipment in any German sports hall to this day.

On the map of Jahn's sports field, the four places to which the officer in Rilke's story sends each of the four parties are: the single bars at no. X, the double bars at no. XI, the pommel horses at no. VIII, and climbing at no. XII. The athletes are supposed to move along the narrow paths, marked as no. III:

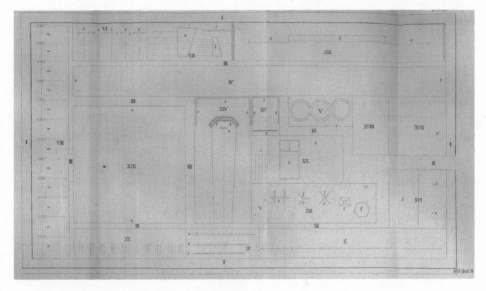

Figure 7.5. *Turnplatz*, or gymnasium

Each of the exercises I had to or rather was asked to perform in my first PE lesson in a German *Gymnasium* can be traced back to Jahn's *Turnkunst*. The warm-ups, called gymnastics in my time, are defined in chapter XIV under the title "Strecken" (stretching). And the *Felgaufschwung* is described in a sub-sub-section of chapter VI, which corresponds to chapter VII in the English translation:

Kapitel VI. Reckübungen
    B. Schwingübungen (86–92)
        1. Der Aufschwung (87–89)
           4te Art (88–89)
               2. Rückwärts (89)

Chapter VII. Exercises on the Single Bar (57–83)
    B. Exercises with Swinging (67–79)
        I. Swinging Up (70–73)
           Fourth Kind (76)
               2. Backwards (76)

As this list shows, Jahn's *Treatise on Gymnasticks* is a truly systematic work. The descriptions of each specific exercise are equally sophisticated. Here is the one on the *Felgaufschwung*, "the upward circle forwards," translated literally from the German original: "Backwards (with feet foremost): the *Felgaufschwung*. The feet are thrown through the pending hang towards the bar in such a way that the belly gets to rest on it." (89)

But what is the pending hang, German *Schwebehang*, or, to quote the English translation, "Hanging in a Suspended Position"? Here is my translation of Jahn's definition:

> 3. *Pending Hang*: the position which the gymnast achieves when he moves his legs, from the hanging on or the resting hang, above the bar in such a way that they remain pending, that is, without touching the bar, neither moving backwards nor forwards.
>
> The pending hang is to be performed first from the earth, and then from the hanging position. (81)

The *Felgaufschwung* is shown in Figure 3 of the following plate from the English version of the book:

Figure 7.6. *Felgaufschwund* (fig. 3)

The finishing exercise I was told to perform is the so-called *Abschwung*, English "swinging off":

2. Der Abschwung (91–92)
   a. reine Abschwünge (91–92)
      1. vorwärts (91)

III. Swinging Off (76–78)
   a. With an Entire Revolution[6] (76–77)
      1. Forwards (76–77)

And this is the description of this exercise, again in my translation, which is closer to Jahn's original than the English version:

3. *The Swinging Off* must always be done with closed legs and feet.
   a. *Pure Off Swingings*; with a complete turn of the gymnast around the axis;
      1. *forwards* from the resting position; also with lifting ...

Even the term *Vorturner*, which the coach of my first gymnastics lesson applied to the student who was supposed to show me the tricks of the trade, is more than a neologism of Jahn's making – it is also a carefully defined social function within his system of gymnastics:

> As soon as a beginning gymnastics institution [*Turnanstalt*] has made some progress, the head coach [*Turnwart*] or gymnastics teacher has to choose ... *Vorturner*, i.e., model gymnasts, out of the most reasonable and the most gymnastics-ready [*turnfertigsten*] students. The model gymnasts have to instruct the newcomers in the preparatory exercises, and, wherever necessary, demonstrate exercises themselves. They must know how to provide assistance, and they have to be on hand whenever any slipping or falling is easily possible in order to prevent any damage. They also have to be so level-headed as to be able to select the appropriate elements from the components of a multi-layered exercise in each case. In supervising younger and weaker students they have to take extra care that the goal, in these cases, is not so much to acquire certain skills, but rather to prepare a general readiness for gymnastics [*Turnfertigkeit*].[7]

So much for the archaeology of my first experience of a PE lesson in a West German gymnasium. I have gone into so much detail in order to emphasize how systematic and detailed Jahn's instructions are. For him, even walking is a great art, "eine grosse Kunst,"[8] and there are no less than three categories of running, two of which have two subsections, and the third one, five.

Jahn's *Turnkunst*

The purpose of Jahn's system is to control, regulate, correct, improve, and – generalizing with Foucault – discipline each and every movement that the human body can perform: stretching, walking, running, swinging, carrying, throwing, slinging, jumping, climbing, wrestling. A few other activities such as fencing, swimming, riding, and dancing are reserved for another book, which, due to circumstances that will be addressed later, Jahn would never write. Since the simple routines of our daily lives were not enough for him, he not only adapted traditional exercise equipment for his art but also invented new apparatuses in order to squeeze every possible permutation out of the complex tensile structure of bones, sinews, and muscles that constitutes our earthly existence. Yet even Jahn's encyclopaedic fantasy could not anticipate all of the possibilities he had created with such simple contraptions as the single and double bars, the pommel horse, or the balance beam.[9] If you have ever watched the discipline of artistic gymnastics at the Olympic Games, you know what breakneck and, in fact, life-threatening extremes these simple structures can induce.

Jahn's *Turnkunst* includes an extensive bibliography on the history and practice of gymnastics and bodily exercises in general, but in the introduction to his book, the author singles out the works of two "forerunners" in particular:[10] Gerhard Ulrich Anton Vieth, *Versuch einer Encyklopädie der Leibesübungen*[11] (Halle: Dreyssig, 1793–94), 3 vols.; and Johann Christoph Friedrich GutsMuths, *Gymnastik für die Jugend, enthaltend eine praktische Anweisung zu Leibesübungen. Ein Beytrag zur nöthigsten Verbesserung der körperlichen Erziehung*. Zweyte durchaus umgearbeitete und vermehrte Ausgabe (Schnepfenthal: Buchhandlung der Erziehungsanstalt, 1804).[12]

Vieth's and GutsMuths's books are contributions to the Enlightenment movement of reform pedagogy that was initiated by Rousseau's *Émile* and completed by such authors as Basedow, Campe, Salzmann, and Pestalozzi at the turn of the eighteenth century. To justify their focus on the physical components of education, both authors quote the old adage *mens sana in corpore sano*.[13] For Vieth, physical exercises had three advantages: "the promotion of humours within their vessels; and the prevention of congestions within these same vessels, ... better processing of humours and removal of useless ones by means of evaporation, [and finally,] permanent renewal of the surrounding air."[14]

This is a purely medical argument based on the age-old concepts of humoral pathology, a theory that dates back to Hippocrates and that GutsMuths quotes as well: "The main cause of our well-being lies in the circulation of humours, and of blood in particular."[15] Yet for GutsMuths, as opposed to Vieth, the purely medical justification for physical exercises is far too narrow; according to him, they must be conceived within the much broader world-historical horizon of Rousseau's critique of culture. I quote the opening paragraphs of his book:

> As long as nature guided man on the leash of instinct and need, he always was in the rigorous school of physical exercise; and without him knowing or intending it, the goal to satisfy nature and instinct coincided with the goal to exercise, to perfect his own body. This is the true *natural* gymnastics.
>
> But when nature guided him over into the region of culture, and when he invented a thousand levers here to satisfy his needs in a more comfortable way, then he surrendered to convenience, comfort, refined manners and often even to fanatic over-excitation. These under-gods softened him, refined him, tyrannized him ... At that point, some wise people of antiquity purposely replaced the earlier natural gymnastics with physical exercises in order to minimize those consequences and bestow more force and flexibility on the citizen's body. That may have been the occasion for the establishment of *artificial* gymnastics for specific purposes; the *military* one, for the formation of the soldier; the *athletic* one, for festive spectacles; the *medical* one, for the healing of physical diseases; but the true one for young and old remains exclusively the *pedagogical* one.
>
> As nature's emulator it replaced that school of strain and effort, into which necessity, with iron rigour, had driven the rough mortal, by opening a training field for the civilized citizen and by trying to do amicably and with friendliness what nature used to do otherwise by force. Only this kind of the gymnastics is the object of this book.
>
> ...
>
> *Gymnastics is work in the guise of youthful joy.* Work because its purpose is anything but an ignoble pastime, but rather the ennoblement of the body. And it should appear in the guise of youthful joy because that joy is so rightfully the cheerful climate within which youth flourishes best. After all, joy is, as it were, the lure by means of which human beings are enticed into the difficult institutions of human life, used to it, bound to it like the

child is being attached to the school desk by means of sweets; so firmly bound that only very few may break the fetters at will.[16]

Gymnastics – or to use the anachronistic term, sports – in and of themselves are not a lure. They are, on the contrary, an activity to which young people have to *be* lured by the promise of youthful joy, because, as GutsMuths explains under the heading "Necessity of Gymnastics, as Proved from the Situation of the Cultivated Citizen, or from the Consequences of our Refined Way of Living:"[17] "A very pressing illness affecting the civilized class of the cultivated world is *idleness, the tendency towards comfort, the aversion to bodily exercise.*"[18]

Eighteenth-century reform pedagogy – like its heirs in our time – always presumes a reluctant subject, and this makes it a paradoxical science of cunning that must use tricks, ruses, and lures to initiate the students' "self-activity"[19] by means of which they can free themselves from the depraved effeminacy of humanity's civilized state.

Jahn adopts the encyclopaedic and systematic structure of Vieth's and GutsMuths's works, but when declaring the necessity of physical exercises he is inspired less by Vieth's medical arguments than by GutsMuth's Rousseauist critique of culture:

> *Turnkunst*, the *Art of Turnen*, is meant to re-establish the lost balance of human culture and education, to align true physical nature with bare one-sided spiritualization, to provide a necessary counter-balance to over-refinement in a regained manliness, and to encompass and capture the whole man in youthful communal living.[20]

The difference is small but substantial. Where GutsMuths writes of "youthful joy," Jahn emphasizes "youthful social life," that is, sports as a form of community-building. Part of this new focus is on the rehabilitation of a form of gymnastics that GutsMuths explicitly excluded from his book, namely, "the *military* one." Thus, Jahn continues:

> As long as man still has a body here below and as long as he needs a bodily life for his *earthly being*, which, without force and power, without endurance and sustainability, without agility and cleverness would waste away to an empty shadow – the Art of Gymnastics will have to remain a main part of human education. It is incomprehensible that this customary art of body and life, this shield and shelter doctrine, this preparation for defensive warfare has been lost for such a long time.[21]

The term *Wehrhaftmachung*, which literally means "to make oneself fortified, ready to resist," but could also be translated as "to arm," "to build up arms," marks the decisive shift from *Leibesübungen* in the sense of Vieth and GutsMuths to Jahn's *Turnkunst*, the shift from such general disciplines as medicine and world history to the much more concrete and contemporary field of politics, or, more precisely, to the politics of Europe at the time of the Napoleonic Wars. In his book *Deutsches Volksthum*, published in 1810, Jahn had opened the chapter on physical exercises with a rueful historical reminiscence: "Since 1648 humility has been the German's greatest hereditary vice; disdaining himself he becomes disdainful, and the people around him disdain him in turn."[22] The reference is to the Treaty of Westphalia, which ended the Thirty Years' War, and which Jahn deemed a humiliating defeat, cause for all Germans to loathe themselves. Hence, Germans were in dire need of being uplifted, encouraged, and strengthened by physical exercises for young people. Now, six years later, and after Napoleon's defeat in the Battle of Waterloo, Jahn pegs his *Turnkunst* to the most recent political and military events of his time. I quote the opening paragraphs of his book:

> Like so many things in the world, the *German Art of Gymnastics* has had a small, unnoticeable beginning. Towards the end of the year 1809, I wandered to Berlin in order to see the entrance of the King. On the occasion of this festivity, a ray of hope emerged for me, and after long years of erring and wandering I made my home here. Love for the fatherland and my own inclination again turned me into the teacher of youth which I had been so often already. At the same time, I had my "German Folkdom" published.
>
> In the beautiful springtime of 1811, first a few, and then more and more students would follow me on Wednesday and Saturday afternoons when there was no school out into the fields and woods. The numbers grew, and we performed youth games and simple exercises. We pursued these activities until the dog days, when an immense number of boys came together, which, however, soon dispersed. Yet there was a core which went its separate way, and which stuck together as regulars in winter, too, and with whom we then opened the first gymnastics area in the Hasenheide in the spring of 1811.[23]

In its very origins, Jahn's *Turnkunst* is tightly linked to the fate of the Prussian state. After Napoleon's decisive victory in the Battle of Jena and Auerstädt, King Frederick William III and his wife, Queen Luise, had fled to East Prussia, first residing in the easternmost city of Memel, and later in Königsberg, a bit farther to the west. And after Napoleon had defeated the king's Russian allies in the Battle of Friedland, King Frederick William was forced to sign the Treaty of Tilsit on 9 July 1807, an event that Jahn, in his book on *Volksthum*, had defined as a reiteration of the humiliating Treaty of Westphalia. Two years later, on 23 December 1809, the Prussian king and the much more popular Queen Luise returned to Berlin, an event that Jahn, looking back from the vantage point of 1816, could define as a new beginning, the beginning of both the Prussian people's and the Prussian state's resurgence that would lead to Napoleon's defeat at Waterloo. It was the fulfilment of a dream, one that Jahn, albeit in veiled form, had already expressed in his book *Deutsches Volksthum*, the foreword to which he had signed 14 October 1808, and for which Jahn coined the new noun *Volksthum*, "folkdom" or "folklore."[24]

Clearly inspired by the energy, exuberance, and pride that the French nation had developed after the French Revolution, Jahn asks a simple question: *Was ist ein Volk?* ("What is a people?"). However not: "What is a nation," because he wants explicitly to avoid this neo-Latin (and thus rather French) term; instead, he replaces it with what he would call an "*ur*-word" from the German "*ur*-language,"[25] the word *Volk*. He asks: "How does a people grow out of singular men to become a people; how out of the milling mass of peoples, finally, mankind?"[26] In short, Jahn tries to define a specific German way of forming and being a people – or, to use a word he despised, a nation – similar to but also clearly distinct from the French model. Thus, under the heading "Popular Festivities," he states: "The object of popular festivities must be tuned to the people [*volksthümlich*], not freedom, enlightenment, reason etc.: These belong to all of mankind."[27]

Instead of the cult of such "mythical antics like the goddesses of reason which the New France summons from the houses of fornication,"[28] Jahn recommends celebrating such events as Arminius's (i.e., Hermann's) victory over the Romans, or Frederick I's Prussian victory in the Battle of Fehrbellin, but also commemorating such sad events as the Battle of Jena and Auerstädt, fought on 14 October 1806. Borrowing a technical term from the Protestant liturgical calendar, he proposes that date be observed as a "day of prayer and repentance."[29]

According to Jahn, each people has its own inalienable character, which means that "the founding day of the universal monarchy [would be] humanity's last day"[30] because it would abolish any distinctions between individual people or states. But the distinct character of these various peoples is not a given – it can be lost, as happened to the Germans, and hence it needs to be retrieved, cultivated, and fostered by the institutions of the state – not just imagined, as Benedict Anderson would have it,[31] but actively produced:

> For me, too, the Prussian state never was the highest form of the art of governance; but, in it, I discovered a drive towards perfecting as well as toward future perfection. For me, it was the core of the splintered

Germany – the youngest and fastest-growing shoot from the old Reich's root, which, since the old days were irretrievably being lost, seemed to rise up as the survivor and substitute of the aging main trunk.[32]

Jahn's book *Deutsches Volksthum*, which encompasses such topics as the uniformity of the state-run administration, the unity of people and state, the Church, the education of the people, the constitution of the people, the feelings of the people, popular literature, domestic life (here he focuses mainly on the high esteem Germans supposedly have for women[33]), and, finally, patriotic wanderings, constitutes a wide-ranging program, in fact, "a state catechism"[34] for the perfection of the Prussian state, and in its wake the rest of Germany as well, which, before Napoleon's victory at Austerlitz and Emperor Franz's abdication in 1806, had formed the Holy Roman Empire. Physical education, not yet called *Turnen*, but placed under the traditional heading *Leibesübungen* (bodily exercises), is an extensive part of the chapter on the education of the people. According to Jahn, such exercises are "a means to the perfect formation of the people" because they prepare the citizen, from childhood on, to become part of the *Landwehr*, the militia:

[A]n autonomous peaceful people, which prepares all male citizens for protective wars, *is a people of male warriors and, in the case of the militia, of warriors in general.* Then, everything joins in the fight, both the inorganic and the organic nature. And against a conqueror who, by his war, has passed a death sentence on a people and intends to execute it in reality, no considerations whatsoever are valid.[35]

Note the distinction between the contingent of all male citizens, and the militia, which does not consist of men alone, but includes women as well, because, as Jahn states: "Even the weaker sex shines in heroism!"[36] In his chapter on girls' schools, Jahn consequently writes: "Physical exercises are not excluded, although they must be practised moderately and femininely."[37] Setting aside this restriction, exercises for girls include "*[s]hooting*, that is, to fire a light rifle; to hit a target reasonably well with a pistol in order not to be proficiently defenceless and not to start at the shot of a gun like geese at thunder – all of this is highly necessary."[38] To create "a noble autonomous people,"[39] a carefully layered system is necessary:

Physical exercises are the preparation in child- and boyhood. In early youth, each man serves three years in the standing army, one year learning the service, the following one practising it, and the third one teaching it. ... Only after all men *fit for war* have become *weapons competent* through bodily exercises, *combative* by means of weapons training, *ready to strike* by means of renewed war games and by always having built up arms, *war bold* through love of the fatherland – only then can such a people be called *able to put up a fight.*[40]

On arriving in Berlin, Jahn proceeded to implement this program. Having studied Vieth's and GutsMuth's treatises, and inspired by his students' frolicking in the fields and in the woods, he conceived his own system of gymnastics complete with a whole set of old and new apparatuses and machines. Since, unlike the old elite of aristocrats, most of his pupils could not afford a horse – a preferred and necessary object for martial exploits since ancient times – he transformed it into the pommel horse, or *Schwingel*, "a horse-like contraption, which, when upholstered, covered with horse skin and made horse-like, is also called swinging[41] horse."[42] To this description, Jahn adds a cautionary note: "To give a completely horse-like appearance to the Schwingel is permitted only if its use is not impaired thereby."[43]

And obviously from watching his students climb and cavort in the branches of trees, he developed idealized forms of these natural shapes: the single and double bars, the balance beam, and scaffoldings supporting ladders and ropes. The goal was universal applicability instead of specialized drills as they had been practised by knights in the Middle Ages or by musketeers in the eighteenth century: gymnastics neither for an elite, nor for underdogs, but for *everyone*, the people as such.

Jahn also invents a new terminology, or more precisely a new language that is structured according to the principles developed in his book on *Volksthum*. Borrowed or foreign words are excluded. This is a general rule, but one that applies to French in particular because, Jahn writes, "to French is to falsify, to emasculate the Ur-force, to poison the language source, to hamper the possibility of further language formation, and total language meaninglessness."[44] Hence, each word must be gleaned from the German *ur*-language, which has two components: Luther's High German, the language of the entire community (*Gesammtsprache*), and the various *Mundarten*, a word that literally translates as "ways of mouth" in the sense of "ways of speaking"[45] and that refers to vernaculars or dialects. For Jahn, both levels of language are necessary because they complement each other: "Without *Mundarten* the language body turns into a language corpse. The written language constitutes the highest advocacy for language unity, Mundarten remain the highly necessary Ur-assemblies of particularity for that purpose."[46]

Probably inspired by Leibniz's "Non-Preemptive Thoughts Concerning the Exercise and Improvement of the German Language," which was published posthumously in 1717,[47] Jahn identifies yet another source for his new terminology, namely the rich vocabulary of the idioms used by various craftsmen and professionals – peasants, carpenters, miners, sailors, hunters, soldiers, and so on – however, only under the condition that these languages have been "kept pure,"[48] that is to say, free from foreign sub- or super-strata. The first and most prominent example of these words is *Turnen*, the new technical term for what used to be called *Leibesübungen*, physical exercises, which was supposedly coined by the gymnasts on the Hasenheide in the spring of 1811.[49] Jahn spends five full pages (xxvi–xxxi) to prove, against all the overwhelming evidence to the contrary, that this neologism has nothing to do with such French words as *tourner* or *tournament*, but rather is "a German Ur-sound [*Urlaut*] which can be heard in several German sister languages, both living and extinct, and which everywhere means to rotate, to round a corner, to bend, to steer, great stirring and moving."[50]

From this neologism alone, Jahn forms more than sixty composita, among them such new adjectives as *turnmüde, turnfaul, turnreif, turnstark*,[51] respectively "tired of," "lazy of," "mature," and "strong for" gymnastics. Newly coined words derived from various German dialects include:[52]

1 from Saxon:
   Reck, "single bar,"
   Riege, "team,"
   Reede, "place where one prepares for an activity,"[53]
   Tie, "place of assembly, socializing, and rest,"[54]
   Schleet, "a wooden bar placed over a shallow pit for balancing";[55]

2 from Swiss:
   Anmann (zu *Vorder- Hinter- und Nebenmann*), "the first person in a team (as person in front, person in back, and neighbour)";

3 from Thuringian:
   Schocken, "the throwing of heavy objects as in the case of skittles balls that are placed in the hand when bowling. On the gym field, where one throws [*schockt*] aiming at a target, only cannon balls of 1–3 pounds are used. Balls that weigh no more than 1½ to 2 pounds are most easily thrown and *schockt*."[56]

In other words, *schocken* is what we now call shotput, and the objects that are thrown or shot in this discipline are nothing but the compact cannonballs of the Napoleonic wars.

Since the words of this new language are strung together not just grammatically but also by alliterations, rhymes, and puns, Jahn's German has its own poetic flair, which is certainly one reason – perhaps the main reason – why so many of his neologisms, and even some of the laws and rules of his *Turnkunst*, are part of the German vernacular to this day. Where GutsMuths constructs a verbose argument about how joy acts as a lure for reluctant gymnasts who do not like to work out, Jahn simply notes: "Where one is having a gymnastics competition with others, all effort turns out to be easy, and all burden pleasure."[57]

The four alliterations in the basic law of his gymnastics are now a common German saying of whose origin in Jahn's *Turnkunst* only a few native speakers may still be aware: "*Fresh, free, joyful*, and *brave* – that is the gymnast's wealth."[58] And under the heading *Turnspiele*, "Matches" or "Games," Jahn declares: "In these games, a sociable, joyful, vitally fresh competition is alive. Here work [*Arbeit*] is paired with pleasure [*Lust*], earnestness with jubilation."[59] Where GutsMuths tries to make an argument, Jahn finds a flashy formulation. And where GutsMuths sees a conflict to be solved, Jahn discovers harmony. To be sure, Jahn does coin the word *turnscheu* to characterize students "shying away" from physical exercises, but the reform pedagogue's problem with reluctant subjects is not his concern. For him, no one needs to be lured into sports because *Turnen* is an occupation so joyful and so liberating that even the clumsiest non-athletic nerd – seeing his or her peers enjoy themselves – cannot help but join in. And because there are enough students who love to exercise, everyone else will be carried along.

What distinguishes Jahn's understanding of physical exercise most fundamentally from that of reform pedagogues like Vieth and GutsMuths is the fact that, for him, *Turnen* is an essentially shared, communal, and – that is to say – *political* activity. Like a modern nation-state, it has its own territory (*Turnplatz*), its own language (exclusively German), and its own general and specific laws (*Allgemeine* and *Besondere Turngesetze*); and these laws even have a spirit, a culture, and an ethics of their own (*Geist der Turngesetze*):

> Good morals [*gute Sitten*] have to work and count more on the gymnastics field than wise laws elsewhere. The highest penalty to administer here will always remain exclusion from the *Turner* community [*Turngemeinschaft*].
>
> The *Turner* who lives and embodies his being properly and in the flesh cannot be impressed upon frequently and insistently enough that no one has to uphold the nobility of body and soul more than he.[60] He least of all can defy a moral imperative because he is more able-bodied. Virtuous

and able, pure and nimble [*ringfertig*[61]], chaste and bold, truthful and fortified shall be his way of being. *Fresh, free, joyful,* and *brave* – that is the
gymnast's wealth. The general moral law is his highest standard and rule.
What disgraces others defiles him as well. To become a model, example,
and paragon – that is what he should strive for. The main instructions to
achieve these goals are: to strive for the highest and most thorough education [*Aus- und Durchbildung*]; to be diligent; to learn something fundamental; not to join in unmanly activities; not to let himself be enraptured
by any seduction, not to seek delights, pleasures, and pastimes that do not
behoove a youthful life. Most admonitions and warnings should, however, always be clothed in such a way that the doctrine of virtue does not
turn into a school of vice.

... One should never hide the fact that a German boy's and young man's
highest and holiest duty is to become a German man and, once having
become one, remain a German man, to work vigorously for folk and fatherland, to become like our *ur*-ancestors, the world saviours. If the goal of
aspirations you set for boys and young men is to mature into honest men,
you ought best to prevent secret juvenile sins. As soon as young people
recognize the archetype of the full manly life, they will cease to squander
the force and time of youth by engaging in narrow consuming pastimes,
lazily dozing away, by rutting lusts and doggishly raving debaucheries.
All education is, however, null and vain which allows the young man to
roam like a will-o'-the-wisp within the barren misery of a delusional cosmopolitanism instead of making him at home within the fatherland.[62]

What Jahn, with a Hegelian formula, calls *Geist der Turngesetze* is
based on two principles: first, the territory of the gymnastics field is
not so much governed by good laws as by good morals; and second,
the severest punishment is exclusion from the community of athletes
and gymnasts. The two propositions complement each other: A community that constitutes itself not by the rule of law but through the
morality of each and every individual – that is, not top down but from
the bottom up – only knows one penalty: exclusion of those who do not
belong. Like a pietistic congregation, the *Turngemeinschaft* is the physical (*leibhaftig*) embodiment of a spiritual community; it is elitist in the
sense that it does not tolerate the slightest aberration from the general
law of morality (*das allgemeine Sittengesetz*); and in its imperative that
each and every one of its constituents, regardless of his social status
or birth, guard "the nobility of body and soul," it is egalitarian. As in
the *Nicomachean Ethics*, the *eudaimonia*, the good luck, happiness, and
joy of the individual, culminates in the *polis* or the *Turngemeinschaft*, a

community, "κοινωνία," of friends for whose members the most desirable thing, as Aristotle said, is to live together: "τοῖσ φίλοις αἱρετώτατόν ἐστι τὸ συζῆν."[63] Jahn's *Turnkunst* is, in other words, an ethics in the Aristotelian sense of this term.

What a privilege it is to be part of this community can be deduced from an implication of Jahn's opening statement. If expulsion is the severest penalty to be administered to the gymnasts, then corporal punishments like flogging, for instance, are implicitly excluded. Already in his *Volksthum*, Jahn had stated: "*Corporal punishments* are unknown to the militia. They are un-German."[64] Two years earlier, on 9 July 1808, the Prussian field marshal and military reformer Neithard von Gneisenau had published his famous manifesto on the "Freedom of the Backsides" (*Freiheit der Rücken*) in the new patriotic weekly *Der Volksfreund* (*The People's Friend*). I quote the opening and the conclusion of this remarkable document:

> Twenty years ago, the word freedom started to resound all over Europe. We are still feeling its reverberations, although there is now a completely different sense implied in this word. Let us avert our eyes from this freedom now, from its many ways and kinds, and occupy ourselves with the freedom of the backsides which is truly not unworthy of an enlightened nation.
>
> Here and there, people still find it impossible to abolish punishments administered by means of the stick and by running the gauntlet in the German military ... People still want to preserve a form of punishment which goes so much and so contradictorily against the standards of our time within the most honourable of all associations.
>
> ...
>
> The *proclamation of the freedom of the backsides*, thus, seems to have precedence over the introduction of the general conscription. If that is not deemed possible, well, then let us abdicate our claims to culture and still seek the motives of good behaviour in wood because we are unable to find them in the sense of honour.[65]

If there ever was a text that marked the shift from what Foucault called the sovereign's power over life and death to the biopolitics of our time, then it is this programmatic statement. The fact that Jahn extends the ban of corporal punishment explicitly to the militia and implicitly to his community of gymnasts is a bold move that not only proves that he understands the latter as a military formation, but also shows him to be far ahead of his time. For in the Prussian legal code, corporal punishments survived up to 1848, when an edict, issued on 6 May, abolished it "as a consequence of the political rights equally bestowed on all subjects."[66]

More specific rules for the *Turner*'s conduct are scarce and basic: he should strive for a thorough and foundational education, avoid engaging in unmanly behaviour, and, most importantly, not let himself be dragged into seductions, pleasures, and pastimes that do not behove a young man. Jahn's art of gymnastics even promises to cure one of the greatest headaches confronting reform pedagogues at the turn of the eighteenth century, provided that two conditions are met. One: all warnings and admonishment are to be phrased in such a way that the school of virtue never turns into a school of vice, which is to say, if I understand correctly, that only positive values ought to be taught, while anything negative, evil, or immoral should not even be mentioned. And two: the highest duty of a young German man is to become and remain a German man. Under these two conditions, Jahn claims, students will not even think of committing secret youthful sins; instead they will engage in service to the fatherland rather than in what Lacan called "the enjoyment of the idiot,"[67] that is, the solitary, anti-communal, asocial activity par excellence: masturbation, not to speak of all other kinds of lust and voluptuousness.

Regarding the fatherland, however, pedagogues must emphasize that it is not an open community but an essentially exclusive one, the opposite of what Jahn refers to as "the barren misery of a delusional cosmopolitanism." Like the *Turngemeinschaft*, the fatherland is defined not only by the people and values it includes, but also by all the strangers it *ex*cludes – by all the others it expels. It is – and perhaps not by accident – the perfect example of what Carl Schmitt, in a famous definition, called the political: "The specifically political distinction, to which political actions and motives can be traced back, is the distinction between friend and foe."[68]

Such xenophobia applies not only to people but to (foreign) words as well: instead of simply stating that a young German man's duty is to become a German citizen, Jahn uses a lengthy paraphrase in order to avoid any allusion to Rousseau's and the French Revolution's concept of the *citoyen* as rendered by the German *Staatsbürger*, a word that Jahn still had used prominently in his 1810 book on *Volksthum*.[69] In that same work, he had spelled out criteria according to which subjects ought to be expelled from the state or the people, two entities that, for Jahn, are one and the same: "A state without a people is nothing, a soulless work of art; a people without a state is nothing, an airy shadow without a body, like the world fleeing Gipsies and Jews."[70] And furthermore:

The right of citizenship must be lost for anyone:
  a) who deserts without being wounded; who is taken prisoner in a dishonest and shameful way; who returns unwounded without his rifle from the battle field;
  b) who gives his word of honour to the enemy that he will not fight against him until he is released from that pledge;
  c) who engages in dishonourable enterprises in his homeland or abroad such as human trafficking, circumcision, gambling, procuring, prostitution, and neck-breaking acrobatics;
  d) who must live on alms;
  e) who is guilty of a crime, or of perjury and adultery;
  f) who, when abroad, defiles his own people's honour;
  g) who goes insane;
  h) who marries a non-yet naturalized non-German woman ...;
  i) who, without permission, enlists in a foreign army; who joins the civil service of a foreign country without asking;
  j) who is able to support a family, is healthy and not without means, and still remains a bachelor.[71]

What Jahn castigates when he speaks of "the barren misery of a delusional cosmopolitanism" is Napoleon's short-lived dream of a unified Europe under French rule. Here, the book comes full circle: having started with the description of the time when the *Turnkunst* was developed under Napoleon's rule, it ends with the wars of liberation, the beginning of Napoleon's defeat:

And, thus, even during the worst of the French time, the love of king and fatherland has been preached and imprinted into the hearts of the young gymnasts. Whoever acts contrary to the German cause or language in a criminal or scornful way, through words or deeds, privately or publicly – that one shall first be admonished, then warned, and, if he does not cease and desist from all his un-German doings, he shall be expelled from the gymnastics field by everyone. No one shall be allowed to come near the gymnastics field who knowingly perverts the German people's essential being [*Volksthümlichkeit*], who loves, lauds, commits, and embellishes foreignness [*Ausländerei*].

Thus, during the gloomy and thundery mugginess of the evil demon [*Valand*], the community of gymnasts steeled, armed, equipped, encouraged, and manned itself for the fatherland. Faith, love, and hope did not relinquish them for a moment. *God never forsakes a German* has always been their motto. During the war only those who were too young or too weak remained at home or idle. During these three years, the institution of the gymnasts [*Turnanstalt*] has brought valuable sacrifices. They rest on the battlefields from the gates of Berlin to the enemy capital.[72]

Already in the introduction to his *Turnkunst*, Jahn states:

> *Military exercises*, even if conducted without rifle, create and cultivate manly grace, awaken and stimulate the sense of order, inure one to obedience and to being attentive, teach the individual to insert himself as an element into a large whole. A well-trained troop of warriors is a spectacle of the highest unity of force and will. Each "Turner" shall mature to become a soldier without being drilled excessively.[73]

This is a well-trained soldier, and one – as the reference to the three theological virtues "faith, love, and hope" indicates – with a spiritual, quasi-religious mission which, codified in a state catechism (*Staatskatechismus*[74]), should be on every pupil's curriculum, and which, with a word that Jahn would have abhorred, we now would call "nationalism."

Consequences

The long-expected moment to attack "the new leviathan who, with his all devouring jaws,"[75] had swallowed the Prussian state in the shameful Treaty of Tilsit, finally came in the spring of 1813, when, while "the French were freezing on their flight from Moscow,"[76] King Frederick William III issued three cabinet orders: the first, "Concerning the Formation of a Military Reserve," on 25 January; the second, "On the Formation of Voluntary Rifle Men, Free Corps," on 3 February; and the third, "General Conscription," on 9 February.[77] Jahn and his assistant, the young Friedrich Friesen, contributed to the formation of the famed Lützow Free Corps, in which Jahn commanded a battalion, but was frequently used as a spy. And he lost his friend Friesen who, as Jahn writes in the introduction to his *Turnkunst*, was "treacherously murdered" on a gloomy "winter night" by "French perfidy" in the mountains of the Ardennes, a martyr for the Prussian and the German cause.[78]

On his return to Berlin in 1814, Jahn immediately resumed his work on gymnastics in the Hasenheide. Finally, there were victories to celebrate: 18 October 1813 – the Battle of Leipzig; 31 March 1814 – the entry of Tsar Alexander I and Frederick William III in Paris; 18 July 1815 – the Battle of Waterloo.[79] And then, finally, the importance of Jahn's work was recognized by the authorities; his efforts were supported by such eminent persons as the Prussian interior minister Friedrich von

Schuckmann, the finance minister Count Bülow, and Chancellor Count Friedrich von Hardenberg.[80] Business was flourishing, *Turnkunst* was blooming.

On 5 May 1816, Goethe notes in his diary a conversation "on *turnen* and academia" with State Councillor Hufeland, visiting from Berlin. And in 1817, he mentions Jahn's *Turnkunst* twice in his conversations with Biedermann, speaking of "the swinging of a particularly well trained *Turner* on the single bars," and concluding: "I value the *Turnerei*, i.e., the art of gymnastics; for it not only strengthens and refreshes the youthful body, but also encourages and toughens the soul and the spirit against effeminacy." And a circular issued by the Ministry of Culture under Baron Karl vom Stein zum Altenstein to the Presiding President of the government recommended "connecting *Turnen* to the totality of all popular education."[81]

But the good days of both the art and its creator Jahn were numbered. After the Vienna Congress, after the book-burning at the so-called Wartburgfest and the murder of the dramatist August von Kotzebue by the student Karl Ludwig Sand, Jahn, the patriot, came under suspicion of being one of the instigators and ringleaders of the rebellious German fraternities, to whose foundation he and his friend Friesen had contributed. Accused of "secret, highly treasonous relations," he was arrested in the night of 13/14 July 1819 and was incarcerated first in the fortress of Spandau and later at Küstrin. And on 2 January 1820, in the wake of the Carlsbad Decrees, the purpose of which was to reign in the liberal and national and hence supposedly revolutionary tendencies in the post-Napoleonic German states, his former supporter, the Prussian minister of both the interior and the police, Baron Friedrich von Schuckmann, issued the following edict: "Since it is His Majesty's grave will that the gymnastics business [*Turnwesen*] be completely discontinued, the Royal Government of the Police has to forcefully make sure that all gymnastics [*Turnen*] simply has to cease." And on 3 March of that same year, the Prussian State Chancellor, Count Carl von Hardenberg, decreed that all gymnastics instruments outside of the municipal areas be removed and destroyed.[82]

Meanwhile, Jahn's supposedly demagogic and treasonous activities were being scrutinized by the Royal Prussian Investigative Commission, which King Frederick William III had appointed as a special court to ferret out any treasonous and other dangerous machinations in his state. At the Kammergerichtsrat (Supreme Court), Councillor Ernst Theodor Amadeus Hoffmann, who wrote fantastic tales as a sideline, happened to be part of that commission. The letters, reports, and decisions pertaining to this case that crossed Hoffmann's desk tell a sad story indeed. Jahn was a divisive figure. Had he not been so charismatic, his *Turnkunst* would never have gotten off the ground. Had he not been so rude and abrasive, he would not have gotten into so much trouble in the second half of his life. In 1803, after getting into a brawl as a student, he had received the *consilium abeundi* from the University of Greifswald – that is, he was kicked out. A dropout from high school and a washout at college, he was nonetheless employed as a teacher at such prestigious institutions as the Gymnasium "zum Grauen Kloster" and Plamann's educational institute in Berlin. When he filed an understandable complaint on 27 September 1819 about having been incarcerated now for almost three months without anyone bothering to tell him why he had been arrested in the first place, he could not help berating the judicial authorities for using a non-German word in their accusation: "I do not know anything about *demagogic* machinations, do not even understand the expression, and have furthermore no idea which linguistic forger might have coined that denomination."[83] The Commission's response, penned by Hoffmann himself, advised him consequently "to await the further progress of his case patiently without making requests which, due to their inappropriate way of writing, deserve a special reprimand."[84]

It is true that Jahn's ideas about the active participation of each and every German in the community of his fatherland were apt to raise suspicion among conservative politicians in the climate of the Restoration after the Congress of Vienna; nonetheless, it is highly doubtful that he was the rebellious republican his detractors purported him to be. And there is little doubt that the way his case was conducted under the leadership of the ministers Schuckmann and Kircheisen was unfair, if not unjust. They were the ones who, despite repeated requests by Hoffmann and his colleagues in the Investigative Commission to let Jahn go, insisted on keeping him incarcerated. Writing for the commission, Hoffmann summed up its findings in a memo, which, as far as I can tell, seems to have been well founded, and which stated

> that no trace can be found that Jahn urged his gymnasts or others to violent rebellion against the government, that the assumption how, in the case of a future revolution, the seed of a German constitution was to be laid by means of the sportive activities, and that Jahn would have had, in fact, that intention, is way too farfetched to justify a criminal investigation and penalty, but that there is an urgent suspicion against him to have expressed himself at sportive activities and on other occasions in a way that could have instigated people's minds against the institutions of the state.

... that the most severe penalty cannot be applied, however:

because the reprimanded passages in his lectures are in no way of a kind to justify such a penalty, and because it is, moreover, not established that these passages did, in fact, arouse discontent and dissatisfaction of the citizens with their government,

because everything else is merely based on hasty allegations, and, finally, because the judges must take into consideration the already sustained long time of arrest.[85]

In the wake of this sober assessment, Jahn was released from prison, but only on the condition, specifically decreed by king Frederick William III,[86] that he be banished to Colberg, Pomerania, and closely supervised by that city's military commandant. And when he was finally acquitted in 1825, he was not allowed to reside near a town with a *Turnplatz* or a gymnasium – hence, he was forced to live far away from the kids he had once trained, or could still have been training on the Hasenheide. He had to wait until 1840 to be rehabilitated by Fredrick William IV, the much more liberal successor to the Prussian throne, who even returned to him the Iron Cross he had earned in the Wars of Liberation. In 1842, the *Art of Gymnastics* was reinstated in Prussian schools, and Jahn was even elected to represent the district of Naumburg in the first German Parliament residing in St Paul's Church in Frankfurt am Main, in 1848. But all of this came too late: Jahn's life and career as an educator and an author had been ruined. Even so, the fame his *Turnkunst* had earned him was to live on. By the end of the nineteenth century, about 280 monuments had been erected in his memory.[87] And in the twentieth century, he was equally celebrated by the fascists in the 1930s, the communists in East Germany, and the democrats in the West.[88]

Thus, the fate of his cause stands in stark contrast to that of his personal life. An essay published in the *Festschrift* for the eminent scholar of German and Indo-European literatures and languages Eduard Sievers, which juxtaposes the traditional humanist gymnasium Schulpforta, Nietzsche's school, to the Philanthropin, which the reform pedagogue Basedow had founded in the eighteenth century, testifies to the triumph not only of Jahn's *Turnkunst* but also of his ideas in general:

If the representatives of humanism, who are the fiercest enemies of philanthropic endeavours, have raised the strongest accusations against the philanthropists in long-winded articles and books, one can only deplore that these opponents never found the time to examine what good the philanthropists have worked – practically and theoretically – for the instruction in German literature and language. If that had been the case, such a shameful state of things as in Schulpforta, an institution, which was considered the prototype of a gymnasium for a long time, and whose institutions were imitated everywhere, would have never occurred. Not only was German literature not included in the curriculum of that institution, one even reprimanded and prohibited the students' private engagement with the German classics, just as, during that time, the famous principal of the school and outstanding representative of classical philology, Illgen, was appalled when an attempt was made to introduce the physical exercises, which had been so popular at the Philanthropien, and which were generally acclaimed, in Schulpforta as well, and when the government in Berlin sent him a pommel horse, which, according to the equally famous philologist Gottfried Hermann, he should not have accepted because the principal of a literary school was not supposed to serve as the groom of a wooden horse.[89]

Thus, *Turnvater* Jahn, the father of German gymnastics, emerged victorious in almost all the battles he had fought. Germany's "reunification" – to use Jahn's expression[90] – was achieved under Bismarck's (i.e., Prussia's) leadership in 1871; his art of gymnastics became a prominent part of the curriculum in German schools; even the study of his beloved German language and literature made it into this curriculum; and, what is perhaps most remarkable, each of these achievements has remained more or less intact to this very day, not to everyone's enjoyment, but as an inescapable fact. His totalizing approach to pedagogy, which encompasses the body and soul not only of the individual, but, above all, of the whole nation, survives in Germany's primary and high school curricula to this day.

One author in whose writings Jahn and his *Turnkunst* loom large is Franz Kafka. In his fragmentary novel *The Man Who Disappeared*, arguably one of the least likable characters of his entire oeuvre is described in these terms:

In contrast, here stood Mr. Green, perhaps a tad more corpulent than Mr. Pollunder, but it was a consistent, mutually supportive corpulence, his feet soldierly clicked together, carrying his head straight up and swaying; he appeared to be a great Turner, a Vorturner.[91]

And in the travesty of a family life that K., the main character of Kafka's fragmentary novel *The Castle*, leads together with Frieda, his future bride, and his two assistants in the role of their children, the double bar and the pommel horse play quite a decisive role. They serve as the scaffold for a hastily erected but completely useless barrier that is supposed to separate the space the head of the community has assigned to K. and his "family," from the classroom the teacher Gisa and her students have a long established right to occupy for their own very different purposes:

> In the morning, they all did not wake up until the first of the schoolchildren had arrived and were standing around the place where they lay, full of curiosity. This was awkward, for as a result of the heat, although now it had given way to a cool atmosphere again, they had all undressed to their underclothes, and just as they were beginning to get dressed, Miss Gisa the assistant teacher, a tall, blonde, handsome girl with a little stiffness in her manner, appeared at the door. She was obviously prepared for the new school janitor, and the teacher had probably told her how to treat him, for even in the doorway she said: "I really can't have this. Here's a nice thing! You have permission to sleep in the classroom, but that's all; it's not my duty to teach the children in your bedroom. A school janitor and his family lying in bed until the middle of the morning! Shame on you!" Well, K. thought he could have said a thing or two about that, particularly on the subject of beds and his family, as he and Frieda – the assistants were useless here, and were lying on the floor staring at the teacher and the children – quickly pushed the parallel bars and the pommel horse together, draped the blankets over both of them, and so created a small room in which they could at least get dressed away from the children's eyes ... Unfortunately, they had forgotten to clear away the remains of their supper, and now Miss Gisa was sweeping it all off the teacher's desk with her ruler. Everything fell on the floor. The teacher wasn't going to bother about the fact that the oil from the sardines and the remains of the coffee were spilt on the floor, and the coffee-pot had broken to pieces; after all, the school janitor would clear it up. Still not fully dressed, K. and Frieda, leaning against the parallel bars, watched the destruction of their few household goods.[92]

Yet one of the most remarkable turns in the reception history of *Turnkunst* may well be the moment when, at the turn of the nineteenth century, two authors tie this art – which, in its very origins, is so closely associated with youthful budding life and the power of the nascent German nation – to death. The hero of Rilke's story "The PE Lesson," Karl Gruber, a member of *Riege* no. 4, makes one last desperate effort and manages, for the first time in his life, to successfully climb to the top of one of Jahn's poles, but only at the price of a fatal heart attack.[93] And the question whether Georg Bendemann, the protagonist of Kafka's story "The Judgment," makes better use of Jahn's system in the end, shall remain open:

> He was already clutching the railings the way a starving man grasps his food. He swung himself over, like the outstanding gymnast he had been in his youth, to his parents' pride. He was still holding on, his grip weakening, when between the railings he caught sight of a motor coach, which would easily drown out the noise of his fall. He called out quietly, "Dear parents, I have always loved you nonetheless" and let himself drop.
>
> At that moment an almost unending stream of traffic was going over the bridge.[94]

NOTES

1 Rainer Maria Rilke, *Die Turnstunde*, in *Werke*, ed. Manfred Engel, Ulrich Fülleborn, Horst Nalewski, and August Stahl (Frankfurt am Main & Leipzig: Insel Verlag, 1996), 3:435–40, quote at 435. Unless noted otherwise, all translations mine.

2 Friedrich Ludwig Jahn and Ernst Eiselen, *Die deutsche Turnkunst zur Einrichtung der Turnplätze* (Berlin, 1816), xxxvi.

3 F.L. Jahn, *Treatise on Gymnasticks, taken mostly from the German* (Northampton, MA: Simeon Butler, 1828).

4 "13. Felgaufschwung und Abschwung vorwärts," that is, "Upward Circle Forward and Swinging Off," Jahn, *Turnkunst*, 94; cf. Jahn, *Treatise on Gymnasticks*, 82, no. XIII.

5 Jahn, *Turnkunst*, 70.

6 Here, the translation differs from the German, which has: "Pure Swinging[s] Off."

7 Ibid., 221–2.

8 Ibid., 3.

9 "Schwebebaum," ibid., 72.

10 Ibid., v.

11 Gerhard Ulrich Anton Vieth, *Versuch einer Encyklopädie der Leibesübungen* [*Outline of an Encyclopedia of Physical Exercises*] (Halle: Dreyssig, 1793–94), 3 vols.

12 Johann Christoph Friedrich GutsMuths, *Gymnastik für die Jugend, enthaltend eine praktische Anweisung zu Leibesübungen. Ein Beytrag zur nöthigsten Verbesserung der körperlichen Erziehung.* [*Gymnastics for Young People Containing a Practical Guide to Physical Exercises. A Contribution to the Most Necessary Improvement of Bodily Education.*] Zweyte durchaus umgearbeitete und vermehrte Ausgabe (Schnepfenthal: Buchhandlung der Erziehungsanstalt,

1804). As the German title states, this is the "second reworked and augmented edition" of a book that had first appeared in 1793, that is, at the same time as Vieth's *Encyclopedia*.

13 Gerhard Ulrich Anton Vieth, *Versuch einer Encyklopädie der Leibesübungen*, new edition (Leipzig: Carl Cnobloch, 1818), 1:10. GutsMuths, *Gymnastik*, ix.

14 Vieth, *Encyklopädie*, 1:15.

15 GutsMuths, *Gymnastik*, 48.

16 Ibid., 1–3.

17 Ibid., 34–64.

18 Ibid., 50, no. 3.

19 "Selbstthätigkeit," a key term of reform pedagogy to which Jahn alludes more than once: Jahn, *Deutsches Volksthum* (Lübeck: Niemann & Co., 1810), 407; *Turnkunst*, 219 and 223.

20 Jahn, *Turnkunst*, 209.

21 Since it is impossible to translate the word play and alliterations of the last sentence into English, here it is in the original: "Unbegreiflich, dass diese Brauchkunst des Leibes und Lebens, diese Schutz- und Schirmlehre, diese Wehrhaftmachung so lange verschollen gewesen" (Ibid.).

22 Jahn, *Volksthum*, 241.

23 Ibid., III–IV.

24 According to Grimm's *Deutsches Wörterbuch*, vol. 12.2: *Vesche-Vulkanisch*, ed. Rudolf Meiszner (Leipzig: S. Hirzel: 1951), 499, it was Johann Gottfried Herder who coined the adjective "volksthümlich" and the noun "volksthümlichkeit." The editor states: "volksthümlich *und* – keit *dagegen schon bei* HERDER" (popular *and* –ity, *however, already in* HERDER). But the sentence "ein schwanken zwischen ihr [i.e. der reimfreien iambischen Übersetzung] und der volksthümlich reimenden manier," ("a fluctuation between it [i.e. the rhyme-free iambic translation] and the popular rhyming style"), which is the only evidence given to prove that claim, is not a quote from Herder's works, but from the editor's concluding report (*Schlußbericht*) to volumes X, XI, and XII of *Herders Sämmtliche Werke*, ed. Bernhard Suphan, vol. 12 (Berlin: Weidmannsche Buchhandlung, 1880) 414. A word that Herder did coin and that may have inspired Jahn is "volkmässig," "appropriate, or, more literally commensurate to the folk, the people." Cf. *Von deutscher Art und Kunst. Einige fliegende Blätter*, in *Herders Sämmtliche Werke*, vol. 5, 1891, 187 and 189; *Von Ähnlichkeit der Mittleren englischen und deutschen Dichtkunst, nebst Verschiedenem, das daraus folget*, in *Sämmtliche Werke*, vol. 9, 429. And since, according to Grimm's *Wörterbuch*, the use of the adjective "volksthümlich" is first attested in Friedrich de la Motte Fouqué's book *Altsächsischer Bildersaal* (Nürnberg: J.L. Schrag, 1818), vol. I, XII, I think it is safe to say that "Volksthum," like

so many other German words, was invented as such and by none other than Jahn himself.

25 Jahn, *Volksthum*, 179–80.

26 Ibid., 4–5.

27 Ibid., 349.

28 Ibid., 354.

29 Ibid., 382.

30 Ibid., 27.

31 Benedict Richard O'Gorman Anderson, *Imagined Communities: Reflections on the Origin and Spread of Nationalism* (London: Verso, 1991).

32 Jahn, *Volksthum*, xi.

33 Referring to part I, section 6, of Christoph Meiners's book *Geschichte des weiblichen Geschlechts* [*History of the Female Gender*], Erster bis Vierter Theil (Hannover: Hellwingsche Hofbuchhandlung, 1788–1800), Jahn writes: "The more universally human a people the greater its homage to the female gender. 'German' ought to be the third holy word which, after father and mother, every little girl should babble in all languages. There has never been a people that has done more for the female gender." Ibid., 432–3.

34 Ibid., 216.

35 Ibid., 306–7.

36 Ibid., 307.

37 Ibid., 263.

38 Ibid., 264.

39 Ibid., 182.

40 Ibid., 314–15.

41 In his book on *Volksthum*, 193, Jahn had used the traditional term *voltigiren*, "equestrian vaulting," for this exercise. Six years later, because all French words were now taboo for him, he coined a new word: "schwingen."

42 Jahn, *Turnkunst*, 36.

43 Ibid., 38.

44 The German reads: "Wälschen ist Fälschen, Entmannen der Urkraft, Vergiften des Sprachquell, Hemmung der Weiterbildsamkeit, und gänzliche Sprachsinnlosigkeit." Ibid., xxii.

45 See chapter III.7 of Jahn, *Volksthum*: "Allgemeine Ausbildung der Muttersprache," [General Formation of the Mother Tongue], 99–100.

46 Jahn, *Turnkunst*, xliv.

47 In paragraph 9 of this essay, Leibniz writes: "I find that the Germans have already elevated their language in all things that can be grasped with the five senses and which are also available to the common man; particularly so in physical matters, as well as in art and in crafts because the learned scholars were almost exclusively occupied with Latin leaving their mother tongue to its own devices, a language which nonetheless was run quite

well by the so-called non-learned as they were following the teachings of Nature. And I would opine that there is no language in the world which speaks richer and stronger about ore and other mines, for instance, than the German. The same could be said of all the other common occupations and professions, of the hunt and hunting, of sailing and the like. Just as all the Europeans who are sailing the world ocean borrowed the names of the winds and many other nautical terms from the Germans, namely from the Saxonians, the Normans, the Easterlings and the Dutchmen." Gottfried Wilhelm Leibniz, "Unvorgreifliche Gedancken, betreffend die Ausübung und Verbesserung der Teutschen Sprache," in *Illustris Viri Leibnitii Collectanea Etymologica*, Hanover 1717, part II, 255–314; quoted here from http://www.staff.uni-giessen.de/gloning/tx/lbnz-ug.htm, accessed 16 January 2019, online version of the publication in *Leibniz und die deutsche Sprache (III)*, ed. Paul Pietsch, in *Wissenschaftliche Beihefte zur Zeitschrift des Allgemeinen Deutschen Sprachvereins*, series 4, vol. 30, 1908, 313–56, 360–71.

48 Jahn, *Turnkunst*, 96.

49 Ibid., iv.

50 Ibid., xxvii. Grimm's *Deutsches Wörterbuch*, s.v. *Turnen*, states explicitly that the word only has "a supposed [*vermeintlich*] Old German root."

51 Ibid., xxvi.

52 Ibid., xli; cf. http://gymmedia.com/FORUM/agforum/11-06-Jahn-Report-32-5-Terminologie-Leirich.pdf; accessed August 2016.

53 Ibid., 237.

54 Ibid., 188.

55 Ibid., 72.

56 Ibid., 121.

57 The German reads: "Da wird alle Anstrengung leicht, und die Last Lust, wo andere mit wettturnen" (Ibid., 211).

58 The German reads: "Frisch, frey, fröhlich, und fromm – ist des Turners Reichthum" (Ibid., 233). Today, the word "fromm" is mainly used in the sense of "pious," "devout" or "religious," but in Jahn's time it still had the old ring of "strong" or "courageous." See Jacob and Wilhelm Grimm's *Deutsches Wörterbuch*, s.v. "fromm."

59 Ibid., 196.

60 Though Jahn advocated the practice of "Turnen" for both boys and girls, his chapter on the spirit of the laws that govern his gymnastics focuses solely on a community of male athletes.

61 According to Grimm's *Wörterbuch*, the German hapaxlegomenon "ringfertig" originally meant "levis, agilis, expeditus," but could later also signify "heiter," cheerful.

62 Jahn, *Turnkunst*, 233–4.

63 Aristotle's *Nicomachean Ethics*, Loeb Classical Library (Cambridge, MA: Harvard University Press: 2017), 1171a.31, 572.

64 Jahn, *Volksthum*, 317.
65 Quoted after Albert Pfister, *Freiheit des Rückens – Allgemeine Wehrpflicht – Öffenlichkeit des Strafgerichts. Drei Etappen auf dem Wege militärischer Entwicklung* (Stuttgart: Deutsche Verlagsanstalt, 1896), 17–18.
66 Quoted after *Meyers Grosses Konversations-Lexikon* (Leipzig: Bibliographisches Institut, 1805–9), s.v. "Prügelstrafe." http://www.zeno.org/Meyers-1905/A/Pr%C3%BCgelstrafe?hl=prugelstrafe, accessed 22 August, 2016.
67 Jacques Lacan, *Encore*, 13 March 1973: "la jouissance de l'idiot." http://staferla.free.fr/S20/S20%20ENCORE.pdf, 65; accessed 7 May 2019.
68 Carl Schmitt, *Der Begriff des Politischen* (Munich: Duncker & Humblot, 1932), 14.
69 Jahn, *Volksthum*, 216–17.
70 Ibid., 18.
71 Ibid., 283–4.
72 Jahn, *Turnkunst*, 234–5.
73 Ibid., xvii.
74 Jahn, *Volksthum*, 216.
75 Ibid., 17
76 Jahn, *Turnkunst*, vii.
77 Ibid., ix.
78 Ibid., viii.
79 Ibid., 212.
80 Ibid., xlvi.
81 This as well as the three preceding quotes by Goethe after Grimm's *Wörterbuch*, s.v. *Turnen*.
82 Biographical details and quotes after Horst Ueberhorst, "Jahn, Friedrich Ludwig," in *Neue Deutsche Biographie* 10 (1974): 301–03, https://www.deutsche-biographie.de/gnd118556622.html#ndbcontent, accessed 7 May 2019.
83 Quoted after Friedrich Schnapp, ed., *E.T.A. Hoffmanns Briefwechsel* (Munich: Winkler, 1969), 118.
84 Ibid., 123.
85 Ibid., 189.
86 Ibid., 199.
87 Hans-Joachim Bartmuss, Eberhard Kunze and Josef Ulfkotte, eds., *Turnvater Jahn und sein patriotisches Umfeld. Briefe und Dokumente 1806–1812* (Cologne: Böhlau, 2008). "Einleitung": 13–17, quote at 14.
88 Ibid., 15.
89 Karl Kehrbach, "Deutsche Sprache und Litteratur am Philanthropien zu Dessau (1775 bis 1793)," in *Philologische Studien. Festgabe für Eduard Sievers zum 1. Oktober 1896* (Max Niemeyer: Halle an der Saale 1896), 374–400, quote at 399–400.
90 "How reunification [*Wiedervereinigung*] should be possible again? is – now – hard to see. May the all-father rule on it [*Allvater mag's walten*]!"

Jahn, *Volksthum*, 114. According to Grimm's *Wörterbuch* (which does not list the quote from Jahn's book), "Wiedervereinigung" was coined in the seventeenth century, but more frequently used only in the second half of the eighteenth century. Thus, it could well be that Jahn was the first to apply it to the history and politics of Germany, where it has played such an important role in the second half the twentieth century.

91 Franz Kafka, *Der Verschollene*, ed. Jost Schillemeit (Frankfurt am Main: S. Fischer, 1983), 112: *Turner* = gymnast, *Vorturner* = model or leading gymnast. It is worth noting, however, that in this same context, Kafka refers to yet another form of sports, in fact, the latest trend of sports in his time. Because Karl Rossmann declines to follow his host Pollunder's daughter Klara to her room, she starts what at first seems a wrestling match, a match that she easily wins not only because of her "sports-steeled body," but above all because she is trained in a brand-new form of martial arts. "'I feel sorry for you,' she says, 'and you are an acceptably pretty boy, and if you had learned Jiu-Jitsu, you probably would have thrashed me through and through'" (91). This is a reference to H. Irving Hancock's book *Jiu-Jitsu Combat Tricks: Japanese Feats of Attack and Defence in Personal Encounter* (New York and London: C.P. Putnam's Sons, The Knickerbocker Press, 1904) , which had appeared in a German translation as early as 1910, just a bit more than two years before Kafka began work on his novel *Der Verschollene*: H. Irving Hancock, *Das Kano Jiu-Jitsu (Jiudo)* (Stuttgart: J. Hoffmann, 1910). The title of this book's last chapter (which I quote in the English original) is: "Touches in the Japanese Science of Attack and Defence – A Summary of the Best Feats for Women to Practise and to Use at Need – Final Cautions to the Student who Would be an Expert in 'Jiu-Jitsu,'" (144), which contains the following timely advice: "Several of the feats that the author has described in the present volume may be learned readily by women, and should be used by them at any time of need and in the absence of their natural protectors ... [E]specially effective for women are the jabs that may be delivered with either elbow in the short ribs of an opponent, or in the soft parts below. If a woman is annoyed by a fellow who steps up to her side in a crowded street it does not come amiss to know how to give him an effective elbow jab in the solar plexus or abdomen. The woman who can do this neatly will save herself from further annoyance" (146–7). Kafka's reference to these passages is ironic, if not cynical: it is not the boy, Karl Rossmann, who "annoys" the girl, Klara. On the contrary, she is the one who attacks. And the whole scene clearly is a replay of Karl's seduction by Johanna Brummer, his parents' maidservant, at the beginning of the novel. As a consequence, the fight has obvious sexual connotations: "'Let me go,' she whispered, her flushed face close to his, he had trouble looking at her so close she was to him, 'let me go, I will give

you something beautiful.' 'Why is she sighing like this,' Karl thought, 'I can't be hurting her, I am not pressing her hard,' and he still did not let go of her." Kafka, *Der Verschollene*, 90. For more on the introduction of jiu-jitsu to Germany, see Sarah Panzer's contribution in this volume, "Importing a German *Kampfsport*."

92 Franz Kafka, *Das Schloss*, ed. Malcolm Pasley (Frankfurt am Main: S. Fischer, 1982), 202–3. Translation based on Franz Kafka, *The Castle*, trans. Anthea Bell (Oxford: Oxford University Press, 2009), 14, however, with some changes.

93 Rilke, *Turnstunde*, 436–40.

94 Franz Kafka, *Das Urteil*, in *Drucke zu Lebzeiten*, ed. Wolf Kittler, Hans-Gerd Koch, and Gerhard Neumann (Frankfurt am Main: S. Fischer, 1994), 41–61, quote at 61.

8 Importing a German *Kampfsport*: The Reception and Practice of Japanese Martial Arts in Interwar Germany

SARAH PANZER

> The presence of mind, self-control, intrepidness, severity towards oneself and chivalry towards others, the full dedication of the entire self earned through judo builds the fighting spirit that marks its disciples throughout their entire lives. It gives them the self-confidence ... that we as a *Volk* so desperately require.[1]

During the latter half of the nineteenth century the twin motors of imperialism and globalization propelled the global diffusion of Western politics, science, industry, art – and sports, the last typically represented by the adoption of cricket across the breadth of the British Empire. The privileged status enjoyed by Western culture invariably reflected too on the sporting traditions and practices of the imperial powers. The evolution of sporting cultures in the age of empire was therefore not simply a matter of leisure and play; it was deeply embedded in the landscape of imperial modernity. In the marketplace of international sports at the turn of the century, the "winners" and "losers" were identified by their ability to conform to a certain set of values and priorities, very often the same priorities valorized within the structural framework of liberalism and capitalism. As a result, the development of modern sports, with their emphasis on increasing efficiency, rationality, and standardization, and the intrinsic value assigned to competition, mirrored the governing principles of the societies that birthed them and encouraged their global transmission. At the same time, the spread of Western sports – under the guise of benevolent internationalism – often meant that local and national sporting traditions were abandoned, delegitimated, or forced to adapt to the new "rules of the game."

Sports therefore open a unique window onto the dynamics by which nations were forced to realign their values against an emerging set of international ethical and ideological norms. This is especially true in the context of German *Sportkultur*, which is often presented as an outlier within the normal parameters of Western sporting history due to the persistence of *Turnen*, with its distinctly political program of mobilizing the disciplined healthy German body in order to unite the German nation, alongside the development of a more recognizably modern international sporting culture.[2] The ongoing tensions between these two competing definitions of sport meant that German sporting culture retained its own national identity well into the twentieth century, and that the association between sports and ethics in the context of modern Germany was often understood in starkly ideological terms as a matter of national cultural integrity.

Yet this did not necessarily mean that self-identified German sportsmen rejected all foreign sports on spec as "un-German"; indeed, the history of the reception of Japanese martial arts within German *Sportkultur* suggests that the standards for judging a sport's "foreignness" were actually much more complex. Although some supporters of jiu-jitsu and judo did highlight the importance of national origins and identities, they consistently used national labels as sliding signifiers – thus the vehemence of the claims that there was a particularly German form of jiu-jitsu – in order to address deeper concerns about the definition and purpose of sport.[3] Various forms of sporting activity and physical training were assessed, not on the basis of where they had originated, but rather by whether they possessed characteristics that could be identified and championed as "German." Questions regarding relative merit in terms of competition, fitness, and practical utility were all deployed in constructing varying definitions of what a true and authentic German sport looked like, but the central problem was invariably an ambivalence about the potential cultural cost of a wholesale acceptance of international sporting norms. These German advocates for jiu-jitsu and judo, most of whom were educated and cosmopolitan urbanites, undeniably understood themselves as modern. What they meant to articulate was not a reactionary rejection of modernity, but rather an alternative framing of modernity that recognized the value of national culture.

Ultimately, what many Germans found alluring about Japanese martial arts – and what ultimately allowed Japanese martial arts like jiu-jitsu and judo to become effectively naturalized as German over the course of the interwar era – was that they were claimed to reflect a more organic or authentic form of ethics than could be found in the other sports of that era, which were commonly represented as excessively oriented towards commercialism, professionalism, and an overly restrictive sense of rationalization. This association between martial arts and ethics in turn reinforced the association between these specific sports and German culture – in other words, they were uniquely ethical because they were German, and they were recognizably German because they possessed this ethical core. Whether they were arguing that jiu-jitsu was an authentically German form of *Kampfsport*, or theorizing about the aesthetic qualities of judo, German writers were intensely preoccupied with the presumed interdependence of national identity and moral virtue when evaluating different forms of sport. In sketching some of the ways in which this relationship was conceptualized during the interwar era, this chapter will offer an alternative lens through which to talk about the allure of ethics in sports: not with respect to the actual praxis and performance of sport, but rather as it relates to the perceived legitimacy and viability of individual sports within the modern global market.

Importing a German *Kampfsport*: Jiu-Jitsu versus Judo in Interwar Germany

German engagement with Japanese martial arts can be fairly precisely dated to the Russo-Japanese War, which many Germans who became involved in jiu-jitsu and judo retrospectively identified as the single most important event in introducing Japanese martial and physical culture to a German audience, in making a "*Völklein*, which up to this point had merely been admired for its splendid lacquer ware" heroic, not only for the scale and sophistication of their newly Westernized military and industrial capabilities, but also for "a physical endurance, tenacity, agility, and strength, as well as an energy, a presence of mind, a determination and a daring, that can only seldom be observed in such outstanding quantity."[4] During the late Wilhelmine era, jiu-jitsu in Germany developed along several parallel trajectories; besides becoming visible as a popular spectacle at circuses, fairs, and popular exhibitions, it was becoming increasingly "accessible" – both to private individuals and to representatives of state agencies – through a variety of academies, mass-produced instructional manuals, and correspondence courses with German master practitioners, the most famous of whom, Erich Rahn (1885–1973), opened his studio for jiu-jitsu in Berlin in 1906.[5]

The individuals who took courses in jiu-jitsu during this era tended to be interested in the discipline more as a form of utilitarian self-defence than as physical exercise or competitive sport. However, a 1909 essay by Martin Vogt established an important precedent for later German engagement with Japanese martial arts; in his *Dschiu-Dschitsu der Japaner – das alte deutsche Freiringen,* he juxtaposed images of standard jiu-jitsu holds and grips with woodcut images from medieval German texts on wrestling, including one illustrated by Albrecht Dürer, in order to make the rather audacious claim that jiu-jitsu more closely resembled authentic forms of German *Kampfsport* than did modern systems of boxing and wrestling, both of which had been so thoroughly modernized and "civilized" as to be essentially foreign to the true spirit of German physical culture. While Vogt never went so far as to suggest rejecting modern sport and returning to unrestricted *Kampfsport,* his evident sympathy for jiu-jitsu, both for its efficacy as a practical form of combat and as a means to reclaim an element of the German cultural inheritance, challenged the presumed intrinsic worthiness of modernization. In addition, by identifying jiu-jitsu as authentically German – in spirit if not in provenance – Vogt's text anticipated later, more radical assessments of its relationship to German culture.

Jiu-jitsu first began taking shape as an independent competitive sport during the 1920s. The National Jiu-Jitsu Association (Reichsverband für Jiu-Jitsu; RFJ) was formed in 1923 and was initially composed mostly of Rahn's students in Berlin, although it included individuals who had studied with Rahn through correspondence courses. In 1924 this group was incorporated into the Deutsche Athletik-Bund, the national association for amateur sport, and in the autumn of 1928, as part of its mission to popularize jiu-jitsu as a mainstream element of German *Sportkultur,* the RFJ established its own monthly magazine, *Jiu-Jitsu Sport.* The first issue printed a mission statement by the editorial staff regarding their envisioned role for the magazine, which was to keep individual regional clubs informed about upcoming events and to tell individual readers about the specific and unique attributes of their chosen sport – with the ultimate goal of popularizing jiu-jitsu. The editors adopted a defiant posture in their statement, referring to public scepticism and hostility from other, more established, organized sporting groups and noting that if jiu-jitsu could find support during "the times of the worst inflation, in that time when sporting activity was nearly impossible," then they could persevere through the "iron will of our sporting community."[6] This set the dominant tone for *Jiu-Jitsu Sport* during the first few years of its existence; most of its articles emphasized jiu-jitsu's innate superiority as a sport while simultaneously bemoaning the German jiu-jitsu community's view of itself as a band of marginalized outsiders. Yet even with this obvious persecution complex, the RFJ did not attempt to coordinate with its counterpart organizations in the United States and Western Europe.

Each issue featured one or two articles submitted by prominent jiu-jitsu instructors across Germany. "Die Entwicklung des Jiu-Jitsu-Sportes" by Rudolf Krotki, an instructor at the Deutsche Hochschule für Leibesübungen, appeared in the first issue; it detailed the short history of jiu-jitsu in Germany, focusing in particular on the need to distinguish more clearly between jiu-jitsu as a practical system of self-defence and jiu-jitsu as an organized sport. Echoing Vogt's argument, Krotki claimed that jiu-jitsu had actually existed, in some undeveloped form, in all pre-modern cultures. Advances in technology in the Western world had made such a system of unarmed combat largely irrelevant, he argued, but the Japanese had successfully "maintained and further developed" the discipline.[7] Krotki credited Rahn as one of the first individuals in Germany to realize the potential benefits of jiu-jitsu, but ultimately critiqued the way in which jiu-jitsu was practised in both Germany and Japan:

> The Japanese treat jiu-jitsu as sport – sport in its ideal form as the development of the body and the training of the spirit. He accepts the methods of self-defence as side effects, but they are simply developed out of the competitive sport and are not taught separately. Our clubs should similarly put sport in the foreground more than we have and practise competitive sparring, the fighting holds, throws, and techniques of falling, and only then – informally – self-defence.[8]

Krotki concluded that the formation of the RFJ, as well as the recent national jiu-jitsu tournaments in Cologne (1926) and Schweinemünde (1927), were evidence that German jiu-jitsu was "on the right track," but admitted that the Japanese were still far superior to their German counterparts, both on an institutional level and as individual sportsmen.

This deference to the Japanese system was repeated towards the end of the article, where Krotki observed that many Germans in larger cities had grown accustomed to the sight of Japanese visitors in universities, factories, and laboratories. He commented approvingly on the success of the Japanese in quickly identifying and adapting the best features of German industry and technology and attributed this to the self-awareness and flexible responsiveness learned through the study of jiu-jitsu: "We should act in the same manner, and hope that the expansion of our sport will result in a similarly agile and quick-witted national community."[9] Krotki therefore advocated that Germans use the Japanese as a model of physical and mental excellence in the same way that the Japanese had once emulated the methods and theories of German science. Ernst Fischer, a leader in Hamburg's jiu-jitsu community, struck a similar note in his article "Jiu-Jitsu, der Sport der Jugend." He echoed Krotki's contention that training in jiu-jitsu led to higher levels of mental and physical awareness, responsiveness, and flexibility. He even went so far as to predict that jiu-jitsu would eventually form "a compulsory element of the general physical development of the youth, as well as for every educated individual" in Germany.[10] Both men – and the RFJ more generally – thus understood jiu-jitsu as a necessary complement to daily life in Germany, but primarily for its value as a modern competitive sport rather than merely as a technique of self-defence.

In the early 1930s, however, jiu-jitsu faced increasing competition for the hearts and minds of German sportsmen from a new source: judo. Developed by Kano Jigoro (1860–1938) and publicly endorsed by Dr Erwin Bälz (1849–1913) as "the ideal form of gymnastics," judo quickly gained a reputation as a physical practice that cultivated in its practitioners not just physical dexterity but also strict self-discipline and moral clarity.[11] The first German club for judo opened in Frankfurt in 1922 under the supervision of Alfred Rhode, a former student of Rahn's.[12] For several years jiu-jitsu and judo coexisted relatively amicably in Germany, most likely because the still relatively small community of instructors and active participants made cooperation necessary if either discipline was to flourish. The first signs of tension appeared in the summer of 1932, when Rhode organized a separate *Judo-Sommerschule* in Frankfurt; this was exacerbated – from the perspective of the jiu-jitsu community – by the founding of a rival organization to the RFJ, the Deutsche Judo-Bund, on 11 August. In tandem with this growing institutional estrangement, a series of articles appeared in *Jiu-Jitsu Sport* during 1932–33 that suggested a steadily widening philosophical rift between the two factions. The timing of this division politically seems to have been entirely coincidental; indeed, *Jiu-Jitsu Sport* and the RFJ remained studiously apolitical during this entire debate.

Jiu-Jitsu Sport covered all of Rhode's activities during the summer of 1932 thoroughly and sympathetically, yet in the September issue an author identified only as 'Gramkau' fired the opening salvo in an emergent debate over the relative merits of jiu-jitsu and judo. The article, "Judo-Dämmerung," described both jiu-jitsu and judo, but focused on one essential point: "Let us be clear that the difference lies only in the rules of combat, not at all in the system itself."[13] This may seem an insignificant critique in retrospect, but it called into question the need for judo as an alternative discipline to jiu-jitsu – if the differences were procedural rather than intrinsic, then all of judo's claims to moral superiority were meaningless. From this starting point, the debate soon turned into a referendum as much on the relative value of native tra-dition and imported innovation as on the respective merits of jiu-jitsu and judo, with both sides claiming that their chosen sport better met the needs of the contemporary German sportsman.

By 1932 the German jiu-jitsu community had evolved its own iden-tity, distinct and separate from similar organizations in the United States and the United Kingdom. Certainly this was due at least in part to the self-consciously provincial tendencies of German *Sportkultur*, inherited from the *Turnbewegung*, which often self-consciously em-phasized the differences, however minor or self-imagined, between the German branch of a sport and its international brand. An article from January 1931 had already made the argument that German jiu-jitsu and Japanese jiu-jitsu were, in effect, two different sports, and that while most other countries had adopted Japanese jiu-jitsu as the model for practice, German jiu-jitsu was a singular and unique disci-pline.[14] Following the events of the summer of 1932, Otokar Klimek expanded upon this idea to draw clear boundaries between the foreign import judo and a form of jiu-jitsu increasingly understood as German. He referenced German jiu-jitsu's roots in self-defence and the early struggle by a few energetic instructors to popularize the sport, and he pointed out that the German jiu-jitsu organizations had few ties to their counterparts in other Western nations, concluding that "the German jiu-jitsu persists relatively isolated from other branches of sport up to the present day."[15] For these men, German jiu-jitsu's uniqueness was a point of pride, a testament to its difficult first years, and a symbol of the continuing evolution of a specifically German – yet still unequivocally modern – *Sportkultur*.

In the February 1933 issue of *Jiu-Jitsu Sport*, Alfred Rhode attempted to explain to an increasingly defensive German jiu-jitsu community why judo could be helpful, even necessary in expanding the commu-nity of practitioners. He agreed with Klimek's assessment that German jiu-jitsu had evolved out of self-defence, but to Rhode this represented a fundamental problem with the sport: "No sport can serve its pur-pose, if its ethical demands come up short. The jiu-jitsu cultivated in Germany seems to me to be based too much on mere self-defence. The moral merits that are inherent to the Japanese method must be adopted by Germany."[16] For Rhode the question of whether German jiu-jitsu was unique and special was secondary to the question of whether it was a ethically instructive discipline; he even went so far as to suggest that judo's prominence was growing internationally because it offered more to its students morally. Yet even in advocating for a greater regard for judo's "moral merits," Rhode still felt it necessary to defend himself against charges that he was acting in an "un-German" way by conforming to the demands of a foreign practice. For all the inroads international sporting culture had made into Germany by the 1930s, the German jiu-jitsu community was still aligning itself under the rubrics of *national* and *foreign* in order to settle disputes.

Franz Dauhrer had the final word on the jiu-jitsu/judo debate in the April issue, with the appropriately titled essay "Nun endlich Schluß mit dieser Debatte!" Dauhrer had little patience with any of the arguments in favour of judo, and he refuted the notion that judo was better because it was more widespread internationally: "If it comes to it, there are a total of about a dozen judo clubs in all of Europe, including Germany, and the United States – that is the entire 'internationalism.' To invoke this pathetic internationalism and to regard it as such should suggest, in addition, a great deal of naiveté and unquestioning obedience to the Japanese gentlemen."[17] Dauhrer's essay dripped with thinly veiled contempt for the moral self-regard of the judo advocates. He referred to the common belief, one once held by many leading members of the German jiu-jitsu community, that the Japanese should be regarded as role models for their superior techniques and ethics. Whereas advocates for judo had used this as a platform when pushing for a transition towards an outright adoption of Kano's system, Dauhrer rejected the basis of the claim itself. According to Dauhrer, "True, Japan is the motherland of judo, the Mongolian conception of a *Kampfsystem* that was originally adopted from China, but Germany is the motherland of German jiu-jitsu, the German conception of a system of unarmed hand-to-hand combat originating and developed in Germany."[18] For Dauhrer, jiu-jitsu was German to its very core and should be regarded as such. This small yet vocal faction of the German sporting community had thus enthusiastically adopted jiu-jitsu as its own – as German. The irony of wielding jiu-jitsu as a shield against the threat of international sport – represented in this context by judo – was apparently wasted on them.

Judo's founder Kano Jigoro visited Berlin for an extended period during the summer of 1933 in his official capacity as the Japanese representative to the International Olympic Committee.[19] Soon after arriving in the German capital, Kano agreed to an interview with the *Völkischer Beobachter* to discuss his understanding of the relationship between sport and the moral spirit of a nation. The resulting article predictably emphasized Kano's stated opposition to both communism and liberalism, but also provided insight into his perspective on the climate of modern sport globally. The interviewer and author of the article, a Dr Walther Schmitt, referred to Kano's conviction that ethics and sport should be intrinsically bound together – an ideal that he put into practice in judo – and that this synthesis of sport and morality had to serve the nation as well as the individual. Kano was quoted thus: "First the

Volk has to be introduced to the idea of the nation, every individual has to become acquainted with the grandeur and the spiritual content of his *Volk*; only then can his love and sacrifice for the nation be demanded."[20] Interestingly, considering the recent debate in Germany about judo's growing visibility, Kano rejected a universal approach to sport as culturally problematic:

> Every *Volk* has its own tradition and culture. It is therefore not possible to establish generally applicable rules in the realm of popular education [*Volkserziehung*]. What has been accomplished in Japan in this area is the close relationship between sport and ethics, a relationship that, as Dr. Kano openly states, is only surpassed by that nurtured in England.[21]

In this respect, Kano would probably have agreed with the members of the RFJ who rejected judo as foreign and therefore as fundamentally incompatible with the particular climate of German *Sportkultur*.

A Philosophy for Living: Judo and the *Körperkulturbewegung*

Even as judo became more widely practised and discussed during the early 1930s, Erich Rahn remained an influential figure. His comprehensive textbook, *Jiu-Jitsu, die unsichtbare Waffe*, was published in 1932; its second edition included, in addition to a string of testimonials by both private citizens and civil service professionals, an official endorsement of his training regimen by Carl Diem (1882–1962).[22] In an article from 1935, Rahn discussed the early history of jiu-jitsu in Germany. He admitted to embarrassment over having participated in gimmicky spectacles at circuses and vaudeville shows, yet he also articulated an endorsement of jiu-jitsu's relevance in contemporary Germany based on a rather stinging critique of the state of modern sport:

> Probably the widespread prejudice against jiu-jitsu, even among sportsmen, will not change until the connection between the sportive and the practical is obvious to everyone. Sport only first becomes "sport" for many when it degenerates, when the entire world watches with anticipation the "matches" of the "champions," when one no longer needs to exert oneself personally but merely to applaud for others. If it is required of these sportsmen that they study the architecture of the human body and to thereby conduct their training rationally, however, too many of them simply refuse.[23]

Rahn wanted jiu-jitsu to be accepted as *Sport*, but not in the way that sport had increasingly come to be defined – that is, in its modern, internationalist form. He instead advocated a version of sport that did not subsist on passive spectatorship and the excellence of the few, but rather demanded the active participation and physical and mental development of the masses. For Rahn, jiu-jitsu represented a practical system of self-cultivation and a non-competitive alternative to international mainstream sports, a stance that aligned his sympathies more with many of the leading members of Germany's *Körperkultur* than with the competitive sportsmen of the RFJ.

The *Körperkulturbewegung* during the early twentieth century is key to understanding the varied philosophies of physical training coexisting in interwar Germany. One factor that has made work on the *Körperkulturbewegung* difficult is the sheer variety of exercise and fitness regimens it encompassed – all from rhythmic gymnastics and bodybuilding to the more esoteric *Freikörperkultur* (FKK) and yoga movements were considered facets of this new "culture of the body." In many respects the movement paralleled the development of competitive sport: both valued flexibility, individualism, and self-determinism; both were predominantly urban phenomena; and both drew their participants from the new urban classes rather than from older patterns of associational culture, as the *Turnvereine* had. The most obvious difference between the two groups lay in their respective attitudes towards the fundamental purpose of physical training. Sportsmen – and women – viewed competition and individual excellence as the ultimate goal, whereas the *Körperkulturbewegung* placed a higher value on the harmonious development of the body and understood competition as counterproductive.[24] With respect to the relative demographics of the two groups, the *Körperkulturbewegung* participants tended to come from the new urban salaried workers whereas the *Sportler* were overwhelmingly more working-class. An additional twist was that the *Körperkulturbewegung* had many more female participants, a phenomenon that was mirrored in many of the jiu-jitsu courses offered in Berlin and other major cities that were either taught as co-ed or specifically aimed at the modern urban woman.[25]

Martin Pampel emerged as one of the leading advocates for judo in Germany during the 1930s; educated and employed as a lecturer at the Institut für Leibesübungen at the University of Leipzig, he was responsible for several articles in periodicals and newspapers that introduced and explained judo for a German audience. His 1935 monograph *Deutscher Kampfsport ohne Waffe (Judo)* argued that judo should function as a model for the cultivation of the German people, both physically and spiritually. Like many others writing about sport and fitness in interwar Germany, Pampel was concerned about what he viewed as the overcompartmentalization of modern life, wherein the individual was divided into "spirit, soul, and body." The solution, according to Pampel, was *Kampfsport*, which created a unified experience for both fighters and audience:

> The impulse towards the highest achievement, towards harshness against oneself, the will for victory, the delight in superiority, the pride of asserting oneself – all of this together gives *Kampfsport* the passion which is capable of sweeping away the enormous crowds of spectators, who represent all educational levels, at wrestling and boxing matches. The popularity of wrestling and boxing matches even in the metropolis is proof that the longing to defeat the personal opponent through direct physical force slumbers in every male creature.[26]

The demands of modern life had created men alienated from their physical selves; *Kampfsport*, properly regulated, sublimated the physical experience of combat into an aesthetic testament to the complete, self-realized individual.

Pampel echoed Rahn's call for a *Sportart* that did not depend solely on competition or on individual excellence, although he did identify a unifying and affirming spirit in the competitive exhibitions and championships that Rahn was so ambivalent about. Ultimately, however, he rejected many of Rahn's more utilitarian claims, such as the applicability of jiu-jitsu to self-defence, as ultimately counterproductive to winning and keeping new participants. He found the reliance on jiu-jitsu's necessity/utility (*Brauchkunst*) to be intellectually disingenuous, because it ignored the reality that most physical activity was done, not out of necessity, but rather out of pleasure; modern individuals learned to swim, not because they feared drowning, but because they enjoyed the sensation of moving through the water. As Pampel understood it, "[t]he epoch, when every physical exercise was necessity [*Brauchkunst*], natural and necessary to the preservation of the species, instinctually done and a requirement for existence in the struggle for survival, lies behind us."[27] Simply put, any attempt to justify physical exercise in terms of utility alone was intellectually dishonest, which is why jiu-jitsu had struggled for so long to find an audience in Germany. Ultimately, Pampel considered judo superior to jiu-jitsu because it provided a transcendental physical and spiritual experience rather than just a dry series of exercises.

Pampel argued for a more esoteric intentionality in support of regimes of physical training, and for this, he found judo uniquely suited. In a passage explaining his philosophy, he suggested that judo had a spiritual and existential component that supporters of jiu-jitsu had never been able to successfully claim for their sport:

> To characterize it as mental-physical is not adequate, because a spiritual element is also contained within it. The adult *Kulturmensch*, sentenced to a continual upright posture while awake, escapes this position with joy at once, so long as he is not yet fossilized [*verkalkt*], whether it is by gliding and floating on the ice, by plunging into deep snow, by jumping, diving, and cavorting in water, or whether it is by Judo on the mats. Perhaps this joyous effect is thusly explained: the upright-standing and -striding person faces merely the objective world, whereas the falling, laying, rolling person, owing to sensations that lay beyond the perceptions of our sensory organs ... aligns himself with the world, no longer feeling that he stands external to it.[28]

For Pampel, then, judo was not merely sport, but rather an entire world view, a lens through which its participants could view themselves in relation to their surroundings. Judo created for its participants a world-embracing, holistic subjectivity that moulded and perfected them physically and morally as individuals, as well as members of a national community.

For all his interest in using judo's more esoteric elements to reform contemporary German sport, Pampel was still acutely aware of the boundaries between the national and the foreign. Supporters of the RFJ rejected judo in favour of what they deemed a specifically German form of jiu-jitsu; Pampel called for judo to be similarly "Germanized." He argued that even though the example of Japan was certainly instructive, "it cannot simply be a matter of adopting a Japanese *Kulturerscheinung* ... It lies with us to build a German practice of judo."[29] In a series of articles published in 1939, Pampel explained more fully what exactly he meant by German judo. He had no intention of "Japanizing" (*japanisiern*) judo, maintaining instead that German judo should not worry about adopting Japanese innovations so long as they "are in accord with our being and our understanding of sport in general and of judo as *Kampfsport* specifically."[30] Specifically, he supported the adoption of the rules of combat used by the Japanese, both because they were logical and enforceable and because they did not pose any threat to a more specifically German conception of sport. He drew the line, however, at the more ceremonial elements of judo – for example, the bow between combatants before a fight – as fundamentally unsuitable for Germans, and suggested a firm handshake as an alternative.

There were nevertheless several key differences between Pampel's understanding of a Germanized judo and the concept of German jiu-jitsu as articulated by the contributors to *Jiu-Jitsu Sport*. The jiu-jitsu faction framed their argument in terms of pride, self-reliance, and national distinctiveness, all qualities supposedly threatened by encroaching internationalist movements and institutions. Pampel, for his part, criticized contemporary German society for its failure to uphold the cardinal moral virtues – including self-discipline, chivalry, and courage – on which it had previously prided itself, and posited that they could be regained through the more widespread practice of judo. Pampel identified a crisis of self-confidence – physical, spiritual, and moral – as Germany's fundamental weakness. In this he separated himself both from the RFJ's self-satisfied and prickly institutionalism and from Rahn's more utilitarian *Körperkultur*, thus sparking a new interpretation of the political utility of Japanese martial arts that owed more to the political traditions of the *Turnbewegung*.

Pampel's conceptualization of judo as both a physical training regime and a form of internal spiritual regeneration found acceptance among other German writers and sportsmen during the second half of the 1930s. Georg Grünewald, the author of a judo manual from 1937, introduced his work with the assertion that "physical education should be a mirror of the *Volksseele*."[31] He repeated Pampel's argument that the instrumentalization of jiu-jitsu as self-defence had hindered a broader acceptance of the discipline because it privileged *Brauchkunst* over "a proper conception of sport." As he pointed out, "[e]ven if some of the exercises could lead to physical education, all of this possible latent value is lost because the practice of the holds is tiresome and then after several weeks the participants stay away and turn instead to a different form of sport."[32] Although the practice of jiu-jitsu could accrue physical benefits to an individual through repetition of the exercises, the image of non-competitive jiu-jitsu was so heavily coloured by the concept of self-defence that many private individuals continued to approach it as such, rather than as a form of training more closely analogous to *Gymnastik* or *Leichtathletik*.

For Grünewald the answer to this dilemma was judo, with its added emphasis on ethical training (*Durchbildung*). Drawing upon his basic assumption that the spirit of a people and their form of physical training should mirror each other, he identified the Japanese as a model of "self-discipline and indestructible pose, courage, chivalry, etc.," arguing that the practice of judo had contributed to "the heroic *Lebensauffassung* of this people."[33] He maintained a clear distinction between judo, "a serious and doughty school of character," and jiu-jitsu as it existed in Germany, "a system of police holds," in order to reaffirm the common understanding of judo as a more spiritually elevated form of martial sport.

It might reasonably be assumed at this point that men like Pampel and Grünewald were merely echoing Kano Jigoro's belief that judo's ethical superiority was its greatest asset relative to other sporting disciplines, yet the broader context suggests otherwise. Kano himself had few articles or essays published in Germany, but in 1937 he contributed a piece to the Berlin arts-and-leisure magazine *die neue linie* in a special issue on Japan. His essay, "Judo, der ideale Sport," primarily addressed the historical context and technical theory behind judo, although he did explain his broader principles in an interesting and revealing paragraph towards the end of the piece:

There exist many opinions as to the goal of physical education, yet I believe that most would agree with me that health, strength, and practical benefits are the main goals. The athletic and track-and-field exercises, which are so strongly promoted across the entire world at present, should be criticized from this perspective. If these exercises are done in such a way as to either mar the harmonious development of the body or to damage the inner organs, then they have nothing in common with our conception of physical education. In my opinion the gymnastic exercises, which are just as common throughout the entire world, fail in two specific ways: they are neither interesting nor practical. Gymnastics should be improved so that every exercise expresses a particular thought, sensation, or natural movement.[34]

For Kano, then, the essence of judo's superiority was embedded in the principle of "maximum effectiveness [*Wirksamkeit*]," not in its moral or ethical principles. For all of his German acolytes' obsession over the spiritual value of judo, Kano himself was much more interested in creating a scientific form of fitness training that in practice would have had much more in common with the spirit of German *Körperkulturbewegung*.

Martial Arts: Jiu-Jitsu/Judo and the *Volksgemeinschaft*

For much of the early twentieth century the German jiu-jitsu/judo community did not involve itself in party politics, even if many of the issues they debated carried a distinct ideological tenor. Indeed, the overall impression of the community's activities and priorities suggests a high degree of continuity between the Weimar era and the National Socialist state. This is not to say, however, that the language used within this literature ignored the broader ideological climate of German society, or that the political institutions of the respective German states overlooked the utility of jiu-jitsu. The National Socialist state's attitude towards associational jiu-jitsu was not measurably different from that of its predecessors; the RFJ was reorganized as part of the general *Gleichschaltung* of all social and athletic organizations, but the group's leadership largely stayed in place, and there was none of the immediate state-directed intervention into its affairs that other civil or sporting organizations experienced.[35] Erich Rahn retained his position as an instructor for the police and military and remained one of the pre-eminent authorities on jiu-jitsu in Germany into the post-1945 era. Moreover, the publications about jiu-jitsu did not change noticeably in their content or in their framing of the central concepts of national and international, traditional and modern. Indeed, rather than challenging or undermining the position of jiu-jitsu and judo in the broader context of German sports and leisure, the Nazi state recognized and incorporated both into its own ideological projects.

In 1937 the Nazi leisure organization Kraft durch Freude (Strength through Joy) released a series of promotional posters advertising some of its offerings in physical education and sport. Most of the posters depicted, in striking graphic images, mainstream forms of modern sport such as swimming, horseback riding, gymnastics, and general physical training (*Leibesübungen*). Included in this series was a poster for jiu-jitsu, a poster that presented jiu-jitsu in precisely the same semiotic code as the other sports – a stylized graphic image on a monochromatic background, with only limited captioning.[36] Jiu-jitsu was thus presented as a known quantity to the German public, essentially equivalent in its ability to be recognized and understood from a single image. In its effective erasure of difference, this poster reflects the extent to which jiu-jitsu had been successfully adapted – and adopted – as German. Significantly, these images were presented in visual language that was unequivocally modernist, which again speaks to the central problem of modernity within the evolving position of Japanese martial arts in Germany.

It was not just the Nazi *Volksgemeinschaft* that incorporated jiu-jitsu into its repertoire of physical training programs; the long-standing ties between law enforcement in Germany and jiu-jitsu were also renewed, albeit in a slightly amended form. The SS, in keeping with its carefully cultivated position as the Nazi state's racial and social elite, incorporated jiu-jitsu as a complement to its other forms of athletic training. Among the seven training groups offered by the SS, jiu-jitsu was placed – along with wrestling and weightlifting – in the category of "heavy athletics" (*Schwerathletik*).[37] This makes it more difficult to assess the number of jiu-jitsu specialists within the SS, because most of the administrative papers refer only to the broader sport grouping. Although additional scholarly work on this topic is needed to offer more concrete conclusions, it does appear that jiu-jitsu was an option for SS officers wishing to expand their physical training, both in the context of personal improvement and as it concerned their status within the military/policing administration of the National Socialist state.

During the summer of 1938, the Deutsch-Japanische Gesellschaft (DJG), an organization devoted to improving mutual understanding and cooperation between the two nations, staged in coordination with the German Youth Ministry (Reichsjugendführung) a tour of Germany by fourteen students selected from eight of Japan's elite universities specifically for their skills in either judo or kendo. Although the DJG had expressed a specific interest in Japanese sport since 1935, the 1938 tour was their first campaign designed specifically to promote them within Germany.[38] The group arrived in Munich on 11 May and spent two and a half weeks touring Germany's major cities, departing 30 May from Cologne on their way to Marseille via Paris.[39] The highlight of the trip was the group's participation in a regional rally (*Gebietsaufmarsch*) of the Hitler Youth in Leipzig, but they also gave public exhibitions of their skills, socialized with the local HJ chapters at special meetings, and visited specially selected sport-related sites in all the cities they toured.

The group was greeted upon their arrival in Munich by Obergebietsführer Emil Klein and Morio Miyamoto, a liaison between Japanese youth organizations and the Hitler Youth, who accompanied the group during the tour.[40] On 13 May they attended a screening of Leni Riefenstahl's *Olympia* at the Ufa-Palast and were guests at a dinner hosted by the Japanese General Consulate at Munich's famous Hofbräuhaus.[41] Their exhibition on 14 May was attended by many of Munich's political and sporting elite and received an enthusiastic write-up in the Munich edition of the *Völkischer Beobachter*: "An appreciative audience ... experienced several extraordinarily instructive hours, during which the sporting merit, as well as the philosophical [*weltanschaulich*] foundation, of the sport of judo was demonstrated in the most impressive manner."[42] After leaving Munich the group travelled to Nuremberg, where they again met with local Hitler Youth groups, gave demonstrations of their respective sports, and did some local sightseeing. After three days in Nuremberg they spent two days in Dresden, with a short excursion to Chemnitz.[43]

The group arrived in Leipzig on 20 May, where they stayed at the Institut für Leibesübungen in Leipzig.[44] They were welcomed by Professor Hermann Altrock (1887–1980), a scholar of the history of sport in Japan.[45] They marched in the HJ's rally on 21–22 May and were officially received by Baldur von Schirach (1907–74) in his role as the Reich's Youth Leader (Jugendführer des Deutschen Reiches).[46] Their active participation was a physical representation of the tour's stated mission – to strengthen the relationship between Germany and Japan's respective youth organizations – and was approvingly noted in most press coverage of the event.[47] The significance of the group's participation in the rally, as opposed to passive spectatorship from the stands, should not be underestimated. The visual impact of Japanese university students marching alongside German HJ members would not have gone unnoticed, either by the other participants or by the audience. For all of the tensions in the German–Japanese diplomatic relationship precipitated by Nazi racial policy, this gesture of creating room for Japanese sportsmen in a Nazi ideological space suggested a more expansive vision of mutual recognition, in this context based on a shared appreciation for sport.

Upon their arrival in Berlin the Japanese students toured the Olympic facilities, then held a training session at the Police Sportverein.[48] Other visits included the HJ's Reichsführerschule in Potsdam; they gave two exhibitions in Berlin, a private one for the Reichsstudentenführung at the Humboldt-Klub on the 25th and a public one on the 26th at the Reichssportsfeld.[49] The public exhibition was coordinated, like all of the similar events on the tour, with the local chapter of the Hitler Youth. The Japanese students first sparred among themselves, after which there were competitive bouts between the Japanese *Meister* and challengers from Berlin's Polizeisportverein. Finally, the German national champion demonstrated self-defence techniques against the European champion.[50]

A report on the public exhibition appeared in the 28 May issue of the *Berliner Tageblatt*; the article, besides recounting the events of the evening, attempted to situate judo and kendo in a broader context for those audience members who were unfamiliar with the sports. The author explained that

> [j]udo, the art of self-defence, and kendo, Japanese sword fencing, are not "sport" in the general sense. They are the expression of a spirit, within which the youth of Japan are raised, a spirit that keeps the glorious tradition of Japanese history alive, and which bears the highest ideals of courage, chivalry, and consistency of character as its banner.[51]

This distinction drawn between sport and judo/kendo, while not explicated, suggested a conception of sport as something more mundane, less symbolically charged. The author, who did not possess any obvious connection to the German community of fans of Japanese sports, was much more drawn to the dramatic kendo bouts than to the judo matches, but his impressions of both disciplines echoed the language of German judo advocates. He described the preparation for the kendo bouts as "ritualistic, calm, and ceremonial," and noted in particular the mutual bow at the end of the bout, in order to "bear witness to the chivalry and courage of the opponent."[52] Interestingly, he compared the kendo matches to "scenes from the duelling floors [*Paukböden*] of German students," which suggests an attempt to render kendo as immediately familiar – even banal – to his audience. This comparison between kendo and the duelling fraternities of Imperial Germany does, however, point to a significant shift in the symbolic weight of jiu-jitsu as Germany prepared for war.

If initial German interest in jiu-jitsu had been spurred by the unexpected success of the Japanese fighting forces during the Russo-Japanese War, the evolution of both jiu-jitsu and judo during the interwar era was characterized by a perceptible "demilitarization," as they were transformed from martial arts (*Kampfsport*) into leisure activities. On the eve of the Second World War, however, the paramilitary side of jiu-jitsu assumed a visibility that it had not possessed since the Russo-Japanese War. In his 1939 textbook on jiu-jitsu and judo, Josef Diwischek framed jiu-jitsu quite literally as a weapon: "Within the many branches of sport, which together can be identified as *Kampfsport*, there are only two that are actually suited as defence and as a weapon against an opponent who does not uphold any rules of engagement or other regulations. They are boxing and jiu-jitsu."[53] With the outbreak of war, many German sporting organizations were forcibly and drastically scaled back, both in terms of financial support and in the scale and frequency of events and tournaments organized.

The tacit ideological consensus of the sporting community – built over the preceding six years – meant that articles published about Japanese sports during the Second World War were more uniform, both ideologically and with respect to the essential nature of martial arts. Rather than continuing the debate over the relative "Germanness" of jiu-jitsu and judo, the wartime literature returned the discussion to the historic nature of Japanese *Kampfsport*. Alfons Mainka, to give one example, described judo as Japan's "secret weapon" in its ongoing military actions in East Asia:

Judo has become the fighting style of the Japanese and demands even from youth full dedication, determination, courage and severity, or the militant bearing that we would also require of our youth through boxing,

wrestling, and martial games. The influence of judo on the strengthening of the military will of the Japanese *Volk* cannot be overestimated. The
naturally small Japanese is able, through the clever application of Judo
holds, to defeat even the physically dominant – larger – opponent. And
in a sporting fight, as in the fate-determining struggles of war, the Japanese man always find the slogan of judo in his heart: "Isame, kuro obi,"
Frischauf, you black belts! From an ominous fate shall you rescue Japan![54]

With this article, German perceptions of jiu-jitsu came, in effect, full
circle: from its initial reception in 1905 as the secret to Japan's victory
over Russia to its transformation into, variably, a form of self-defence,
a competitive sport, a physical training regimen, a moral philosophy,
and finally back to its original identity as an explicitly martial art. This
transformation was duly noted by the Allied powers, which banned
jiu-jitsu and judo, along with boxing, wrestling, and other "military
and para-military sports," during the postwar occupation of Germany;
the ban lasted until 1950, whereupon the indefatigable Erich Rahn
promptly reopened his Berlin academy.[55]

Conclusion

In making the case for jiu-jitsu and judo, German supporters of these
disciplines specifically identified and claimed their essential qualities –
whether the efficiency of jiu-jitsu or the moral aesthetics of judo – as
German. Explicitly or implicitly, these claims rested on the presump-
tion that Japanese martial arts were distinct in their moral qualities
from other sports as currently practised in Germany and in Europe
more generally, and that it was precisely these attributes that marked
them as necessary for the cultivation of a more authentically German
modern *Sportkultur*. The process of introducing and adapting Japanese
martial arts to Germany during the early twentieth century should
therefore be understood as a process of selective appropriation, as well
as naturalization. In this way, German sportsmen were able to claim
the ethical or physical attributes of these sports as, quite literally, their
own. Given that this rhetoric came at a time when German national
self-confidence was at a low ebb, its appeal should be obvious. Yet it is
also significant that these were martial sports and were quite explicitly
discussed and represented as such; for all the talk of self-restraint and
chivalry in this literature it is undeniably clear that the appeal of these
particular sports was also embedded in the contemporary German
fascination with the *samurai* and *bushido*.[56] Martial arts were successfully naturalized as *Kampfsport* during this era because they offered

the immediate allure of sports as a form of personal cultivation – both physical and mental – as well as an ethical component that addressed German anxieties about the continued viability of national culture in an age of internationalism.

NOTES

1 Martin Pampel, *Deutscher Kampfsport ohne Waffe (Judo)* (Leipzig; Berlin: B.G. Teubner, 1935), 24.
2 Christiane Eisenberg, *"English sports" und deutsche Bürger: Eine Gesellschaftsgeschichte 1800–1939* (Paderborn: Schöningh, 1999); Allen Guttmann, *From Ritual to Record: The Nature of Modern Sport* (New York: Columbia University Press, 2004). See also Kittler, "A Well Trained Community," in this volume for a more extended discussion of *Turnen* as a system designed to "control, regulate, correct, improve, and ... discipline each and every movement which the human body can perform."
3 Jiu-jitsu developed as a method of unarmed combat brought to Japan from mainland Asia and cultivated by the samurai; its basic principles involve manipulating an opponent's balance and physical pressure points in order to subdue or injure him or her. The mantra often repeated in reference to jiu-jitsu is that "victory comes from surrender"; this refers to the various techniques used in the discipline to turn an opponent's strength or advantage against them, as opposed to attacking them directly. Throws, joint locks, pins, and holds are all common techniques used in the discipline; by contrast, karate and other Asian martial arts utilize kicks and strikes much more extensively, with the ultimate goal being either to bring the opponent into submission or to cause enough pain to force a surrender. Judo is a modern derivative of jiu-jitsu. Although the technical distinctions between jiu-jitsu and judo are somewhat more complicated than space here permits, there is a very clear difference between the two words in their Japanese context. The word 'jitsu/jutsu' suggests a more mechanical technique, whereas 'dô' literally means "way" and is mostly used in reference to religious or ethical doctrine (e.g., Bushidô = Way of the Warrior).
4 Martin Vogt, *Dschiu-Dschitsu der Japaner – das alte deutsche Freiringen* (München: Carl Aug. Seyfried & Comp., 1909), 5.
5 Klaus-Dieter Matschke and Herbert Velte, *100 Jahre Jiu-Jitsu/Ju-Jutsu und Judo in Deutschland (Eine Chronik von 1905 bis 2005)* (Vierkirchen: Schramm Sport GmbH, 2005), 37.
6 "Zum Geleit!" *Jiu-Jitsu Sport* 1, no. 1 (October 1928): 1.
7 Rudolf Krotki, "Die Entwicklung des Jiu-Jitsu-Sportes," in *Jiu-Jitsu Sport* 1, no. 1 (October 1928): 2.

8 Ibid., 2.

9 Ibid., 3.

10 Ernst Fischer, "Jiu-Jitsu, der Sport der Jugend," in *Jiu-Jitsu Sport* 1, no. 1 (October 1928): 3.

11 In Bälz's words, Kano had "won for jiu-jitsu a moral side and cultivated it in that he taught the strictest self-control, not only in regard to the physical but also in relationship to the character." Erwin Bälz, "Einführung zur deutschen Ausgabe," in H.J. Hancock and Katsukuma Higashi, *Das Kano Jiu-Jitsu (Jiudo)* (Julius Hoffmann Verlag: Stuttgart, 1906), xiv.

12 Bernd Wedemeyer-Kolwe, *"Der neue Mensch." Körperkultur im Kaiserreich und in der Weimarer Republik* (Würzburg: Königshausen & Neumann, 2004), 308.

13 Gramkau, "Judo-Dämmerung," *Jiu-Jitsu Sport* 5, no. 6 (September 1932): 3.

14 "Japanisches und Deutsches Jiu-Jitsu," *Jiu-Jitsu Sport* 3, no. 10 (January 1931): 3.

15 Otokar Klimek, "Judo-Dämmerung," *Jiu-Jitsu Sport* 5, no. 8 (November 1932): 5.

16 Alfred Rhode, "Warum Judo?" *Jiu-Jitsu Sport* 5, no. 11 (February 1933): 6.

17 Franz Dauhrer, "Nun endlich Schluß mit dieser Debatte!" *Jiu-Jitsu Sport* 6, no. 1 (April 1933): 3.

18 Ibid., 3.

19 In addition to his role in revitalizing Japan's historic sports, Kano played a critical role in integrating Japan into the growing international sporting community. He formed the Imperial Japanese Amateur Sports Association (*Dai Nihon Taaiku Kyôkai*) in 1911, which became the central body responsible for selecting the members of Japan's Olympic squads. He was the first Asian member of the IOC and accompanied the Japanese team to Stockholm, Antwerp, Los Angeles, and Berlin, where he successfully won the 1940 Games for Tokyo. Although ambivalent about judo's representation in the Olympic Games, he did advocate for its inclusion as an exhibition sport in the Los Angeles and Berlin Games. Judo was set to premiere as a competitive sport in the 1940 Tokyo Games; after their cancellation, the sport remained off the official schedule until the 1964 Olympics, also in Tokyo. Inoue Shun, "The Invention of the Martial Arts: Kanô Jigorô and Kôdôkan Judo," in *Mirror of Modernity: Invented Traditions of Modern Japan*, ed. Stephen Vlastos (Berkeley: University of California Press, 1998), 163–73.

20 Dr Walther Schmitt, "Exz. Professor Dr. Jigoro Kano in Berlin," in *Völkischer Beobachter (Norddeutsche Ausgabe)* no. 168 (17 June 1933), Erstes Beiblatt.

21 Ibid.

22 Diem had recently been promoted to General Secretary of the German Sports Committee for Physical Exercise (*Deutsche Reichausschuss für Leibesübungen*) and was a key figure in negotiating the divergent visions

offered by *Sport* and *Turnen*. He is perhaps best known today for his role in organizing the infamous 1936 Berlin Olympic Games. For recent work on Diem, his importance to the history of German sport, and the controversy surrounding his role in the Olympic movement, see Wolfgang Benz, ed., "Erinnerungspolitik oder kritische Forschung? Der Streit um Carl Diem," *Zeitschrift für Geschichtswissenschaft* 59, no. 3 (2011).

23 Erich Rahn, "Jiu-Jitsu, die unsichtbare Waffe," *Westermanns Monatshefte* 80, no. 9 (1935): 97.

24 For more discussion of this, see: Wedemeyer-Kolwe, *"Der neue Mensch,"* 334.

25 Marga Garnich, "Jiu-Jitsu als Selbstverteidigung im Dienste der Frau," *Velhagen & Klasings Monatshefte* 51, no. 6 (February 1937): 629–33.

26 Pampel, *Deutscher Kampfsport ohne Waffe*, 2.

27 Ibid., 13.

28 Ibid., 23.

29 Ibid., 20.

30 Martin Pampel, "Judo auf Japanisch," *Kraftsport. Illustrierte Wochenschrift für Schwerathletik* 3, no. 16 (19 April 1939), 14.

31 Georg Grünewald, *Judo Kampfsportschule* (Kempten im Allgäu: Otto Oechelhäuser Verlag, 1937), 3.

32 Ibid., 5.

33 Ibid., 7–8.

34 Jigoro Kano, "Judo, der ideale Sport," in *die neue linie* 8, no. 5 (January 1937): 2.

35 Eisenberg, *"English sports" und deutsche Bürger*, 341.

36 Heinemann Lothar, "Jiu-Jitsu mit Kraft durch Freude" (Berlin: Verlag der Deutschen Arbeitsfront, 1937). Bundesarchiv Plak 003-018-007.

37 Berno Bahro, *Der SS-Sport. Organisation, Funktion, Bedeutung* (Paderborn: Ferdinand Schöningh, 2013), 93.

38 Protokoll über die 1. Sitzung des Sportausschusses am 14.12.35. BArch R64IV 57, 36.

39 Abschrift 30.5.38/We. Rundreise der Japanischen Sportlergruppe vom 12.–30. Mai 1938. BArch R64IV 57, 6–7.

40 "Japaner Gäste des Reichsjugendführer," *Völkische Beobachter (Münchener Ausgabe)*, No. 132 (12 May 1938), 6; "Japanische Judokämpfer in München," *Münchener Neueste Nachrichten*, No. 132 (12 May 1938), 6.

41 "Japaner zeigen ihren Kampfstil," *Münchener Neueste Nachrichten*, No. 133 (13 May 1938), 16.

42 "Jiu-Jitsu – Judo – Kendo. Einzigartige Vorführungen japanischer Studenten in München," *Völkischer Beobachter (Münchener Ausgabe)*, No. 137 (17 May 1938), 8.

43 "Besuch aus Fernost. Japanische Sportstudenten als Gäste der HJ," *Dresdner Neueste Nachrichten* (19 May 1938); "Japanische Jungsportler. Siebzehn japanische Sportstudenten besuchten Chemnitz," *Chemnitzer*

Tageszeitung (22 May 1938); "Nippons Jugend in Dresden zu Gast," *Dresd-ner Neueste Nachrichten* (20 May 1938).

44 "Japanische Studenten in Leipzig," *Berliner Börsen-Zeitung*, No. 237 (22 May 1938).

45 One of the more interesting documents to emerge out of the aborted 1940 Tokyo Olympics was a two-volume collection of lectures on Japanese culture by staff at the University of Leipzig, published in 1937 under the title *Japan und die XII. Olympischen Spiele 1940*. The preface was contributed by Ambassador Count Mushakoji, and Altrock wrote the introduction. For more on Altrock, see Hans Joachim Teicher, "Altrock und Diem – zwei vergleichbare Biographien," in *Der deutsche Sport auf dem Weg in die* Moderne, ed. Michael Krüger (Berlin: Lit Verlag, 2009), 375–84.

46 "Japanische Gäste der Hitlerjugend. Sie nehmen am Gebietsaufmarsch in Leipzig Teil," *Neue Leipziger Zeitung* (20 May 1938).

47 "Baldur von Schirach spricht zu Sachsens HJ," *Leipziger Neueste Nach-richten* (22 May 1938).

48 "Japanische Sportstudenten in Berlin," *Berliner Börsen-Zeitung*, No. 243 (26 May 1938); "Vierzehn japanische Sportgäste," *Berliner Tageblatt*, No. 243–4 (25 May 1938).

49 "Japanische Sportstudenten in Berlin," *Deutsche Allgemeine-Zeitung*, No. 243 (26 May 1938).

50 Programm für den Deutsch-Japanischen Gemeinschaftsabend am 26.5.1938. BArch R64IV 57, 8. "Deutsch-japanischer Gemeinschaftsabend," *Deutsche Allgemeine-Zeitung*, No. 245 (28 May 1938).

51 "Erziehung im Samurai-Geist. Japanische Studenten führten Judo und Kendo im Reichssportfeld vor," *Berliner Tageblatt*, No. 248–9 (28 May 1938), 7.

52 Ibid.

53 Josef Diwischek, *Jiu-Jitsu und Judo. Mit 131 Ill* (Wien: Ostmärkische Zeitungsverlags-Gesellschaft, 1939), 5.

54 Alfons Mainka, "Judo, der japanische Nationalsport," *Politische Leibeserzie-hung* 8, no. 1 (18 January 1941), 12.

55 Matschke and Velte, *100 Jahre Jiu-Jitsu/Ju-Jutsu und Judo in Deutschland*, 52.

56 This phenomenon, which first emerged during the Russo-Japanese War as a means of explicating Meiji Japan's successful modernization, departed from earlier forms of European engagement with Japanese culture in its insistence that the German and Japanese national cultures were similar enough as to be mutually recognizable and thus potentially transferrable. Sarah Panzer, "Prussians of the East: Samurai, Bushido, and Japanese Honor in the German Imagination, 1905–1945," *Bulletin of the German Historical Institute* 58 (Spring 2016): 47–69.

9 The Ethics and Allure of the Foul in Football

ANNETTE VOWINCKEL

When I was a child my family used to watch football whenever a European or World Cup took place. My father would cheer for the German team – not fanatically, for he is a rather calm person, but in any case unconditionally. My mother, in contrast, would scold anybody playing foul, no matter which team the player belonged to. When Germany won the World Cup in 1974 (I was eight years old) my father was enthusiastic even though the Dutch had played a better match; my mother, however, stuck with the attitude that football (as much as watching football) is somehow uncivilized: as if to confirm her aversion, all male family members got drunk that day. As a child I tried to reconcile the two views: I wanted the German team to win as long as they played a fair game. It took several decades for me to accept that fouls are not "evil" in ethical terms but are integral to any football match, and that eliminating them might lead to football being fair but boring. Less ethics (in the sense of distinguishing between "good" and "evil") enhances football's specific allure (defined as the ability to cause a state of complete immersion).

To unfold my argument, I will first explain the official rules regulating foul play in football. I will then discuss some paradigmatic cases of foul playing. Third, I will explain why any Platonic approach to football involves a contradiction in terms and why we are well advised to draw on an Aristotelian notion of performative action in order to grasp the allure of football. I take a brief look at football fan culture and address its specific partiality when it comes to judging foul play. I will then present my conclusions.

FIFA Rules Regulating the Foul

In the late fifteenth century William Shakespeare used the term "foul play" in order to describe behaviour that differed from "fair play" as just and honourable conduct. Today, the terms "fair" and "foul" play commonly describe the opposition between a practice that conforms with the rules of a sport and one that violates those rules.[1] Common forms of playing foul in sports are, according to Sigmund Loland, "cheating," the "professional foul," and "play-acting." Loland defines cheating as using "means outside of the rule system of a sport" and thus producing an "unfair exclusivity."[2] To restore justice, the competition itself must be restored – for instance, through a free kick and the attribution of moral blame to the cheater. Loland speaks of a professional foul if a player "violates the rules intentionally and openly and accepts the penalty with the rationale of a long-term advantage for him or her, or for the team."[3] Play-acting, in contrast, is a way of pretending that one has been fouled and "has been developed into an art for some players."[4] While I do agree with Loland that there are different categories of foul playing, I will argue that it is not merely a violation of the rules but also part of the particular allure of sport, and I will take football as an example.

According to FIFA rule no. 12 ("Fouls and Misconduct"), a direct free kick is awarded to the opposing team if a player commits any of the following offences: he/she charges, jumps at, kicks or attempts to kick, pushes, strikes, or attempts to strike (including head-butt), tackles or challenges, trips or attempts to trip a player of the opposing party.[5] It is further forbidden to hold an opponent, to "impede an opponent with contact," to spit at the opponent, and to "handle the ball deliberately." These offences are likewise followed by a direct free kick for the opposing team.

Further sanctions depend on whether a foul was committed carelessly, recklessly, or with excessive force. A foul is careless if the player "shows a lack of attention or consideration when making a challenge or acts without precaution"; it does not need to be sanctioned any further. A foul is reckless if the player "acts with disregard to the danger to, or consequences for, an opponent"; such a foul must be cautioned. Finally, "excessive force is when a player exceeds the necessary use of force and endangers the safety of an opponent"; a player using excessive force "must be sent off."[6]

In 1970, FIFA introduced the red and yellow cards in order to visibly mark the difference between a careless, a reckless, and an excessive foul. In times of black-and-white television the referee would pull the yellow card from a shirt pocket, and the red card from a pants pocket, which made it easier for the audience to tell one from the other. In German the red card was thus named *Arschkarte* (butt card), a term that has since migrated into colloquial language – meaning, that somebody who was shown this card had bad luck.

Cautionable offences are, among others: delaying the restart of a play, dissenting from the referee by word or action, not keeping enough distance from an opponent, "feigning injury or pretending to have been fouled," committing a foul or handling the ball "to interfere with or stop a promising attack," and "verbally distract[ing] an opponent during play or at restart."[7] Sending-off offences are: deliberately handling the ball in order to prevent the opposing team from scoring, making a serious foul play, spitting at any person, using "offensive, insulting, or abusive language and/or gestures," and drawing a second caution in one and the same match.[8]

In theory, the rules are clear; in practice, they severely challenge the referee's faculty of judgment, for he/she has to rate not only the visible action but also the player's (supposed) intention. The referee cannot read thoughts and so must rely on intuition and experience. This is particularly tricky when, for example, a careless foul leads to a severe injury of the opposing player or the referee suspects a dive.

Besides listing what is forbidden in football, we can further distinguish various "narrative" categories of the foul. These categories are not defined by the rules; rather, they are based on common sense and framed by the situation in which a foul is committed. Most of all they are part of radio and television commentators' repertoire – thus, audiences are very familiar with them. The first category is the *offensive foul* (German: *Stürmerfoul*). Unless things get too brutal, this kind of foul is ordinarily regarded as having been committed in the heat of the battle. In the eye of the beholder (especially the fan of the offensive team), it is a rather trivial offence because the aim is not to hurt or cheat the opponent but to score a goal – and scoring goals is, after all, the main task of an offensive player.

The second category is the *professional foul* (German: *taktisches* [tactical] *foul*, which seems even more accurate) It is often committed in the midfield in order to disrupt an offensive move on the part of the opponent and to gain time for rearranging the defence.[9] The tactical foul often involves pulling the shirt or crossing the opponent's way and seeking physical contact. In the moral hierarchy of the foul it ranges somewhat lower, for it seems more unfair or pettier, in any case more calculating, than an offensive foul emerging in the heat of the moment. The so-called emergency break is a step up from the tactical foul, and since it is by nature brutal, it is often sanctioned by a yellow or red card; in the penalty area it naturally prompts a penalty.

The revenge foul differs substantially from the former three: it can be any kind of inappropriate action such as hitting, kicking, pulling, biting, or verbally offending the opponent. It is widely considered to be a rather despicable kind of foul because taking revenge – especially out of frustration – contradicts the idea of fair play.

The accidental foul, by contrast, can result from a lack of body control or from a false estimation of space and speed. Interestingly, the body language of any foul is usually that of "sorry, I didn't mean to" (indicated by a gesture of raising both hands over the head), even if it was not accidental. So in a strict sense we have to distinguish between the "real" accidental foul and the feigned accidental foul. In the ethical hierarchy, it ranks somewhere in the middle, for it is not evil but reveals a certain amount of physical incompetence, or a character flaw.

The least controversial category of the foul seems to be the *violent foul*: a player hits, kicks, or bites an opponent, and anybody would agree that this kind of action is intolerable. Yet as we will see, what is tricky here is that it is sometimes not clear what has prompted the violent foul. It may be an unacceptable outburst of violence, but it may also be a very human reaction to a verbal or physical insult.

Last but not least, we should mention the dive – a very special kind of foul. According to Wikipedia, a dive is "an attempt ... to gain an unfair advantage by falling to the ground and possibly feigning an injury," and a dive in the penalty area must be sanctioned. Even if there is no physical contact between the offensive and the defensive player, the referee still needs to guess whether the defensive player has stumbled or has gone down intentionally. Any misjudgment may lead to a severe distortion of the game's result, not least because the average number of goals scored is rather low in football (since 1954, the average number of goals in a World Cup game has been 2.84).[10]

Players who admit that they stumbled without interference from the opponent are candidates for fair play awards. In 1997, Robbie Fowler of FC Liverpool got a penalty after being tripped by Arsenal London's goalkeeper David Seaman. Fowler protested the referee's decision, and when the referee refused to change his mind Fowler kicked the ball so "sheepishly" that it bounced off Seaman's torso – with the result that, as a commentator had it, Liverpool's "Jason McAteer, one of life's logical positivists ... fired it unsheepishly into the goal."[11] Fowler was a candidate for a fair play award precisely because nobody expected him to do what he did: "You always contest a penalty award against you. You never dispute a penalty award in your favour."[12]

Some Outstanding Examples of Foul Playing

On 9 July 2006, France met Italy in the final of the FIFA World Cup in Berlin's Olympic Stadium. After 109 minutes (and way into extra time), French team captain Zinedine Zidane struck Italian Marco Materazzi in the chest; he was red-carded and left the football ground only minutes before ending his career as a professional footballer. Italy won the subsequent penalty shootout 5–3 and won the cup. When asked why he attacked Materazzi, Zidane remained silent. It was only a year later that Materazzi gave his version of what had happened. In his account he pulled Zidane's shirt, and the Frenchman said, "If you want my shirt I'll give it to you at the end." Materazzi answered, "I prefer your whore of a sister," leading to the head butt in question. Zidane neither confirmed nor denied this account.[13]

In the absence of this explanation Zidane came across as a violent and uncontrolled offender who attacked his opponent for no obvious reason. Interestingly, most of the French population took Zidane's side. And not only the French sympathized: Zidane was elected best player of the championship. Even if there was no alternative to sending him off, anybody would agree that Zidane had good reason to react to Materazzi's verbal insult (assuming that his account was correct). In fact, Zidane's attack was memorialized with a bronze statue raised in front of the Centre Pompidou in Paris in 2012. In the end, what seemed at first like a vicious attack contributed substantially to the making of a hero: not only was Zidane the best player in the tournament, but he had selflessly defended his sister's honour without shouting it from the rooftops. He was entirely rehabilitated and is today the manager of Real Madrid.

The professional foul is always good for storytelling, too. During the 2010 World Cup, a match between Uruguay and Ghana was tied 1–1 when Luis Suárez committed a handball only one minute before the end of extra time. He was sent off, and Ghana was awarded a penalty kick, which Asamoah Gyan missed. When Uruguay won 4–2 after 120 minutes, Suárez was celebrated as the hero of the match and insisted that the "hand of god" had been at play – he was, of course, citing Diego Maradona, who had scored a goal using his hand during the 1986 World Cup.[14]

Another famous professional foul was committed by Michael Ballack of Germany during the 2002 World Cup: he stopped Korean Chun Soo Lee in midfield, knowing that he would be cautioned and that a second yellow card (he had received one in a previous match) would banish him from the final against Brazil. FIFA subsequently modified the rules: now, a player will be banned from the final only if he is sent off in the semi-final, but not for receiving two yellow cards in different matches.[15] It is interesting that a player who is cautioned or sent off after a professional foul is often labelled a hero – not only by the fans, but also by international commentators: the foul is not interpreted as a malign action, but rather as an act of self-sacrifice for the team.[16]

My fourth example is Dutch Arjen Robben's dive during a match against Mexico in the World Cup of 2014, which, along with various other dives, informally won him the "Golden Dive Award" on YouTube and the nickname "Flying Dutchman."[17] Interestingly, Robben admitted several months later that it was a dive, explaining that he thought he was going to be kicked but the Mexican player pulled back his leg at the last moment.[18]

My final example is as exceptional as Zidane's head-butt. During a match against Italy, Luis Suárez of Uruguay (already mentioned above as the "hand of god") bit his opponent Giorgio Chiellini on the shoulder; since the referee did not see the incident, Suárez was neither cautioned nor sent off. Yet, basing their decision on video evidence, FIFA subsequently banned him for nine international matches and from any football-related activity for four months.[19] In Hans Ulrich Gumbrecht's view, there was something so brutal about the biting that it challenged the boundary between (animalistic) nature and (domesticated) culture, and it is the very nature of sport to challenge this boundary.[20]

The five incidents described here have these things in common: they made it to the headlines, and they were spectacular. Some of them are historic in the sense that they prompted public debate and even a change of rules on FIFA's part. However, most fouls are ordinary in the sense that they lead to a free kick without drawing any further attention. Whenever a referee misjudges a situation, some people call for video review, on the assumption that it will result in more fairness on the football pitch. Yet there are good reasons to limit the use of video to very special situations such as Luis Suárez's bite. One reason is that even video is limited, in that it documents only what we see and not what we hear; Materazzi's insult against Zidane, for example, would not have been recorded unless the entire stadium had been stuffed with directed microphones. Second, video interrupts the flow of the match – which is why, for example, the use of instant video is limited to two appeals per match in American football as well as in German football, where instant video was introduced in 2017.

In my view, however, the most striking argument against the use of video technology is that it goes against the ultimately contingent nature of football. Misjudgment on the part of a referee not only is human but also guarantees that the allure of football ranks higher than its ethics. In fact, in the entire history of football, there has never been a match without a foul. Playing foul is not forbidden (as it is forbidden to steal), nor does it indicate the player's moral inferiority. It is a design element: we may or may not like it, but it *defines* football for players as well as for audiences in stadiums and living rooms. To unfold my argument,

I will play through the Platonic and Aristotelian approaches to football respectively and argue that only the latter helps explain the specific allure of football.

A Platonic and an Aristotelian Approach to Football

Plato is always a good reference when it comes to philosophical reflection on sport, and John Zilcosky in his contribution to this volume has shown in detail how reading Plato (and studying his biography) helps us understand wrestling.[21] However, I will not discuss here Plato's reflections on sport as a form of educating the human body and soul. Rather, I will try to apply Platonic ideas to different kinds of sport, taking his theory of forms as a starting point. The central assumption of this theory is that anything that exists in the "real" world is a materialization of an abstract idea. For example, every table that we can touch or have our breakfast on resembles the *idea* of an ideal table; it may resemble this idea more or less accurately, but it never does so perfectly, for it is only one particular table and thus "accidental."[22] In the realm of sport, the ideal performance would be one that accords perfectly with the rules (in team sport) or a particular form (e.g., in gymnastics). But of course it matters whether we are referring to an individual discipline that strives for perfection – such as ice dance, synchronized swimming, or dressage – or are reflecting on team sports like football, basketball, or hockey, where the task is to win by scoring the most goals.

Grasping synchronized swimming in Platonic terms is astonishingly easy: there is an idea of beautiful, harmonious, and synchronous physical action, and the closer the actual performance gets to this ideal the better it is (performances are scored on a scale of 100, rating artistic impression, execution, and difficulty).[23] The athlete attempts to train his or her body with the result that physical energy is transformed into (near-)perfect movements controlled by the athlete's soul. In fact, it is the soul that educates the body, not vice versa: "the good soul, by her own excellence, improves the body as far as this may be possible."[24] Anybody exercising sport excessively will end "by becoming a hater of philosophy, uncivilized, never using the weapon of persuasion, – he is like a wild beast, all violence and fierceness, and knows no other way of dealing; and he lives in all ignorance and evil conditions, and has no sense of propriety and grace" (this comes astonishingly close to my mother's opinion of football).[25]

Applied to football this would mean that it is the players' task to shape physical action by virtue of moral reflection. The "idea" of football would not be to score a maximum number of goals and thus win the game, but rather to avoid violating any rules – most of all, to commit no fouls. The ideal football match would be one without free kicks, cautioning, and send-offs, without players tripping, diving, or spitting. The referee would not have to read the players' minds, for there would be no misbehaviour, just elegant and well-executed moves towards the opponent's goal and likewise elegant and nicely executed moves in order to prevent goals on the part of the defensive team. Needless to say, such a game has never taken place and will never take place, even though some fans of FC Barcelona rightly think that their team has come pretty close.

Many people would argue that a football game is more attractive if ugly fouls are avoided, and that a good team will win matches by playing beautiful and intelligent football rather than by scoring goals at any cost. Yet when an uninspired and very defensive Greek team won the European Cup in 2004, manager Otto Rehagel (nicknamed "Rehakles") defended his team by saying that "what's modern is the team that wins" ("modern spielt, wer gewinnt"). Thus, even if we agree that FC Barcelona plays football more beautifully than the Greek team of 2004, we still need to recognize that there are different styles and philosophies of football, and only very few players would prefer to lose elegantly over winning with luck and/or chutzpa.

In any case, in the real world there is no such thing as an ideal match in a Platonic sense, not only because no player is perfect but also because referees need to strike a compromise between strictly applying the rules and letting the game flow. If they blew the whistle for every single foul committed, the flow of the match would be permanently disrupted (and in any case no referee can observe twenty-two players simultaneously). What happens on the pitch is thus the result of various checks and balances, and to be a good referee one must acquire a good sense of what needs and needs not be sanctioned: this is exactly why he or she can apply the advantage as long as the offensive team does not lose the ball.

A Platonic approach to football seems to be unimaginable, whereas an Aristotelian approach offers some insights into the aesthetics of football, both as a team sport and as a media event, given that Aristotle's philosophy is not about abstract ideas but about phenomena that appear to the senses. Plato's ideology is strictly deductive (or top-down in the sense that abstract ideas rank higher than real-world phenomena), whereas Aristotle allows for inductive arguments as well. Applied to football this could mean that Plato would first work out a set of rules to which the players would have to submit, while Aristotle would watch a large number of matches and adjust the customary rules until they work best – and this describes the history of modern football more accurately than any abstract or deductive approach.

Let us start with the specific aesthetics of football: it can be a pleasure to watch the moves of a single player, and it can be even more of a pleasure to watch scenes of felicitous interplay involving two or more players. But this is not what I am interested in. Football is an aesthetic sport primarily in the sense that perception of it is based entirely on what *appears to the senses* – on the vision and hearing of the spectators, and on the haptic sense of the players. What counts on the pitch is not whether a player intended to score a goal, but whether he *did* score a goal; not whether a player intended to trip an opponent, but whether we saw her tripping; not whether a player has a beautiful move in mind, but whether that beautiful move was completed. Likewise, referees have to make decisions based on what they see, and this is particularly tricky when a player is cautioned or sent off – as mentioned above, these decisions require reading the player's mind. The radical dependence on the visible is, furthermore, an element shaping the audience's experience. Yet audiences often see what they *want* to see. What the fans of one team see as a brilliant move may look like a foul to the fans of the other team. Such judgments are based not just on visual perception but also on the assumption that one's own players have better intentions than those playing for the opponent (I will address the fan phenomenon below). Likewise, it does make a difference whether a team is cheered or booed by its fans in the stadium, and whether fans sing songs or remain silent.

Second, football as a team sport is deeply rooted in social reality. On the one hand it assigns particular roles to particular team members: the goalkeeper, the striker, the midfielder, the back. The more diverse the team the better the narratives accompanying its play, for example in the context of globalization and its impact on team structures. In August 2016, the twenty-nine players of the first-team squad of FC Liverpool were of thirteen nationalities; only eleven were British citizens.[26] The twenty-four players of Juventus Turin were of twelve nationalities, among them only seven Italians,[27] and even the twenty-nine players of Bayern München were of ten nationalities, including eleven German citizens.[28] Likewise, a national team is more alluring when different roles are assigned, for they come with narratives as well. A case in point is the Boateng brothers, who were born in Berlin to two different German mothers and the same Ghanaian father: Kevin-Prince, the older, plays for the national team of Ghana, while Jérôme, the younger, plays for

Germany. Thus a match between the two often prompts commentaries on the family situation, sometimes even drawing on the biblical story of Cain and Abel.[29]

Even if all players on a team were of the same nationality and ethnic background, football would still be a play with assigned roles. The captain, for example, is usually a more experienced and rational character, while a younger teammate may be more of a hotspur; others will serve as comic relief or mediator. The performative character of football also becomes clear in the gestures we see on the pitch. A player committing a foul, for example, often lifts her arms in order to indicate either that it was no foul or that she did not commit it on purpose. A player scoring a goal will physically express his joy, be it by cheering the corner flag, taking off his shirt, or doing a somersault. Even the showing of a red or yellow card is a kind of performative action on the part of the referee, not to speak of Zinedine Zidane's head-butt or Arjen Robben's dives – these were first-rate elements of a virtual drama.

Hartmut Böhme has argued that football, like a good play, resembles life proper:

> Take the victims suffering from injury or being fouled; the birth of new heroes, the fall of the kings; the meteoric rise of a new prince; the braves of a defensive battle; the courageous spearheads breaking through defensive bulwarks; a coruscant genius; a goalkeeper crazing adversary strikers; indomitable team helots; the great directors; the abdication of strategic rulers of the past; the victories of David. The erroneous verdicts of the battle-judges. Luck conspiring against a team. The divine second of a decisive kick. The overwhelming rebellion against defeat. The triumphal zero gravity of a sovereign victory. The patient wait for the adversary's mistake. The dull victory of the mean over a furious rival. Confusion and overview. The incredibly perfect move. The tenacity of one's own team. – They are figures not only of the game but of life inasmuch as life is agon. And agon is life.[30]

The third level of Aristotelian perception addresses the media coverage of football. A stadium holds several tens of thousands of fans; the final of the 2014 World Cup reached one billion viewers on television.[31] On a phenomenological level we could thus argue that football is mostly a TV sport. However, television substantially alters our perception: the visual totality of the stadium is being replaced by an edited version that synthesizes the perspectives of dozens of cameras. Television provides close-ups, repetitions, and slow motion, and the "real" acoustics are eclipsed by the voice of a commentator and thus narratively framed in a way that we may or may not like (it is possible but rather uncommon to switch off the loudspeakers). The result is a zero sum game: what we lose in terms of atmosphere or even authenticity may be made up by the gain in detail, (subjective) proximity, and background information.

For mass audiences, football seems to be the most attractive of all athletic disciplines, and there are various ways of explaining why. Hans Ulrich Gumbrecht has argued that it provides a perfect opportunity to get "lost in focused intensity," but this is likewise true for any other kind of athletic performance.[32] K. Ludwig Pfeiffer has argued that it is the specific constellation of group size, space, and motion that makes football so attractive.[33] Ralf Adelmann and Markus Stauff have explained that televised football is more than just football because it generates a knowledge and narrative of its own kind.[34]

In any case, it is clear that football has aesthetic, social, and media dimensions that can only be grasped if we assume that "real" football appears to the senses; that it is performative rather than abstract; and that striving for perfection will ruin a match rather than do justice to the idea of football. German football coach Alfred Preissler once put the Aristotelian idea of football in a nutshell by stating that "all theory is grey – essential is [what's] on the ground" (Alle Theorie ist grau – entscheidend is auf'm Platz).[35]

Now, what does all this tell us about the allure and ethics of the foul? First, in a "Platonic" football match no fouls would occur, yet this match exists only by way of abstraction. In a real game the foul is *what appears as a foul* – to the referee, to the players on the opposing team, and to the fans of the team whose player was fouled. Through televised repetition, we can check whether the referee's decision (or non-decision) was plausible. But in many situations, even a slow motion playback will not answer the question properly, for neither the referee nor the fouled player nor the audience in the stadium or in front of the television set can read the player's mind.

Thus any attempt to distinguish between a careless foul, a reckless foul, an excessive foul, and no foul at all will be framed by a plausible narrative, drawing on the foul as a performative action. Likewise, a player can use a foul as a means to design the game. He or she can trip a player when not observed by any of the referees; turn a mere stumble into a dramatic plunge; stand up quickly and continue playing; kick back; start an argument; wait for the medics to come and then get up quickly; or admit a dive a year later. Whatever he or she does will be part of a narrative.

On the face of things, it would seem that the resulting narratives also provide moral judgments. Sanctions are immediate, and their aim is not to prompt insight on the part of the player but to maintain order for the game's sake. A pitch is not a court, and playing foul is part of the specific allure of football, which provides scenes like Zidane's head butt or one of Robben's dives, which we may or may not like but which we cannot do without – at least if we assume that a game of football is not framed by the idea of justice but by the idea of allure. Any attempt to "overmoralize" a match in the sense of "seeing things as moral issues that aren't"[36] clashes with the idea of sport as spectacle, unless the spectator is a "purist" who "wants to see it played in the best way possible" and hence without any violation of the rules.[37]

One exception must be made: there is a sharp line between a regular foul and an attack threatening the opponent's physical health. When I started to investigate rather uncommon cases of foul I quickly found a collection of the "ten worst fouls in history" on YouTube. I strongly recommend that you not watch them, for the pictures are haunting and make us aware of how fragile a human body can be. A foul leading to severe injury will be judged by a sports court, not a referee.

The Fan's Perspective

A football fan is never a neutral observer. To better understand the fan's perception of the foul, it is helpful to take a look at Arndt Pollmann's phenomenology of the football fan – in particular, at his distinction between the "real" fan and the nine different types of "fake" fan, for the real fan will naturally have a double standard for a foul depending on who committed it – which is not necessarily true for one of the other prototypical fans, namely the social, the moralist, the aesthetic, the politically correct, the defiant, the opportunistic fan, the fan on trial, the British football fan, and the hooligan.[38]

The social fan, as opposed to the "real" fan, is one who visits the stadium or watches a match because his or her friends do so; the politically correct fan loves to cheer the best African team in a World Cup, while the defiant fan likes to play the *enfant terrible*, for example, by cheering a German team in an Italian restaurant. The opportunistic fan always cheers the winning team, and if **his** own team is about to lose, it's not **his** team anymore. The fan on trial checks what it is like to be a fan of various teams. The British fan is hyperbolic and identifies with his club to the point that he can hardly distinguish between the club and himself. The hooligan is a follower of political theorist Carl Schmitt, in that he distinguishes between friend and foe in real life as well as on the pitch, interestingly without really caring about football.

Most interesting in our context are the moralist and the aesthetician, for they address football's ethics and allure respectively. The moralist fan loves fair play, hates too much physical commitment, and suffers from incorrect decisions on the part of the referee – they agonize him "as much as an undeserving equalizer, let alone match-winning goal."[39] In contrast, the aesthetician among the fans loves sophisticated moves and rejects unfair plays by either team: "They perch on the beauty of the game, rave over complex relays and a divine feel for the ball. After a grim battle like the match between the Netherlands and Portugal during the World Cup of 2006 – with four send-offs and uncounted yellow cards – you can hear him mourn: 'If this goes on I'll stop watching.' A real fan would handle such free-floating aesthetes with care. Whoever is only interested in the grace of sports is well advised to relocate to rhythmic gymnastics or maybe dressage."[40]

In contrast to "false" fans, "real" fans stick with their team through good times and bad, no matter whether it plays good or bad football. They desperately want the team to win, and "a football match is a good, a stirring, a passionate, a beautiful and intelligent match, if and when one's own team – supported by chanting fans – manages to defeat the opponent by exercising skill, power, ruse, and rigor."[41] Unlike the moralistic fan, the real fan does not care about a foul as long as it is committed by his own team, and unlike the aesthetician, the real fan doesn't care about beauty as long as his team wins.

Most people watching football, however, do not match any of Pollmann's prototypes, neither the various false nor the real fans. They drop in for World Cups and drop out after the final. They passionately support their national team in case or as long as it takes part in the competition. This is obviously harder for fans from Libya or the Philippines than for fans from Spain or Brazil. They may be indignant about any foul, and in the absence of their own they will probably want the better team to win. Yet even for neutral fans a spectacular foul will add to football's allure.

Conclusion

While rules define the idea of football, the most intriguing moments in real football result from their violation. Football's attraction, like that of many other team sports, is predicated on the fact that it allows us to stay on the surface. It is stuff for repetition, close-up, and slow motion, as in the case of Arjen Robben's dive in the match against Mexico. Football causes adrenalin rushes and heated debates, as in the case of Luis Suárez's bite. Although the rules sanction foul playing, the foul is an integral part of the game. The rules decide victory and defeat, they are part of football's particular allure, and sometimes they unexpectedly produce heroes like Zinedine Zidane. Imagine a match without a foul: my mother would love it; I would walk away.

NOTES

1 Sigmund Loland, "Fair Play," in *Routledge Handbook of the Philosophy of Sport*, ed. Mike McNamee and William J. Morgan (London and New York: Routledge, 2015), 333.
2 Ibid., 343.
3 Ibid., 344.
4 Ibid.
5 "Laws of the Game 2016/17," International Football Association Board (IFAB), 81, http://www.fifa.com/mm/Document/FootballDevelopment/Refereeing/02/79/92/44/Laws.of.the.Game.2016.2017_Neutral.pdf.
6 Ibid., 81.
7 Ibid., 85–6.
8 Ibid., 87.
9 Warren P. Fraleigh confirms the existence of the "professional foul" but denies that it is, at the same time, a "good foul." See Fraleigh, "Why the Good Foul Is Not Good," *Journal of Physical Education, Recreation and Dance* 53, no. 1 (1982): 41–2; idem, "Cheating," in *The Bloomsbury Companion to the Philosophy of Sport*, ed. Cesar R. Torres (London: Bloomsbury, 2014), 341–3.
10 See "WM 'Statistik' Tore pro Saison," http://www.weltfussball.de/statistik/wm/1.
11 David Lister, "Football Hero in Honesty Shock," *The Independent*, 26 March 1997, http://www.independent.co.uk/voices/football-hero-in-honesty-shock-1275119.html.
12 Ibid.
13 "And Materazzi's Exact Words to Zidane were ...," *The Guardian*, 18 August 2007, https://www.theguardian.com/football/2007/aug/18/newsstory.sport2.
14 "World Cup 2010: The Hand of God Belongs to me, Says Luis Suárez," *The Guardian*, 3 July 2010, https://www.theguardian.com/football/2010/jul/03/world-cup-2010-hand-god-suarez.
15 "World Cup 2010: Fifa Changes Rules to Prevent World Cup Final Bans," *The Guardian*, 20 June 2010, https://www.theguardian.com/football/2010/jun/20/fifa-rules-world-cup-2010.
16 For example, Frank Hellmann, "Michael Ballack: Die Tränen des tragischen Helden," *Frankfurter Allgemeine Zeitung*, 25 June 2002, http://www.faz.net/aktuell/sport/michael-ballack-die-traenen-des-tragischen-helden-159751.html.

17 For example, "Arjen Robben Wins the Golden Dive Award," *YouTube*, 14 July 2014, https://www.youtube.com/watch?v=9gllC9qkM1o.

18 "Netherlands 2–1 Mexico – World Cup 2014: Arjen Robben Admits 'Diving,'" *Huffington Post*, 30 June 2014, http://www.huffingtonpost. co.uk/2014/06/30/netherlands-2-1-mexico-arjen-robben_n_5542635.html.

19 See "FIFA World Cup, Third Biting Incident," *Wikipedia*, last modified 15 August 2016, https://en.wikipedia.org/wiki/ Luis_Su%C3%A1rez#2014_FIFA_World_Cup.2C_third_biting_incident.

20 Hans Ulrich Gumbrecht, "Der Biss von Luiz Suárez," *Neue Zürcher Zeitung*, 1 April 2016, http://www.nzz.ch/meinung/kolumnen/ momente-des-fussballs-der-biss-von-luis-suarez-ld.11011.

21 See John Zilcosky, "Wrestling, or The Art of Disentangling Bodies," in this volume.

22 See Kurt Flasch, "Zur Rehabilitierung der Relation. Die Theorie der Beziehung bei Johannes Eriugena," in *Philosophie als Beziehungswissenschaft*, ed. Wilhelm Friedrich Niebel and Dieter Leisegang (Frankfurt am Main: Heiderhoff, 1971), 13; cf. Johannes Scotus Eriugena, *Periphyseon* [*De divisione naturae*], ed. A. Jeauneau (Dublin: Dublin Institute for Advanced Studies, 1968), 505 D and 490 B.

23 Cf. "Fina Synchronised Swimming Manual for Judges, Coaches & Referees," http://www.zwemfed.be/sites/default/files/FINA_SY_ MANUAL_13_17.pdf.

24 Plato, *The Dialogues of Plato translated into English with Analyses and Introductions by B. Jowett, M.A. in Five Volumes*, 3rd ed., revised and corrected (Oxford: Oxford University Press, 1892), http://oll.libertyfund.org/ titles/767#Plato_0131-03_1518.

25 Plato, *The Dialogues*, http://oll.libertyfund.org/titles/767#Plato_ 0131-03_1634.

26 See "First-Team Squad," *Wikipedia*, last modified 31 August 2016, https:// en.wikipedia.org/wiki/Liverpool_F.C.#First-team_squad.

27 See "Current Squad," *Wikipedia*, last modified 2 September 2016, https:// en.wikipedia.org/wiki/Juventus_F.C.#Current_squad.

28 See "Current Squad," *Wikipedia*, last modified 6 September 2016, https:// en.wikipedia.org/wiki/FC_Bayern_Munich#Current_squad.

29 Philippe Ridet, "Les Boateng Abel et Caïn du Mondial," *Le Monde*, 22 June 2010, http://www.lemonde.fr/sport/article/2010/06/22/les-boateng-abel-et-cain-du-mondial_1376875_3242.html.

30 Hartmut Böhme, "Idole und Bälle. Fußballkultur und Fetischismus," in *Am Ball der Zeit. Die Fußballweltmeisterschaft als Ereignis und Faszinosum*, ed. Rebekka Ladewig and Annette Vowinckel (Bielefeld: Transcript, 2009), 166 (author's translation; German: "Da sind die leidenden Opfer der Verletzung und der Fouls; die Geburt des neuen Helden, der Sturz der

Könige; der kometenhafte Aufstieg des jungen Prinzen; die Heroen der Abwehrschlacht; die kühnen Spitzen, die das Bollwerk durchbrechen; das aufblitzende Genie; der seine Gegner zur Verzweiflung treibende Torwart; die Heloten der Mannschaft, die unbezwinglich sind; die großen Dirigenten; die Abdankung des herrscherlichen Strategen der Vergangenheit; der Sturz der Favoriten; die Siege Davids. Die schicksalhaften Fehlurteile der Schlachten-Richter. Das gegen die eigene Truppe verschworene Glück. Die göttliche Sekunde, in der durch einen Kunstschuss alles entschieden ist. Das unbändige Aufbäumen gegen die Niederlage. Die triumphale Schwerelosigkeit eines souveränen Siegs. Das geduldige Lauern auf die Fehler des anderen. Der glanzlose Sieg des Durchschnitts gegen einen furiosen Gegner. Die Verwirrung und die Übersicht. Der unfasslich perfekte Spielzug. Die Beharrlichkeit der eigenen Linie. – All dies sind Figuren nicht nur des Spiels, sondern des Lebens, insofern das Leben Agon ist. Und der Agon Spiel.")

31 See "2014 FIFA World Cup™ reached 3.2 billion viewers, one billion watched final," 16 December 2015, http://www.fifa.com/worldcup/news/y=2015/m=12/news=2014-fifa-world-cuptm-reached-3-2-billion-viewers-one-billion-watched--2745519.html.

32 See Hans Ulrich Gumbrecht, *In Praise of Athletic Beauty* (Cambridge, MA: Harvard University Press, 2006), 51.

33 K. Ludwig Pfeiffer, "Der seltsame Attraktor des Fußballs: Gruppe, Raum, Bewegung," in *Am Ball der Zeit*, ed. Ladewig and Vowinckel, 25–36.

34 Ralf Adelmann and Markus Stauff, "Die Wirklichkeit in der Wirklichkeit. Fernsehfußball und mediale Wissenskultur," in *Querpässe: Beiträge zur Literatur-, Kultur- und Mediengeschichte des Fußballs*, ed. Ralf Adelmann and Markus Stauff (Heidelberg: Synchron, 2003), 103–21.

35 See Wade, "Alfred Preißler: 'Grau is alle Theorie ...!'" 24 May 2002, http://www.schwatzgelb.de/2001-05-24-helden-adi-preissler-grau-is-alle-theorie.html. Collections of football citations also ascribe the sentence to Otto Rehagel, then manager of Herta BSC Berlin, who once said that "the truth is on the ground" (die Wahrheit liegt auf dem Platz); see, for example, "Fußballzitate – eine Sammlung, wenn auch keine vollständige," http://fussballzitate.de/index.html; "Fußball Tippspiele," http://www.mathematik.uni-ulm.de/~wwthimm/bl-tip/zitate.html.

36 C.A.J. Coady, *What's Wrong with Moralism?* (Malden: Blackwell, 2006), 1, quoted in Michael W. Austin, "Sport as a Moral Practice: An Aristotelian Approach," *Royal Institute of Philosophy Supplement* 73 (2013): 37.

37 Stephen Mumford, *Watching Sport: Aesthetics, Ethics, and Emotion* (Abingdon: Routledge, 2012), 14; Carwyn Jones, "Spectatorship – Watching and Following Sport," in *Routledge Handbook of the Philosophy of Sport*, 401–10n1.

38 See Arnd Pollmann, "Fußballgott, erbarme dich! Fan-Sein als ekklesiogene Neurose," in *Am Ball der Zeit*, ed. Ladewig and Vowinckel, 139–41. Carwyn Jones has developed a similar scheme; see Jones, "Spectatorship," 403–8.

39 Pollmann, "Fußballgott," 139 (author's translation; German: "Moralisten sind Anhänger des Fair-Play, verabscheuen jeden allzu harten Körpereinsatz und sonstige Unsportlichkeiten. Fehlentscheidungen des Schiedsrichters quälen den Fußball-Moralisten ebenso wie ein unverdienter Ausgleichs- oder gar Siegtreffer. Der Moralist will nicht, dass 'seine' oder irgendeine bestimmte Mannschaft siegt. Nein, die bessere möge gewinnen.")

40 Pollmann, "Fußballgott," 139 (author's translation; German: "Sie setzen allein auf die Schönheit des Spiels, schwärmen von komplexen Ball-Stafetten und göttlichem Ballgefühl. Im Anschluss an eine erbitterte Fußball-'Schlacht,' wie man sie bei der Weltmeisterschaft 2006 z.B. zwischen Holland und Portugal zu bestaunen hatte – vier rote und unzählige gelbe Karten – hörte man den Ästhetiker klagen: 'Also, wenn das so weitergeht, dann guck' ich nicht mehr!' Man hegt als echter Fan eine gewisse Vorsicht gegenüber diesen bindungslos flottierenden Schöngeistern. Wer allein an der Anmut des Sports interessiert ist, dem wird man raten wollen, sich bei der rhythmischen Sportgymnastik oder vielleicht beim Dressurreiten umzuschauen.")

41 See Pollmann, "Fußballgott," 142.

PART V

Coda

10 Swimming

KARIN HELMSTAEDT

Part I

It was forty years ago, in July of 1976, that the dream was born. I sat as a small girl on the floor of our den, bare legs outstretched, fingers clutching the green shag carpet. Canada's Nancy Garapick was churning her way to Olympic bronze in the 100 metre backstroke in Montreal – a mere three hours away from where I sat.

Her exploits, at only fourteen, seemed very remote on the small black-and-white television screen. But when she stood on the podium in her oversized terrycloth bathrobe, next to East Germans Ulrike Richter and Birgit Treiber, I could feel my mother, a Maritimer like Nancy, radiating the pride of many Canadians. "I'd like to go to the Olympics one day," I said, not even knowing what it really meant. "You could," said my mother, her eyes fixed on the grainy screen. "But what would I do?," I asked. She looked at me resolutely. "You could swim," she said.

My father had been a swimmer before fleeing his native East Germany – so perhaps it was a logical choice. Two years later my younger brother and I joined our local swim team in Kingston, Ontario. I jumped into the pool and never looked back.

Thus, so innocently, in a local twenty-yard YMCA pool, began the long, arduous quest for excellence. And although it would be years before I could articulate it, the allure of that sporting prowess was already exerting its force. Fun and games in the early days, and the weightlessness, are like the insect bite that first infects you. Then, with increasing focus on stroke development and speed, it's all about how to move efficiently through water. Local swim meets gave way to larger, regional competitions, times improved. Ribbons in white, blue, and red for early age group competitions cluttered my bulletin board, later on trophies had pride of place on my shelf.

With varying levels of skill, and endless enthusiasm, our first coaches taught us what to do in the water: how to execute efficient strokes, to breathe and undulate with the ease of a porpoise, to hone our bodies into a hydrodynamic ideal. How to make the water your ally. Workouts increased in frequency, early mornings became the norm, parents driving us through the frozen winter darkness so we could hit the water at 5:30 a.m. The endless line on the bottom of the pool. How to push your limits, hold that stroke, blast off that turn, reach for that wall. How to fight the soreness and fatigue, and then do it again, and again, and again.

We learned cheers and motivational slogans to counteract the repetitive drudge: No Pain, No Gain – Go for 1T! I excelled at the individual medley, the all-rounder event in swimming consisting of butterfly, backstroke, breaststroke, and front crawl. The 400 metre version is a punishing race – requiring endless repetition, flawless change-overs between strokes, rock solid endurance. Goggle marks dented our faces well into first period at school. Eyelids grew heavy. By the 3:40 bell it was time to head back to the pool. Switch on that radio tune in my head. My blonde hair took on a metallic, chlorine sheen.

At fourteen I qualified for my first Junior Nationals in Halifax, Nancy Garapick's hometown. Nerves had entered the game, the pressure to perform was often visceral. My gut one long, serpentine spasm as I stepped up to the block, I felt that queasy state of being both competitor and outside observer. After a 400 I.M. my stomach was twisted into hypoglycaemic knots. It would take hours for the cramps to subside, hours to consume even a small portion of food. But the effort had brought me forward. My coach was satisfied. The race went on.

Fast forward to 1984: for five days at the Etobicoke Olympium for the Canadian Olympic Trials, I tasted the thrill of having it all fall into place. Of personal best performances that had me mixing in the ready room for finals – as if in a vaccuum – with the country's best. As a rural talent from a small team, I missed the Olympic ticket, but my performances earned me National Team carded status and the promise that in four years my time would come. At the Los Angeles Olympics – marked by a Soviet-led boycott – Canada shone in the pool. Olympic hardware glinted in the sun, and the allure of podium glory brought funding – both government and corporate – pouring into our sport.

It was a heady time, and the will to swim with the best in the world was a potent draught. It had to be, because stepping onto the international deck was where the innocence stopped. Not only did the reality of coach–swimmer dynamics pose some real challenges for a teenage girl, but our Eastern European competitors were formidable, and the leitmotiv of East German dominance in women's swimming – already more than apparent in 1976 in Montreal – was willingly ignored. All the while we were being trained according to what many of our coaches understood as the "East German model," which meant upwards to 20 kilometres a day during heavy training periods, plus weight training. All the repetition, all the pain and sweat were intended to make us unflinching, unfaltering racing machines, and we willingly embraced the role. It became a point of pride to be tougher than the rest, to never give up. We adopted battlefield postures, right arm raised with a triumphant fist in the air after victory, one's own or that of a teammate, and the primitive surge of adrenaline and endorphins – the fearlessness, when the cocktail was just right – were what I imagined a warrior must feel.

At that level, we had to push much further and hold out much longer for any pleasure. It often came right on race day, after we had tapered down the kilometres and shaved our bodies until they were smooth as silk – arms, legs, back. After months of high-volume training, the practice of "taper and shave" allowed us to "feel" the water in a state of abnormal rest, in a state of heightened sensitivity; the rush alone upon entry into the water was enough to shave tenths, even seconds off a personal best time. This was the intoxicating trip en route to the climactic surge to the wall, the sensation of cold molecules sliding over warm skin, of the medium supporting you, allowing you, for precious seconds, to feel no pain. Like a natural drug.

But internationally we were trying to keep up with an opponent that was using *chemical* ones. At the World Aquatic Championships in Madrid in 1986, we witnessed a clean-up of historical proportions, with East German women winning thirteen of sixteen events. Rumours were rife that their performances were powered by steroids, but beyond acknowledging they were indeed doing *something* better than we were, our coaches stuck doggishly to the mantra of "you just have to be tougher" and "no negative thinking." All the positive thinking in the world didn't change the hard facts of the world rankings, however, and it didn't help when coaches denigrated our performances – and our commitment – as not good enough. This rankled me, and I questioned what was happening, even did research on the GDR's sporting miracle machine. Its scouting, selection, and scientifically monitored training programs with specialized sport schools were well documented, and clearly superior. Outside of a few powerhouse club teams, our nation's elite seemed to rely largely on a lucky alignment of circumstances: a favourable combination of talent, motivation, support, and logistics with a decent pool and a skilled coach. Many did well even without all these elements – but still, too many factors were left open to chance.

In 1988 Swimming Canada changed its policy for Olympic selection, which until then had been automatic for the top two swimmers in each event, and top four with alternates in the 100 and 200 metre freestyle for relays. But in 1988, qualification standards were calculated from world best times. In the women's events many of these were held by East Germans, and were scintillatingly fast, which resulted in some qualifying times well under the Canadian record.

At Olympic Trials in May of 1988 I placed second in the 200 I.M. but was off the qualifying standard by several seconds. In fact, the overall Olympic team selection was so small that second-chance trials were held in August. In hindsight, our "East German model" training regime was the downfall for me at this point. Endless miles in the water and a brutal weight program drove my blood lactate levels to the highest I had ever recorded. The real East German model, with its legions of scientists, and its "U.M." ("*unterstützende Mittel*" or "supporting means" was the euphemistic label assigned to the anabolic steroids used in the GDR's state-ordered doping plan), would have recognized the exhaustion, the overtraining, and compensated accordingly: with rest, with drugs. So how could we measure up when *our* model was one of devastatingly fragmentary understanding?

The Canadian Olympic swim team travelled to Seoul with multiple vacant spots. With the Soviets and the East Germans back on the scene, our women mustered a bronze medal in the 4x100 medley relay. It was a jarring and frustrating end to my own Olympic dream. But 1988 saw a whole nation's dream crumble when Canada's gold medallist and 100 metre dash world record holder Ben Johnson tested positive for steroids, lost his medal, and disgraced the nation. What followed was a federal government inquiry, led by Ontario Appeal Court Chief Justice Charles Dubin, that exposed rampant use of performance-enhancing drugs in Canadian sports such as track and field and weightlifting, and that resulted in Canada revising its drug-testing policies and procedures. The "shocking" revelations during the ninety-one days of Dubin Inquiry testimony blew away any residual belief that Canadians were the good guys. Although it put Canada at the forefront of the battle against performance-enhancing drugs, many athletes were on the fence as to whether it had been a good thing for sport. For officials in East Germany, where the government was in cahoots with testers to make doped athletes appear "clean," it must have been a strange comedy indeed.

I spent the next few years feeling chronically numb and disillusioned – questioning why, when there was so much smoke, no one had looked for the fire. Because the rumours were there for a reason. And patterns, properly observed, can expose those reasons.

Not long after the fall of the Berlin Wall I moved to France. As a student and a budding journalist, I continued my questioning on European turf. Meticulous descriptions of state-sponsored doping in the former East Germany based on Stasi files and archives were gradually coming to light. And just as China's female swimmers and athletes were taking over the world ranking lists in their turn, the rumours were confirmed.

What followed were years of research, interviews, articles, and travel to sporting events, as well as a prize-winning documentary film and a follow-up book. East Germany was steadily coming to terms with its past, and during that process, I spoke to doctors, historians, coaches, parents, and former athletes. I interviewed countless victims of State Plan 14.25, under which girls as young as ten had been given anabolic steroids. Many of them had later been cast off by a system that promoted only its best. As I tried to come to terms with my own disappointments, I came to deeply understand the physical and psychological consequences, sometimes irreversible, of a drug-powered training regime – the ideological constraints of Communist East Germany, the human variables affecting the system, how some had found the strength to resist, and how others could not. By 1998, when pilot doping trials of doctors and swim coaches involved in the system began in Berlin, I had moved to Germany to cover the story first-hand.

Turning this story into an acceptable truth has been a slow process. In Germany, the trauma it has caused is ongoing. The multitude of stories – painful, disturbing, too often tragic – and the sufferings they have brought to light are reason enough to question the power of a sporting allure that has led entire governments to instrumentalize athletes to an almost science fictional degree.

Yet it is fascinating to observe, within German society, and society as a whole, just how fervently we wish to will it all away. To ignore the well-documented facts and believe again in the myth of the athlete as a moral and physical ideal, as an ambassador of national pride. Meanwhile doping scandals have erupted and re-erupted in country after country: China, the United States, and most recently Russia. A level of fatigue – the very antithesis of the allure we find so enticing – has set in around the topic. We now know, thanks to unfaltering research by German sport historians, that organized and government-endorsed doping was rampant in West Germany as well, and that countless politicians, officials, and coaches *on both sides* were in the know. But where was their moral obligation to the athletes in the 1970s and 80s? Why were these authorities, world swimming governing bodies first and foremost, not more concerned with the actual welfare of their charges? And why were the few who dared voice their discontent so callously branded as poor sportsmen? Instead of letting the West in on the doping hoax decades earlier, the very "class enemy" that Communist East Germany so vilified did its best to emulate the GDR's pharmacological success. It's all there, in the ethic-less ethics committees and the reams of articles. The Rio Olympics of 2016 were a case in point of how the thrill and excitement of sporting glory supersede the farce that many of the races have become. "Doping journalists" and doping researchers are an unpopular lot, always trying to expose the tarnish on the shine, yet, given the toll that doping has taken on sports and athletes across the board, what is the moral alternative?

So should we just accept the widespread drug use in so many sports, such as international cycling? Because indeed, you don't get through a Tour de France without them. Can we afford to explore the idea of a "clean" league and a league that allows for performance enhancement? Should athletes be allowed to choose? It seems to me that the problem of the level playing field would arise regardless, given discrepancies between countries in terms of financial means, access to substances, medical expertise, and so on. And in such a scenario, how can we realistically encourage our children to partake in high-performance sport, when the physical consequences could be dire?

It is sobering to concede that years of revelations, scandals, confessions, documentaries, and articles – even the well-meant anti-doping measures – have had so little effect on the overall "cleanness" of sport – quite the opposite. But even as the International Olympic Committee tries to mop over its greatest ethical crisis yet, the fundamental problem of the narrative we use for sport comes into relief. The allure at this point is as treacherous as the seductive force that the word itself implies. We – society, governments, sport federations, and the media – have for too long demanded a double standard in that we insist on the performances as relentlessly as we insist on the squeaky clean, shiny athlete. Yet the will to impose ethical regulation and controls carries with it the risk of destroying the very thing that makes sport so enigmatically gripping: the raw unpredictability of the athlete as a surging force of speed, strength, and precision; that moment of transcendence that we as spectators, as fans, as cohorts, share, fists in the air.

So perhaps the overriding question is, what purpose is sport to serve? Is it to provide the enthralling charm of the fairy tale, the distraction, the entertainment factor intrinsic to the glory? This, of course, appeals to our coarser instincts. Or do we favour a more humanistic perspective that encompasses excellence as a noble pursuit, sport as a physical benefit with broader societal implications, and failure as an acceptable element of the game? It is a constant challenge – as an athlete, as a citizen – to be confronted with the baseness of one's own human impulses. And perhaps this hard-wiring is the crux of every choice made in the rush of desire to win. In de Coubertin's words (so deftly quoted by Charles Stocking),[1] "sport produces beauty because it creates the athlete, who is a living sculpture" – an aesthetic ideal – viewed from the outside. But in battle, in the real test of mettle, the honest heart is anything but beautiful.

Part II

It came to me out of the blue. Quite literally, the azure waters of the Mediterranean, as I watched my seven-year-old daughter frolic on a remote beach in southeastern Crete. Nearly two years earlier she had joined the beginner ranks of – irony of ironies – a former East Berlin swim team. As I contemplated the potentially daring experiment we had embarked upon, I watched her play, oblivious to anyone around her, bobbing and plunging, otter-like, in the warm shallows. I knew that if I called her she would be reluctant to leave her element.

The thought occurred to me: what if I could get that back? Get back to the time when it was all about child's play – about loving the water, the weightlessness, the feeling of limbs in sweet suspension? Before the pressure, before the pitting ourselves against one another, before the awakening of killer instincts and the advent of expectations. Because our drive grew out of that feeling of mastering a skill and a flow of movement – it's the reason we even want to get in there and do it again.

Over the years post-competition, I was one of the few of my close female swimming cohorts who actually stayed in touch with the water. Some of my best friends steer clear of it altogether – refusing to go near a pool, even reluctant to venture into the lake, taking a few strokes at most before turning back to dry land. Their achievements in the sport paralleled or even exceeded my own, yet their desire or even their *need* to be in the water was somehow irreversibly quelled. There had been too much drudgery, too much monotony, too much abuse. Nowadays they opt for running, a more grounded mode of training that allows for full awareness of one's surroundings, even conversation. But when it came to exercise I had to stay true to my element, initially out of a vague compulsion to hang on to the familiar, to keep competing, through a season of triathlons and a stint with Masters swimming. Later, more sporadically, to maintain some semblance of conditioning but also because, after all the years spent devoted to one sport, this was what my body could not forget, my truest and deepest skill. Occasionally I was reminded of this while stroking towards the middle of a lake, with an expanse of water on all sides and the freedom to gaze at the waterline – trees, cloud, and sky. Sometime I would stop to hang suspended just below the surface, contemplating the shimmering silver line of transition between elements.

The transition from life as an athlete to life without the twice-daily fix of kick boards and pull-buoys is a curious and often difficult process. For me there was always a need, yet at the same time, the more I realized how duped we had been by international competition, a refusal. So when my son was old enough to swim I deliberately kept him away from pools. We opted for European handball, a group sport that focused on different skills and that allowed for play. But when I sat in the bleachers watching a game, I felt like the proverbial fish out of water: other parents who came from a handball background surged with excitement, muttered and shouted as if their offspring's entire life depended on the outcome. I felt out of place. In those sweaty gyms, I had forgotten where my home was.

The kind of open water freedom I sought every summer in lakes was bound by the seasons, so when I made the decision to get back in the water, after a more or less ten-year hiatus from pools, I had to get back to the sharp reality of chlorine. I did this, on the one hand to get back in touch with the scene for my daughter's sake, but on the other to attempt to shake off the years of drifting media fatigue, and to recall why I had devoted so much of my life – hundreds and thousands of hours – to such a sublime activity, only to have the delight driven out of me. To resavour the pleasant shock of submersion in cool water, of slow motion activation, old neural pathways firing into action, the deep muscular memory of familiar stroke patterns reawakened. I joined a team of enthusiastic Masters, planned training times into my busy schedule, was both delighted and distraught at how quickly behavioural athlete "ticks" could return. The not so pleasant shock was the pain involved in this endeavour. Muscles and tendons remembering an elasticity they now struggled to replicate. A dormant shoulder injury reawakened. This was not a mere summer dip, but this was not a race. It was a journey to where the feeling of addiction had begun.

I also had to give myself a goal. After six months of training, I travelled to one of the most remote places on the planet, to the northeastern tip of the Arabian Peninsula. The Musandam Peninsula is an exclave of Oman, marked by dramatic fjord formations as the Al Hajar Mountains plunge into the waters of the Strait of Hormuz. The longest fjord there meanders 17 kilometres inland, its craggy, inhospitable landscape supporting only a handful of fishing villages. I joined a group to swim these waters and for six days embarked on an aquatic exploration that was as much about finding an old, familiar tempo as it was about discovering a breathtaking part of the world *from the water*. Leisurely coastal swims, circumnavigations of islands, and brisk crossings let me experiment with pace, finding the flow and reforging that old alliance with salty water as a medium, a force, and a friend.

There were other friends to enrich the experience: dolphins, waiting for us daily, at the mouth of the fjord, their sleek, shining bodies describing endless arcs over the glare of the water's surface. Their movements were slippery, effortless, inviting. Their tireless enthusiasm for cavorting in the wake of the boat fascinated me. This was *real* play: rolling repetition, revelling in the pliable support of an aqueous playground, savouring speed achieved with almost imperceptible adjustments of muscle and connective tissue, sheer glee at a lightning swift change of course, deep delight on the plunge into luminous green depths.

As I stroked along the shell-encrusted coast one afternoon, marvelling at fish, spiny urchins, and corals some 3 metres below, another creature rose from the sloping sea floor like a broad black bed sheet. My startled intake of breath thwarted by the water, my body contracted slightly, instinctively willing itself to flatten on the surface, like a film of oil. I floated, transfixed, then nudged myself ever so slightly around to come face to face with a giant mobula ray. My mind raced through a rapid interrogation as to whether or not I was in danger as the beast lifted its diamond-shaped body to consider me at an angle, revealing the brilliant white of its underbelly. And there we were, suspended in the shallow depths, in a gently undulating balance, caressed by the remnant of a Persian Gulf stream. Like a mirror image of awe we shared a moment, both beings inquisitive, shy, all fibres extended in a mysterious inner matrix of aquatic trust. Such a massive creature, poised in mid-flight, still but for the slightest lilt of a coastal current under its wings. A moment later, the obsidian prongs of its eyes had seen enough, and it flashed away into the depths, leaving me to marvel at such split-second recruitment of muscle fibre, at such mind-blowing precision and efficiency of movement. It was a sublime encounter with perfection – this animal made for navigation through water. My whole body tingled, acutely aware of how we can only aspire as human beings in this element, but the exhilaration intrinsic to the effort is glorious.

And after four days, as I crawled through glassy morning waters, breathing rhythmically to a magnificent mountain mirror image, a waterline, cloud, and sky, I thanked the elements that in some way the experiment had worked. The rush returned: a lifting, as breath and velocity were suddenly effortless, and every pull had the sole purpose of clean propulsion. Focused, but no goal in sight, just the sweetness of straight ahead, unhindered, into the blue. There *is* a pure place, in water, in space, and it's worth coming back to the heart to find it.

NOTE

1 See Charles Stocking, "The Allure and Ethics of Ancient Aesthetics: Hellenism in the Modern Olympic Movement," in this volume.

Contributors

Marlo A. Burks is a scholar of German literature. She is the translator of *Hugo von Hofmannsthal: Writings on Art / Schriften zur Kunst* and is currently working on a monograph on the aesthetic experience in fin-de-siècle Vienna.

Grant Farred's most recent books are *The Burden of Over-Representation: Race, Sport, and Philosophy* (Temple UP, 2018) and *Entre Nous: Between the World Cup and Me* (Duke UP, 2019).

Hans Ulrich Gumbrecht is the Albert Guérard Professor Emeritus in the Departments of Comparative Literature and of French and Italian at Stanford. A decade ago, he published an aesthetics of spectator sports under the title *In Praise of Athletic Beauty* (Harvard UP), and he is proud that this book has been translated into eleven languages. Since his beginnings at Stanford, in 1989, he has been helping the university's American Football department in its recruiting activities.

Karin Helmstaedt is a Canadian broadcast journalist and presenter based in Berlin, Germany. She was a member of Canada's National Swim Team from 1984 to 1988.

Wolf Kittler is Professor in the Department of Germanic, Slavic, and Semitic Studies, and in the Comparative Literature program, at the University of California, Santa Barbara. He has taught at the universities of Erlangen-Nürnberg, Freiburg im Breisgau, Konstanz, Munich, and Cornell. His publications include books on Franz Kafka and Heinrich von Kleist, and articles on literature, philosophy, the history of science, techniques, law, warfare, and media from antiquity to the present.

Rebekka von Mallinckrodt is Professor of Early Modern History at the University of Bremen. She has published widely on early modern sports and body techniques.

Sarah Panzer is an Assistant Professor of Modern European History at Missouri State University. Her research focuses on the sociocultural dynamics of the German–Japanese relationship during the first half of the twentieth century.

Sofie Remijsen is Lecturer in Ancient History at the University of Amsterdam. In 2015, she published a monograph on the end of Greek athletics in late antiquity.

Charles Stocking is Associate Professor of Classical Studies and core member of the Centre for the Study of Theory and Criticism at the University of Western Ontario, and associate member of ANHIMA (Anthropologie et histoire des mondes antiques) in Paris, France.

Annette Vowinckel is a specialist in the cultural and media history of the twentieth century. As head of the Department for Media History at the Center for Contemporary History, Potsdam, she recently published a book on the cultural history of photojournalism. Further information at www.annette-vowinckel.de.

John Zilcosky is Professor of German and Comparative Literature at the University of Toronto and is the author, most recently, of *Uncanny Encounters: Literature, Psychoanalysis, and the End of Alterity*. In 2017, he was awarded the Friedrich-Wilhelm-Bessel Research Prize of the German government.

Index